200 Themes for Devising Theatre with 11–18 Year Olds: A Drama Teacher's Resource Book

200 Themes for Devising Theatre with 11–18 Year Olds: A Drama Teacher's Resource Book

Jason Hanlan

methuen | drama
LONDON • NEW YORK • OXFORD • NEW DELHI • SYDNEY

METHUEN DRAMA
Bloomsbury Publishing Plc
50 Bedford Square, London, WC1B 3DP, UK
1385 Broadway, New York, NY 10018, USA
29 Earlsfort Terrace, Dublin 2, Ireland

BLOOMSBURY, METHUEN DRAMA and the Methuen Drama logo are trademarks
of Bloomsbury Publishing Plc

First published in Great Britain 2024

Cover design: Ben Anslow

A catalogue record for this book is available from the British Library.

Library of Congress Cataloging-in-Publication Data
Names: Hanlan, Jason, author.
Title: 200 themes for devising theatre with 11–18 year olds :
a drama teacher's resource book / Jason Hanlan.
Other titles: Two hundred themes for devising theatre with 11–18 year olds
Description: New York : Bloomsbury Academic, 2024. |
Includes bibliographical references and index.
Identifiers: LCCN 2023030889 (print) | LCCN 2023030890 (ebook) |
ISBN 9781350279636 (paperback) | ISBN 9781350279643 (hardback) |
ISBN 9781350279650 (pdf) | ISBN 9781350279667 (epub)
Subjects: LCSH: Drama–Study and teaching (Secondary)
Classification: LCC PN1701 .H365 2024 (print) | LCC PN1701 (ebook) |
DDC 792—dc23/eng/20230831
LC record available at https://lccn.loc.gov/2023030889
LC ebook record available at https://lccn.loc.gov/2023030890

ISBN: HB: 978-1-3502-7964-3
        PB: 978-1-3502-7963-6
        ePDF: 978-1-3502-7966-7
        eBook: 978-1-3502-7965-0

Typeset by RefineCatch Limited, Bungay, Suffolk
Printed and bound in Great Britain

To find out more about our authors and books visit www.bloomsbury.com
and sign up for our newsletters.

CONTENTS

ACKNOWLEDGEMENTS

*'The play's the thing, wherein I'll catch the
conscience of the king.'*

To the thousands of students and teachers of drama everywhere who continually remind us that drama is about a truth which connects us all.

My daughter, Naomi Bunyan. A talented illustrator who unfolded my ideas onto the cover of this book so precisely. Grant Bunyan, for his excellent and original design work on the icons used throughout the book.

My friend and colleague for many years, Mark Lovejoy, for the energy and support you have always so willingly shared.

My mother, the wonderful storyteller who embroidered the facts which kept us all connected.

My wife, Monica, for time, inspiration and peace.

A BIT ABOUT ME

I qualified as a drama teacher in 1994 and went on to teach in two large comprehensives in the UK, as head of drama and later Performing Arts. Along the way I worked as an LEA advisor for drama and a teacher trainer. Alongside teaching I worked as a senior moderator/examiner for 15 years. Mostly though, for the Past 28 years, I've been a drama teacher in British secondary schools and, more recently, internationally.

My first book, *200 Plays for GCSE and A-Level Performance*, published by Methuen in 2021, is used extensively as a resource for drama teachers seeking the best published materials for their students.

This book is a tool for selecting and making connections between thousands of stimuli in a focussed, teacher-friendly format. It brings together stimuli from art, music, media, history, dance, theatre and literature in a package to stimulate devising with students from 10 year olds to college and beyond . . .

PART ONE

1

Why Devise?

Drama is a creative art form; like a painting, we can admire and enjoy its form, but some of us will be inspired to paint our own. To suspend disbelief for a moment and seize the opportunity to say something.

For me true devising is a collaborative group response resulting in the creation of an original piece of theatre. It doesn't begin with a script but with an idea, a response to a stimulus and a desire to say something.

It's an enrichening process that helps us make sense of our world and to dream of possibilities. It enables us to question what we can't understand or accept and to set this before an audience who have come to share. The young have a hunger, a fire for this kind of art; it's in their nature.

How does it compare with scripted work? To me a big difference is its seemingly, fleeting existence. A script is solid, known and revered, whereas devised work is a response without such form and therefore can appear to students, in some way, less valued. We study and learn a script. For its performance we build our character based on an author's intent and the director's vision. With devising we ask students to create a performance on a blank sheet, requiring the involvement of an entire creative team from the outset.

The original stimuli should be experienced by the entire group at the same time. Directors become facilitators, working with the techies, costume, set, makeup designers and ensemble as one. Making decisions and choices together. In this way students become personally invested in the piece and the ownership is total. The emotional investment in the work will often result in its creators needing to be the performers, with the final piece being something they realise together.

Devising is an enriching process and something all students of drama should experience. Your role as their teacher is to give the blank sheet a heading, a beginning, something inspiring, something that matters! The role of this book is to provide that inspiration in an easily accessible format, so that you may kindle that fire.

2

About This Book

To write a *list* of 200 topics for devising drama would be simple. After all, pick a noun, any noun! Pick an adjective or even a verb for that matter! The list would be endless ... and pretty pointless. Take for example the noun 'War'. Given to students as a stimulus this solitary noun; a state of armed conflict is not enough to work with. It's too little, too much, too vague and way too confusing. But give it a frame, a focus and the possibilities start to become less daunting. Without guidance students will eventually find their own focus, but not before wasting valuable time on negative disagreement rather than discussion. Give them a stimulus like 'War through the ages' or 'Families during wartime' and the focus becomes sharper. Introducing patriotic songs of the times and some of the poetry and propaganda, showing them newspaper articles from the time, letters from soldiers, paintings and film footage, provides younger students in particular with ready-made characters and emotions, enabling them to feel like a soldier, a wife or child at home. Read what they read, dance as they danced, to feel something of what they felt ...

Devising as a group requires a high level of collaboration and a strong framework. If either is lacking, any creativity often descends into flights of wild fancy and a myriad of dead ends; where excellent ideas are lost or diluted in an often awkward attempt to tie everything together to fit a story. As an examiner I've seen work where the students have quite obviously fought for three months and finally compromised over a contorted story which allows for 5 different 'remarkable' ideas to have a disjointed presence. A piece which doesn't flow, or flows like a soap opera with an often mundane and highly predictable storyline. Where artistic vision is lost, confused or simply paying lip service to the given title.

Conversely, the best devised work I have seen has been where students were given inspiring stimuli, presented through a variety of media with clear guidelines, including an awareness of shared responsibilities and skills.

Over 28 years I have been lucky enough to see many passionate, powerful performances from students who have worked with a topic that engaged them through focussed research-based practical experimentation. This always begins with a teacher, who grabs their attention and enables them to stay focussed and passionate, spending time preparing and having the right materials and ideas for their student. This book is a collection of such materials and ideas with ready-made frameworks for teachers, enabling students to make important connections and devise meaningful theatre on 200 topics. Divided into two parts, Part One contains 9 chapters exploring aspects of devising and Part Two the 200 topics.

Devising is often seen as the 'easy, fun bit' of drama. Enjoyable yes, but it's never easy. Even writing about it is confusing! I began easily enough, with what I knew worked, and then, because I'm a teacher, I tried to categorise and give an order to the 200 topics. I found myself looking at eight categories which were: *Conflict.* We're always involved in some kind of conflict and it makes for good theatre! *Faith and belief.* Historically, it's what much of the conflict has been about! *The human condition.* Birth, death and love and everything in between! *Human behaviour.* Those things we do to each other. *Our world.* Its past, present and future. *Science and technology.* From the plough to Facebook. Fake tans to fake news. *Power and authority.* Who has it, how they acquire it and hold on to it, and those who are powerless. And finally, *Human expression.* How we express ourselves.

As I worked I realised it was impossible to categorise in such a formal fashion, it's all connected; all linked; wonderfully, historically, scientifically, spiritually, artistically and confusingly! I realised I was in danger of compiling an overdose of inspiration. What was needed was a strong, clear starting point for each topic, offering as much or as little stimuli and research opportunities as needed to spark the creation of meaningful theatre.

The result is 200 highly focussed, stand-alone, yet interconnected topics, to make us sit up and pay attention. The things we talk about, that don't go away, that make us laugh, cry, protest and more. 200 things that matter.

With scripted work, we ask students to communicate the meaning of the playwright. When devising, we ask them to create and communicate meaning. Let's not begin by confusing them with vagueness or information overload! A stimulus should excite and offer possibilities not dazzle, confuse and confound.

Before introducing the topic/stimulus to students, it is important to involve the group in workshops/games that get them thinking and moving in sympathy with the chosen topic. For example, before a unit on Homelessness or Poverty offer a workshop on status and play control games.

The introduction or presentation which follows the workshops can take a number of forms. With some it may be a thought-provoking quote or statement which sparks meaningful debate/discussion. Indeed at times, insightful or provocative words in an intimate, sensitive environment are enough to get the process started. With other groups/topics there may be a need for a well-prepared, stimulating presentation (PowerPoint/Prezi or short film montage, perhaps with music) to present a theme. With larger groups or where a whole class is working on one topic, I create an installation in the drama space to stimulate the senses as the class enters. I try to make it as multi-sensory as the subject allows, with students prepared, and able, to enter the space engaged and ready to suspend disbelief. Sometimes it's enough to simply ask students to describe a feeling or emotion. Each topic and group should be considered separately. I would never, for example, introduce subjects like, *Body image* (070) or *Suicide* (059) with an installation. You know your students.

The purpose of this book is to provide as much or as little as you need to enable your students to begin the creative process.

With Unit 006 'WWI The Home Front'. Having previously played Control and fear games, students entered the space which was scattered with paper poppies over white sheets around the performance area. Music of the era played, and videos projected on the walls and ceilings. Later students were shocked by mortar explosions (SFX) and flashes of light followed by Soldiers' prayers and poetry. I present this with teacher(s) in role, but if that's not your thing, consider recruiting older students to assist. Allow moments where students are left to explore the space and interact with the materials, in their own time. I believe students who share an experience are less likely to argue and prone to have a similar vision/intent.

Depending on the age of the students, any shared experience should be thought provoking, perhaps even shocking them into a reaction/discussion. As part of the stimulus package for each group, in addition to the materials shown for presentation/installations, I include relevant newspaper articles, images, research, stories, plays and movies. There is also a section providing song/music and examples of where dance and other art forms have been used to express similar ideas. Finally offering differentiated suggestions on genre, practitioners and how their style/methods could be incorporated, including suggestions on how design students can use their skills to inform and contribute to a finished piece.

Groups should **not** be given *everything* and certainly not all at once. A steady drip feed of material/stimuli, using only what they need, allows for more development of ideas and is less overwhelming.

When I talk about 'multi-sensory', I realise it's not entirely possible to re-create the smell or taste of war, but we can make very strong associations. Some topics lend themselves better to a range of senses. (See emotion memory workshops in Chapter 8.) Use the tech at your disposal, make it relevant, make it real.

I am also very aware that not all drama departments and spaces are created equal. However, we are all in the business of enabling students to suspend disbelief and know what can be done with the resources available.

This book provides a multitude of ideas for 200 topics. But remember it's a 'guide' to '*Stuff that works*' not 'The be all and end all'.

Each topic is numbered and clearly indicates (links) to other themes, encouraging students to think synoptically and create relevant and meaningful theatre. The links are also useful for planning and progression.

Each topic is presented in the following way:

Topic number 001–200	Topic title. *'A referenced quote to start a discussion'*	
♣♣	**Suggested group sizes/makeup and age appropriateness.** With devising, the size and make up of a group will affect methods and final product. Age can be dependent upon the subject/stimulus being explored with maturity and sensitivity playing an important role.	
⚑	This section is about *introducing* the topic, through an installation or a discussion, a questionnaire, a shocking fact, a headline or a statistic. Sometimes a well-placed question is all a group needs to run with an engaging idea, at other times they will need more. **Workshops/games:** Starter suggestions to warm students toward the chosen theme. Explained in Chapter 8. **More controversial:** Usually a single sentence or fact (the devil's advocate), to encourage more able students. An *extension task* for the more adventurous! **Questionnaire:** Where appropriate, compile a fun questionnaire for each group, based on their topic. I may suggest a few questions but the idea is, you know them better. Encourage students to answer individually, only sharing later.	
☼	This section contains tasks and suggestions. Where to look and what to look for. Many of these are excellent for personal research/homework. **Look at:** Steers students to a specific, relevant area connected with the topic. **Research:** Suggests people, places and things connected with the topic. **Search for:** Sometime we need help seeing through the vastness of it! The web can lead us all down the wrong path sometimes. In this section I give exact wording to help refine searches, helping students narrow it down and stay focussed. **Look at the language:** This section examines how words are often used or misused in everyday speech/media, giving students different perspectives. The way we manipulate a word could be the key to the title or the inspiration for a piece. **What the papers say:** Headlines and stories. How the press handles the topic. Suggested articles. Any suitable resources newspapers may offer on the topic. Facts, statistics, and the less obvious, but worth thinking about . . .	
Stimulus	🎭	Some props/artifacts/images are instantly recognised by an audience and carry a simple message or meaning like: authority, love, peace, danger. However, what I am referring to here may never feature in a performance, its function being to start a conversation or trigger an emotion, which may inspire a piece of original theatre. By encouraging students to engage with, examine, explore, research and even invest emotion in an artifact is a hook to grab their attention and hold it throughout what can be a lengthy process.
	📖	Three suggested novels and/or reference books connected directly or indirectly with the chosen topic.
	📝	One piece of poetry which resonates on one or more level with the topic.
	🎭	Three different plays that share themes with or raise questions about the subject. It may be the whole body of work or selected scenes.
	🎞	Suggested movies/TV series. Note that film/TV may not be directly about the subject. It may simply be of the same era or genre or contain specific relevant scenes. Relevant documentaries and YouTube videos. All movies carry ratings. It is not suggested you show entire movies, only selected relevant scenes.
	♫	Songs/music to inform, and inspire. It could be the lyrics or simply the rhythm. Try not to simply be influenced by the lyrics. Often there is more to it. Mood/atmosphere or just the music itself. At times lyrics lead the devising simply because they are compelling or emotive. I often find that just music can complement instead of becoming the narrative. At times a song is included for its ironic value (juxtaposed) . . . Could be simply a background sound. A great source of emotive music scores can be music from the movies. Atmospheric/powerful and sensitive with no lyrics.
	🎨	Paintings, sculptures, photography and installation relevant to the topic. Simply symbolic, or a direct response to the theme. A painting or sculpture could also inspire the set design.

	Based on what my students and I have done or what I have seen as a visiting examiner/moderator. Some will be straight advice on production/practitioner/genre. In some I describe something I've been involved with or seen which has been particularly memorable. In some cases there will be more than one style/practitioner suggested, to present a piece. Where appropriate, I have suggested practitioners or theatre companies whose work is relevant. Also included here are ideas about staging, set, lighting and costume.
	An assessment of the risks from a teacher's perspective. What to look out for and what to guard against. From physical dangers to causing offence to other faiths/beliefs. Students' personal experiences with death, and their age/emotional development, influence their ideas on the subject. The media is full of images of death. A student may have experienced death of a family member or friend, even a pet and we as teachers have to be sensitive to this before considering topics which may even touch upon it. Know your students, in this respect you are the expert!
	This section helps teachers make connections quickly for teaching, extra inspiration/extension tasks and planning. I do not name every possible link. At times, everything links! I have listed those which have a potential to work as an extra stimulus.

3

Choosing The Right Topic/Theme

Knowing your students

This book gives 200 topic suggestions, some quite specific, for example historical events like *Hiroshima*, whilst others like *The Heart* are open to much wider interpretation. However, all 200 carry suggested multi-sensory stimuli to provoke those important first emotional responses and discussions that lead to successful collaborative devising. But, what to choose?

It should be something that matters, something your students care about. A topic which engages, that makes them curious or indignant, thoughtful and fired up! Remember it has to sustain their interest throughout what can be a lengthy process. If it doesn't engage them, think how their audience might feel!

I've always been inspired by images and music but for some it could be a quote, a piece of literature or newspaper headline that fires the imagination. Within every group there will be students who are moved/inspired in different ways. For this reason, I suggest a range of stimuli for every topic, not to set before a group hoping there will be something for everyone, but with the selective sensitivity that knowing your students affords you.

With devising, students should feel free to explore confidently as performers or technicians. and in order to achieve this you must *know your students*. If you have taught them for years, you will know them enough to at least understand group dynamics and individual abilities. If they are new to you, as is often the case, it is vital that you get to know them as quickly as possible in order to select appropriate themes and stimuli which enable real group collaboration.

I talk a lot about *knowing your students*, but how does this relate to devising? Some of the topics are age sensitive with each of the 200 listed carrying suggested age ranges. However, you are best placed to judge the appropriateness of a subject and not solely based on age. Who is in the group? You must be sensitive to their capabilities and their vulnerabilities. Of what they could do and what they should never do! What to expose them to and what to protect them from.

There are difficult, highly sensitive topics, which should not be *given* to students, rather offered as part of a choice, when they begin to look in that area. I included a number of highly sensitive issues because we need to offer choices on subjects that can touch our lives. In particular with older students, such material should be there for you to share with them if they so choose.

Just as allowing students to have free rein in choosing any script they want to perform is to invite calamity, so it is with devising, perhaps more so! *'The whole world and everything in it'* may be inspiring, but it's also a mind-numbing overload. We should provide a strong supportive framework for students or risk them simply getting lost in the vastness of it all. Without such a framework, students are often drawn to sensation for its own sake, producing confusing and often tasteless art.

To begin with, who do you have in the room? What are their *abilities*, and just as important, their *affinities*?

Ask them:

1   What have they done before?
2   What are they passionate about?
3   What are they studying in other subjects?
4   Do they have a knowledge of the techniques used for the making of Drama?
5   Can they use these techniques to communicate meaning to an audience?
6   Do they know why playwrights use the techniques they do?
7   Can they name any practitioners associated with these techniques?
8   What are their preferred style/genres?

The Skills Audit

Part of knowing your students is what I call the *skills audit*. Most of them are keen to perform, but what else can they do? Often a student's skill in another area can lend itself to theatre and enhance both the piece as a whole and their individual performance. Students seldom volunteer what they do in other subjects. Why would they? The skills audit is a way of uncovering those extra skills/interests that could contribute to an interesting piece of theatre. Some skills very obviously lend themselves to theatre, others less so. Students with an identified skill or talent often possess confidence, and this in itself is transferable and enabling. The *skills audit* explores the idea that students can bring other skills to Drama, ones which they may never otherwise reveal. During the audit it is important to explore how the various skills within the class can be sensitively exploited by a group seeking to make their own artistic statement with their chosen topic. So, what might these skills be? The acrobat, the ballet or street dancer, singer, musician, amateur magician, parkour runner, martial arts student, juggler, tightrope artist. Those with another language, sign language. The technicians, designers, artists, carpenters, costume designers and makers, DJs and rappers – they all have transferable skills.

Not all students will exhibit a skill, they may instead have an affinity, a passion, or an expertise. Creating meaningful theatre as a group is about taking risks. Like all risk taking, it's daunting. The comfort students feel when using their own expertise in a performance or devising context can help overcome nerves and embolden artists, who in turn help and inspire others. The mantle of the expert! Confidence is infectious, some students only need the example of others.

Your students are imaginative, creative, artistic, emotional, empathetic, generous, agile, adaptable and multi-talented. Often they just don't tell you! So ask them: What other things do you do? At times they will be reluctant to share, especially if it's a new group, but they will eventually really warm to it. Encourage students to show you and the class what they can do. Get them to make a list of their skills in their drama journal (Chapter 7) which, apart from including the skills they acquire throughout the course, should also proudly proclaim the skills they bring and share. I strongly believe that when first introduced to devising, students should work within their personal realm/comfort zone before expanding into wider society.

4

Devising Techniques
(A Simple Set of Rules)

'OK class. This is my favourite part of drama. You are about to start creating your very own pieces of theatre! You have total creative freedom. This is what you're going to do!'

It's every drama teacher's dilemma. The contradiction of giving a format or even guidance to creative freedom! The great appeal of devising is that sense of creative liberty, the freedom to take on a subject close to your heart and say something. But close to whose heart? and what exactly are you going to say, and how? and to whom? Even working alone we can become distracted, diverted, lose direction and sight of the very thing that inspired us. The sheer amount of great ideas, the endless flow of information, opinion and vision. Great intentions can become diluted, frustrating and ultimately, tiresome. Multiply this by a group of 4 or 5 talented students with free rein and they end up wasting time and doing very little with a lot, when they should be doing a lot with a little. Based on personal experience, I have set out below, a series of techniques which, whilst encouraging the free flow of creativity, retain the sharp focus required for successful theatre.

Games and exercises. Even when we have a definite topic, the problem with creative freedom is where to begin. For me it's what all good drama begins with: a game or workshop to get them in a frame of mind which suits the chosen topic. Drama teachers have their favourites and in Chapter 8 I have detailed the ones I have used with the 200 topics.

Introducing the topic. If students have a shared experience, they will have shared ownership of the work they are developing right from the start. This should excite/provoke them, to ensure their final piece will do the same for their audience. Each topic carries suggestions on how to achieve this.

Initial responses. When students react to the stimuli, whether as shared feelings, improv, dance or artwork, it should all be recorded. Allow a fixed, adequate time frame for this. (See *Streams of consciousness*.) Make time for quiet contemplation or rowdy responses, all the while recording the energy and emotions of those initial reactions. There must always be *adequate* time for this response. Avoid at all costs situations where their reactions have to wait until next week! They should never go home or to their next lesson without having had time to reflect and record.

A great fun exercise used by *Frantic Assembly* is to put together a *questionnaire* for each student, based on their topic. It is a gentle, disarming way of gathering information based on personal experiences which the group then shares. The questions '*Have you ever . . .?*' Or '*Describe a situation where you . . .*', etc, lead to light-hearted, shared experiences and comparisons. This should be done before any research as it is about students' individual experiences/thoughts and feelings.

Research. Students should be given time for focussed research, which they conduct independently over a period of time. (As homework.) Each of the 200 units contains areas for directed research. The more students know about their chosen subject/material, the more empowered their imaginations become. Try giving each member of a group a different task (or in pairs) for homework so that 'class time' is about collaborative making. Each task can be taken from the highlighted sections – **Research: Look at: Search for: Look at the Language:** and **What the papers say:** But also consider the art, literature and music research areas listed. Extension tasks could involve students investigating the **links** and exploring the connections between theirs and other students' work or from the sections entitled, **More controversial.** In this way each member of a group comes to sessions with a different view of the chosen topic/stimulus. This brings fresh energy and material with which to devise. Students come wearing the *mantel of the expert* and this empowerment transcends the whole process.

Practical exploration. The fruits of student research should be explored practically through rehearsal/workshops as part of an almost simultaneous process, with them entering sessions ready to discuss and try out/improvise shared yet juxtaposed ideas. A group's dynamic is a vital source of energy in any collaborative creation.

Style. Consider style at an early stage. We should prepare our students with a working knowledge of a number of theatrical styles/genre and practitioners/ theatre companies. Groups should develop and research those that really interest them and for which they have a talent (Chapter 7). Encourage them to explore a number of the elements of the theatre, like mime, movement, stillness, sound, music and lighting. Creatively experiment with staging and levels. Don't be afraid to move away from naturalism, instead working to create strong visual images through physical theatre.

Drip feed. Students often grab the initial stimulus idea and fly with it. However, there are times when they require new energy or simply refocussing. Each of the 200 topics contains suggestions of relevant literature, music, movies, plays and paintings as well as newspaper articles and suggestions about language. I suggest that these are drip fed as necessary to keep the interest/energy levels high.

Feedback. As the process continues, encourage students to watch other groups' rehearsals and feedback their understanding of what is being created. Feedback should be a part of the process and offered at regular intervals. Remind students of their original artistic intention and ask if the feedback they're receiving suggests they're still on course.

Write it down! What do we want to say? Establish the group's 'artistic intention' and put it on paper as soon as it becomes apparent. Encourage students to write down all decisions. Apart from making notes and sketches during the process (Chapter 6), it can be useful to film sessions and the ideas they try out. Explore individual objectives within the group. Why do they want to make this piece? Get them to write it down and then share. Based on this they can record a group statement of artistic intent.

Consider your audience. By asking, who will they be? What students want to say to and show them, and how do they want that audience to feel once they've sat through the performance?

Time management. Too much time can be the enemy of devising! Students should know they have a performance date and that time is not necessarily on their side!

Best practice. Expose your students to some of the great contemporary devised work available. Including designers (Chapter 7).

Streams of consciousness. Give students a blank piece of A3 paper. Place a photo/image in the centre. This could be a photo of a person, newspaper picture or a photo of a chosen artifact. Having looked at/studied their photo they should write down (or draw) what the image says to them. Write/sketch without rules or direction, no *Spelling, Punctuation or Grammar*, just record on the sheet: words, memories, smells, feelings, emotions . . . When the sheet is full (allow time). Remove the image. What is left should be a jumble of words, sketches, scribbles with a blank square/rectangle in the middle. Students should consider everything on the paper and respond with a word or phrase which best sums it all up. This should be written in the blank space and is the response to the original image. The start of the story or a title. How would you represent this in a tableau? This process could be straight from image to a physical response but writing it down can be a useful stage as well as a way of recording the direction of a piece.

Artificial Intelligence. There is a place for AI to act as a tool for further generating/combining and generally experimenting with students' own ideas. Improvisation prompts using keywords from Apps like ChatGPT can be fun and spark new ideas/directions for students. (See Unit 162.) As with any search your input prompts should be precise. Scaffold a story/ Freytag.

Using improvisation. Improvisation is often seen as a way of '*getting a laugh*', and whilst it can be entertaining in its own right, it is not all that improv is about. Improv should not be used exclusively, rather as another important tool for actors. It can be used to explore meaning in a given text but also as way of exploring a stimulus/idea in the devising of new work. Improv is fun but it should come with rules. Train your students to have a good set of improvisation skills, accepting change, being able to accept each other's ideas, to be chivalrous with fellow performers and to say 'yes'. Avoid blocking or asking questions. Always trying to physicalise, using the body to *show* instead of vocalising helps free the imagination.

Hot seating. As a way of developing a character, establishing motivation, feelings and emotions. Don't get bogged down with story/plot.

Experiment. With devised work, a *story* may only begin to emerge as rehearsals progress but also consider that with some work the *story* will not be the '*be all and end all*'. Encourage students to use contrast and juxtaposition, allowing their audience to view things from a different perspective, to feel challenged, perhaps even uncomfortable. Try using humour, where perhaps none is obvious. Play around with time, using flashforward/back. Use multi-role with serious intent. Break the fourth wall, use choral speaking and/or narrative. Third person narration. Narration of movement, narration of intent through monologues/soliloquy. Play around with pace and pause. Try stillness and silence to explore tension. Challenge your students by asking what happens when they introduce music. Encourage them to consider movement, highly choreographed and stylised work? Encourage them not to get bogged down with the plot or involved in writing page after page of dialogue. Require them to get physical and use space/ levels, to take an idea and perform it in a small confined space, then in a much larger one. Look at how gestures get larger, proxemics change and the dynamics alter. Experiment with design, sound and lighting and consider different forms of staging.

Designers should contribute to the initial response and planning stages just as the performers do. Responding as designers/technicians. As each stimulus means something different to each performer, so it is with designers. They should be part of every discussion and rehearsal, recording what works and what does not.

The joy of devising is all about inspiration and creative freedom. Inspiration is everywhere, it is our job to ensure students don't overdose on it. Encourage them to get up and do a lot with a little, to be focussed and honour their ideas.

5

Examples
(Case Studies)

In this chapter I take eight specific examples from the list of 200 topics and give a personal insight into the process my students went through to create a unique piece of theatre in each case.

Each study should be read in conjunction with the relevant numbered unit.

Unit 007 Hiroshima

The quote was: *'The genius of Einstein leads to Hiroshima'* (Pablo Picasso – Spanish Artist).

I worked with a group of fifteen 17-year-olds.

A significant factor was that the students had studied this event as part of their history syllabus.

There is a lot of photographic evidence of Hiroshima and Nagasaki along with many eye-witness accounts (as with all images of death, be sensitive to each individual in the group).

I wanted the stimuli to focus on the speed and initial silence before the almost total destruction, enabling the students to feel a sense of shock and wonder, followed by horror.

In the lesson immediately before, I involved the group in body sculpting and soundscape workshops.

First session. I began with an empty studio with chalk outlined bodies on black stage blocks which we had lightly dusted with talcum powder and ash. When the students had all entered in silence under very low lighting, I used a quick flash of light and brought in dim lights to reveal the body outlines, before projecting images of Hiroshima after the bomb. A SFX of a high wind was slowly replaced by *Threnody to The Victims of Hiroshima* by Krzysztof Penderecki.

I left the lights low, lit candles and we sat in silence to remember the dead. After ten minutes I asked each student to record in writing or sketches, their thoughts/feelings about the event. They then shared one meaningful sentence each.

I asked the students to stand and hold hands. They were then asked to blink their eyes, before informing them that it was during just such a blink that 80,000 people were wiped out at Hiroshima.

I shared images of newspapers from the time, in particular how the Japanese papers had reported the bombings. We then considered that a second bomb was dropped on the city of Nagasaki 3 days later, killing an estimated extra 74,000 men, women and children. The clock on the wall was stopped at 8:15. Bob Dylan's *A Hard Rain A-Gonna Fall* played as images were projected on the walls of the moment everything stopped. Including: the piles of bodies, the flattened city, the remaining dome. The real shadow images of bodies on walls. From the projections of the black nuclear shadows of Hiroshima, students assumed tableau positions and brought the victims to life.

Students were given specific research to undertake as homework. Some looked at the National Archives special topics pages, others, the website for the Hiroshima Peace Memorial. Two of the more musical students were given the *Hibaku Piano* to research. Others were asked to research The Ground Zero 1945 collection of paintings by the survivors. And the bronze sculpture '*Wind of no Return*' by Hisashi Akutagawa. Another pair looked at how the world's press covered the events of 6 August 1945. '*A Noiseless Flash.*'

All research/homework was shared with the class during the next lesson. Four groups of varying sizes formed and took different aspects of what they felt and knew about Hiroshima. One group of four were most moved by the images of victims on the walls after the blast and gave them names, a family, history and lives. From this a profound piece of theatre took shape. Another group used dance and brought the same 'shadows' to life. Some excellent and very moving work was done using the highly stylised movement (slow motion), exaggerated facial expressions and the stylised mime of practitioners like Lecoq and Berkoff in particular.

See suggested literature, music, movies in Unit 007.

Unit 033 Mirror, mirror

Quotes used: '*If art reflects life, it does so with special mirrors*' (Bertolt Brecht – German poet, playwright).

'*The mirror is my best friend because when I cry it never laugh's* (Charlie Chaplin).

'Life is like a mirror, we get the best results when we smile at it' (Unknown).

I began with 5 groups of four 13-year-olds. We started by playing the game 'Mirror images' with simple daily routines and building to more complex. We also used repetition exercises.

I set up a number of mirrors in the drama space. Including a long dress mirror and some smaller hand-held. I asked students to take a long good look in a selected mirror. To study what they saw. How did they feel and who or what was looking back at them? Had they chosen a full mirror or a smaller one. What was the difference? Looking at the whole of your reflection and surroundings or just your face.

We talked about our reflections and how similar/different they were from ourselves.

During this session I gave out a questionnaire about their favourite 'selfie'. We considered that our image is never far away from us, whereas in history, images of ourselves were less common. The class talked about how our selfie image was different, that mirrors somehow lent another dimension.

As research-based homework students were asked to look at various superstitions attached to mirrors in different cultures, Narcissus, the history of mirrors and to find images of mirrors as portals. Students also investigated links with other units: Old wives' tales, Fairy tales, Beauty, Dreams and Nightmares, Body image and Eating disorders.

In the second session, students presented their findings to the class.

After each student had presented their research and taken notes they returned to their groups. From discussion and practical experimentation one group split into two pairs. This perhaps came from the original mirror-image games. One pair worked on a beautiful piece which involved a mirrored dance performance to Arvo Pärt's *Spiegel im Spiegel*. The pair began by walking to a mirror in a dance studio and watching each other, tie ballet shoes and put hair up, before building to a dance. They finished by leaving and switching off the light.

Another group worked on the idea that mirrors can transport us to parallel universes where we are opposite/different versions of ourselves.

One group looked at soliloquies shared with a reflection. Others looked at the role of mirrors in movies.

Another pair looked at a completely different person looking back at us, using the mirror to communicate with the departed.

One pair was inspired by Michael Jackson's *Man in the Mirror*, working with the idea that the reflection brought about change in the man himself.

Some groups used a frame to signify the mirror with a performer/s on either side, whilst others found this too confining. Interestingly no groups wanted to use small hand-held mirrors. One group experimented with using projections as reflections but kept returning to the problem that 'it wasn't a reflection and didn't work'. I have seen an excellent piece working with the distorted images of a broken mirror, which for safety reasons used projections.

A group of four worked on body image issues based on the mirror.

See suggested literature, music, movies in Unit 033.

Unit 067 Alzheimer's and dementia

Quotes used: *'Alzheimer's disease locks all the doors and exits. There is no reprieve, no escape'* (Patti Davis – American Author, daughter of Ronald Regan).

I worked with mixed pairs of 14-year-olds

Students warmed up with repetition exercises and soundscape workshops. We then played memory games. With older students, emotion memory work can be significant.

I placed the following artifacts on a stage block under a single spotlight. An hour glass, a wedding ring, a bunch of wilted flowers, an old family photograph, a hand mirror, a wallet/purse, a hat, a wristwatch, pen and paper and a pair of glasses. It acted as a memory test at first but more importantly as links into old age/elderly relatives.

I used Frantic Assembly's Chair duet workshops to create physical bonds between pairs. One young and patient, the other elderly and needing guidance. We followed this with a sensitive discussion about older relatives. We talked about memory. I asked, 'Have you ever forgotten what you were about to say, why you went into that other room? Imagine being like that all the time, forgetting people, places, memories slipping away, lost in a fog. Even forgetting who you are, who you were.'

Students were given specific individual research topics. Dr Alois Alzheimer and his research into mental illness. Alzheimer's Society. The 'Forget Me Not' Project. US Against Alzheimer's. Alzheimer's Association. alz.org. The MOMA Alzheimer's project and investigate the work and life of Artist and Alzheimer's sufferer William Utermohlen. *'Conversation Pieces.'* Students also investigated the links with other units like: Old age, Death, Assisted Suicide, Mental health, Family photos and The stranger.

My father (who had Alzheimer's) wrote everything down, on his doctor's advice. Reading it back now reminds me it was a stream of his consciousness. I use stream of consciousness with students as a starting point writing about their oldest relatives' memories.

As a class we watched the video by NIH 'How Alzheimer's changes the brain' (YouTube).

We worked on emotion memory and grief (Stanislavski).

Working in pairs, students were inspired by the personal statements of sufferers and their relatives, literature and sections from the selected films.

Much of the work focussed on the relatives and how they lose their loved ones. One pair used highly stylised movement (slow motion) with exaggerated facial expressions, to show sufferers swimming through a fog (Berkoff).

We had been to see *Lovesong* by Abi Morgan (Frantic Assembly), as a result duet work was very prevalent in some pieces.

Two students created a pair of shared soliloquies based on their initial work with streams of consciousness and emotion memory.

One pair worked on how music evoked memories and emotions. They used Neil Young's *Helpless* and through projected images and dance they replayed memories, let them fade and become fewer until the screen went blank.

See suggested literature, music, movies in Unit 067.

Unit 087 The heart

Quotes used: *'The heart is forever making the head its fool'* (François de La Rochefoucauld – French Cardinal).

Working with older students (15+) in small groups of 2–4.

Workshop. Soundscapes. Using the heartbeat (Iambic pentameter) we used drums and movement to walk through '*If music be the food of love play on*' (*Twelfth Night*), because they had been studying the play in Literature. There are many sonnets which would work with the iambic pentameter. Feel the heartbeat. di-DUM di-DUM di-DUM di-DUM di-DUM.

I projected images of the heart in advertising. *I ♥ New York etc.* . . . and the heart as a symbol of a healthy lifestyle.

The *Oxford English Dictionary* has an entry of 15,000 words for the word *heart*. Most of these are as metaphors. We explored some of them as a class.

We also **Looked at the Language**: A Heart of stone, of glass, of gold, of a warrior, of a devil, of a woman, of a child. A constant and universal metaphor. It can be hard, dark, soft, set on, broken, torn, shattered, given, melted, won and moved. Instructed to think with our heart, to give of it, to feel with whilst all the while looking after it.

Directed **research** included: Why the ancient Romans made such a big connection between the heart and love. The American Heart Association. The British Heart Foundation. Early anatomical studies (da Vinci) to modern prints. The work of Chanelle Walshe. Search for images of the heart. Now search for images of the heart as a metaphor ... Discuss differences/similarities. Students also investigated the links with other units like: Fairy tales, Love, Grief, Divorce,

The list of songs about the heart is almost endless but an interesting exercise is to get students to select their current favourite, then those of their parents and grandparents. What has changed?

The heart as a metaphor was the most popular focus for the students. The more adventurous had some quite abstract ideas and ran with the idea of the heartbeat and physical theatre. Some were very literal using red filters/ lighting and SFX; the first thing an unborn child hears; the heart monitor and flatlines. Others looked at a broken heart both in love and literally. One group looked at how Shakespeare used the heart in his works, representing love, jealousy, bravery, cowardice, sorrow, life, patriotism etc. . . .

With such a vast amount written, sung, painted and performed about the heart, I found it useful to get students committing their artistic intent to paper at once as many found it difficult staying focussed and keeping it simple.

See suggested literature, music, movies in Unit 087

Unit 117 Aberfan

Quotes used: *'The past is a foreign country: they do things differently there'* (L. P Hartley – British novelist).

'Tip Number 7, at Aberfan became a symbol of corporate negligence towards the working classes' (Unknown).

'Buried alive by the National Coal Board' (A father of an Aberfan victim).

'The angel of death has been abroad over the land' (John Bright – British Radical and Liberal statesman, in his 1855 speech opposing the Crimean war).

I worked with students aged 11+ in small mixed groups. On other occasions I have worked on large ensemble pieces.

I have a personal connection to this piece. I was eight when tip 7 buried Pantglas Junior School,19 Miles down the valley in a similar junior school in Pontypool. Drama work I have been involved in about that day has always been through a child's eyes, with music/singing and poetry being a large influence.

Workshops. Status, confinement and *control games.*

Included in the small stimulus presentation was an NCB: (National Coal Board) recruitment poster, the images of the children's coffins, a candle, a doll/teddy bear, a toy car, Primary school desk and chairs, a school clock stopped at 9:13 am.

Directed **research** included looking at the findings of The Aberfan Disaster Tribunal Report.

The National Library of Wales Education Services. https://hwb.gov.wales. What the Papers said: The original article in the *Weekly Merthyr Express*, and in the world of art; the *Cofiwch Aberfan Mural* 2020. *Aberfan* by Dorothie Field. *Partially Buried* by James Rielly. The sculpture *21. 10. 1966*

144 9:13AM by Nathan Wyburn at the Rhondda Heritage Park S.Wales. Students also investigated the links with other units like: Death, Coal, Class, and even The Titanic as a way of looking at how the working classes suffered in that and other disasters.

Students shared their findings and recorded each other's work. We also gathered in one place all the terrible statistics they had found.

As a class we watched *Aberfan – Valley of Sorrow.* (1966) British Pathé. And *The Price of Coal* by David Alexander (YouTube).

Aberfan: The Fight For Justice BBC Cymru Wales.

The Netflix series *The Crown* Season 3, Episode 3) also has a disturbing account of the events and what followed. We also listened to parts of the album *Cantana Memoria* by Karl Jenkins

I found a really useful teachers' resource: TES Aberfan – the story of a disaster. https://www.tes.com

Groups also investigated how badly the families were treated as the NCB tried to dodge responsibility in the years that followed. The tribunal found the NCB entirely responsible for the disaster. Yet no one was ever prosecuted or even lost their job over what happened.

Docudrama was the favoured genre with most students. Perhaps due to the amount of material available in this form. Ensemble work, examining class and justice produced strong pieces drawing comparisons with disasters like the Titanic and Grenfell. We did not focus on individual stories, rather looked at the vastness of it, then focussed on the lost children. For older students. Dance piece/physical theatre. Projected images (Eddie Ladd).

See suggested literature, music, movies in Unit 117.

Unit 126 Domestic violence

Quotes used: *'Domestic violence is an epidemic, and yet we don't address it. Until it happens to celebrities'* (Nelsan Ellis – American actor and playwright).

'Culture is no excuse for abuse' (Davinder Kaur – British author).

I worked with a mixed ability group of 15-year-olds. I strived to ensure a gender mix of students who were comfortable with one another.

I introduced the topic with the workshop *That hurt* and played some *control games*, using boy/girl pairs wherever possible.

The class worked with a 'happy family' making a freeze frame of a wedding photo. They observed a slow disintegration of the relationship. Establishing normality, then introducing levels of tension. (Discussions on what parents/adults/partners argue about.)

In workshops, tension was developed into conflict with students creating soundscapes of violent actions and words.

Directed **research** included: Looking at high profile celebrity couples cases.

How domestic violence is reported by different newspapers.

Students researched statistics in their own town. Domestic violence against men.

How the police (The Law) deals with domestic abuse, historically and today.

Cultural excuses made for violence against partners. Domestic violence and art.

Songs about domestic violence. Students also investigated the links with other units and were surprised at just how many and varied they are, from PTSD to Commedia dell'arte.

A great resource is Art-sheep.com domestic violence with a link to twelve very powerful videos/works. (Watch them first and select according to your students.)

The class looked at the work of Italian artist and activist aleXsandro Palombo whose paintings use Marge Simpson, Wonder Woman and Wilma Flintstone as victims of abuse from their partners.

Two students discovered during their research into *domestic violence and art*, the Mexican artist Alberto Penagos, who has created a series of works entitled 'Violence against women'. From this work on suffering one group concentrated their piece on a mime about facial expression and how pain and silent suffering exists behind the façade of many happy families.

Another group's research led them to watch a piece from *France's Got Talent* 2018. Dakota and Nadia dance against domestic violence on YouTube. Well worth a watch, in particular for physical/dance pieces. The music industry has much to say on the matter and students were greatly influenced by some very powerful music videos available.

Much of the work was stylised and highly choreographed. There was a strong use of music and dance. Soundscapes. Minimalist sets were the popular choice.

Others went for *realism*. Kitchen sink drama (Pinter). With hidden tension, pauses and threatening silences.

One group focussed on the much less discussed domestic violence against men.

A very memorable piece involved an elaborate Punch and Judy set with a Commedia dell'arte style look at violence.

See suggested literature, music, movies in Unit 126.

Unit 153 The Moon

Quotes used: *'He made the moon to mark the seasons'* (Psalm 104:19).

'Everyone is a moon, and has a dark side which he never shows to anybody' (Mark Twain).

'O, swear not by the moon, the inconstant moon' Romeo and Juliet, Act2, Scene2 (Shakespeare).

Our nearest neighbour and a source of wonder for all ages!

A memorable piece for me, was with a large ensemble of 22 11-year-olds. I began by turning the drama space into a kind of planetarium and showing Moon 101 National Geographic available on YouTube.

Research included: Asking students to find five facts and five myths about the moon.

How the moon affects our behaviour.

The moon's symbolism, signs and meanings in different cultures.

Images of the moon. Articles about the first moon landing Apollo 11 in 1969.

More controversially some students researched: Lunatics and the moon, full moon and evil/werewolves/pagan worship.

Students shared their research findings to the group and everyone took notes. I presented my own facts (as needed). For example: 'It' controls the tides, our moods, and eclipses the sun. Written about, sung about, painted, prayed to, sworn by. 'It' measures the months and changes shape, 'it's' always there. Everyone who ever lived, walked beneath 'it'. 'It's' haunting, symbolic, beautiful and different every night. My challenge was simple: 'So what would you say about "it" in a piece of theatre?'

As a class we considered the moon in art and music. Students also investigated the links with other units like: Old wives' tales, Witchcraft, Mental health and the Sea.

Another excellent starting point is to search for *The NASA Gallery* and look for *Moon Facts*.

Students tasked with looking at the Moon in music came up with: *Dark Side of The Moon* by Pink Floyd. *Walking On The Moon* by The Police and *The Whole of the Moon* by The Waterboys. There are many more and I reminded them of classical pieces like Beethoven's Moonlight Sonata.

Students were fascinated by moonlight and used projections, and gobos to illuminate the space. Dance/physical theatre using the light to highlight the power of the moon over the tides/nature were a popular idea with classes talking about the moon in *A Midsummer Night's Dream*.

We talked about Pagan rituals too but by far the most popular with young students was our fascination with the moon as a destination.

They created a simple yet affective lunar surface and with music, dance and projections, performed a beautiful piece of theatre based on the moon waiting for man to return . . .

With such a vast subject, in particular for younger students, I found there had to be a definite focus, especially for large groups.

See suggested literature, music, movies in Unit 153.

Unit 187 Surveillance society

Quotes used: *'Under observation, we act less free, which means we effectively are less free'* (Edward Snowden – American whistle-blower and former National Security Agency contractor).

'We should not be comfortable or content in a society where the only way to remain free of surveillance and repression is if we make ourselves as unthreatening, passive, and compliant as possible' (Glenn Greenwald – American journalist, lawyer and writer).

I worked with a group of 14- and 15-year-olds in small mixed groups of 3 and 4.

For my first introductory lesson I had used the schools CCTV camera to film my drama class lining up outside the studio. I played it back to them whilst playing *Every Breath You Take* by The Police.

I asked the students if they were aware of how many CCTV cameras they walked past over the weekend. I asked if they felt the cameras were simply protecting them: or was there something more sinister? In 2020 there were approx. 5.2 million CCTV cameras in operation in the UK. In the US the figure is far greater. Then there's your multimedia connections! Think those are one-way?

What does your profile look like? What is Big Brother's name? MI6, Alexa, Microsoft, McDonalds, Amazon? We had some very interesting conversations and it appeared that most students were quite comfortable with mass surveillance.

Research homework included: What is metadata? Look at the work of Trevor Paglen (Photographer). Look at Surveillance Art. artandsurveillance. com

What is the history of CCTV? Where did it start and why? Explore how CCTV is used to curb antisocial behaviour in your local area.

More controversially, how did mass surveillance during the COVID pandemic help to keep us safe?

Look at your government's explanations of how CCTV is used in your community.

What is Government data collection? Are traffic cameras for our safety or to raise money?

The first session feedback of their research findings revealed that they were now far less comfortable with the whole idea of 'being watched!' The overall question was 'Do *they* really need to know so much about *me*?' Opinion was divided on mobile phones and the collection of metadata.

I asked them to read the BBC article by Ivana Davidovic, dated 18/11/2019, 'Should we be worried by ever more CCTV cameras?'

As a group they looked at how differently people behave when they know they're being watched and used some simple movement-based work to highlight the differences.

The students were struck by the chances of misinterpretation of what is seen and the visual aspects more than the recording of our data. (Left for another time perhaps!) The result was a very bold project . . .

An open air performance on the sports field was recorded by a high up CCTV camera from a fixed perspective. The angle ensured that the faces of most of the performers were not seen. The performance was of an apparent argument and ensuing violent fight. The audience watched it on a large screen and were asked to answer questions on what they had seen (not heard). The group then entered the studio and re-performed the same piece. Seen from the new angle, with music it became apparent it was a dance and not a fight. Audience surprise and reactions (which had been filmed) were projected on the backscreen before the dance had finished! Point made . . .

See suggested literature, music, movies in Unit 187.

6

Keeping a Devising Log Within Your Drama Journal

The Drama Journal

The journal is a vital tool in all drama classes and never more so than when it becomes the sounding board for group devising work.

I've always given drama students a plain artist's sketchbook. Their first ever homework is to cover it with 'What the theatre means to me'. What comes back can give you a real insight into each student. From the brightly coloured collage of theatre publicity to the blank question mark.

For all students, regardless of age, the journal is a place to reflect and self-evaluate. Do I mark it? I make a point of regularly looking at it, jotting pencil notes in margins to show I have read their work, that I'm interested in it, but I don't give grades. Suggestions and positive feedback, but never a number or letter. Assessment rather than evaluation, leaving that for the final piece . . . They can sketch, write rough notes/plan, whatever they want. It's theirs. My only requirement being, that it is regularly updated.

The journal should be treated as a working notebook and present at every session, with students accustomed to using and sharing them.

Aside from a list of the skills they will be expected to cover during the course, I also encourage students to write about those skills they bring to your classes (see Chapter 3 'The skills audit').

The Devising log

I distinguish the devising log within their drama journal by asking students to turn it over and start from the back; keeping them separate yet linked.

Students should record their initial response to the stimuli followed by detailed documenting of the creation and development of ideas, including analysis and evaluation of individual contributions to the process and how they wish to communicate meaning in the final piece.

This can be in the form of notes, sketches, work and details of discussion within the group, mind maps, photos of work in progress, role on wall, hot seating, stream of consciousness etc. Details of their personal research and where it led them. Feedback and their reactions/responses. A List of the skills, passions of the group. . . what they want to say.

I have ten essentials regarding the devising logs, that all students:

1   record their initial response to any given stimulus,

2   get the dramatic aims of the piece down on paper,

3   start thinking about the audience early on,

4   answer the question, 'What is the point of the piece?',

5   record how they have developed the piece in each rehearsal,

6   list research: sources and results, style/genre, structure and form,

7   get into the habit of analysing and evaluating their own work and that of others at every stage of the process,

8   comment on what has worked and what hasn't,

9   reflect upon the process they have been through in order to develop and refine their initial ideas and intentions into a final devised piece. Both as an individual and as a group,

10 foster a willingness to share these notes/observations.

Getting into the habit of making notes each step of the way will make it easier to write up the whole process if required for a presentation or a written exam. It is worth bearing in mind that students who enter devised work for exams will be required as part of their entry to show a working journal or log which will need to cover the entire process. Such evidence will need to show teacher supervision and authentication.

Including video journals within the logs, whilst very useful, is not a replacement, devising demands, your intentions, original ideas and thoughts to be in writing.

7

Styles and Practitioners
(Referred to in Part 2)

Styles

In order to create provoking, interesting art it is important to experiment with different styles of performance. Considering a stimulus for your students with a performance style in mind enables more informed decisions about artistic intent and what they want their audience to experience. It is useful that they have a number of styles in their repertoires, with which to experiment. Through improv with different styles it will become apparent which will work best for exploring their chosen theme. They may want to go for the very theatrical, involving many different dramatic techniques, or a piece of physical theatre using movement and non-verbal communication. Students should become familiar, through their own research, with an increasing range of dramatic styles.

Below is a list of some suggested styles/genre.

Absurd. European, using multiple features to express a tragic theme through comedy. Anti-literary, anti-theatre.

Comedy. Intended to make an audience laugh, funny, amusing and satirical in tone, usually with a happy ending. However, comedy can be used to relieve tension or make an audience laugh before shocking them. Brecht's Tickle and Slap (Spass).

Commedia dell'arte. Usually improvised comedy with stock characters. Stylised, recognisable costumes and characters, mask and exaggerated gesture, panto/slapstick, 'lazzi', originated in 15th-century Italy.

Epic. Didactic drama avoiding illusion. Using '*Gestus*'; *alienation effect*, to distance the audience from emotional involvement; Brechtian; the absence of realism; political.

Expressionism. A modernist movement. European and later USA, the depiction of emotional experience rather than physical reality.

Forum. Boal. Theatre of the Oppressed. Using theatre to achieve socio-political aims. Audience interaction exploring different options to deal with a presented problem or issue.

Immersive. Theatre which relies on audience immersion such as promenade or performance art, audiences become part of the performance itself.

Melodrama. Usually a sensational plot, highly emotional and dialogue led, over sentimental, using music and exaggerated love, revenge and lust, plot over character.

Metatheatre (Metadrama). Theatre which draws attention to the fact it is unreal by the use of a play within a play for example, or reflecting comedy and tragedy together.

Naturalism. Late 19th- and early 20th-century European movement. The creation of a perfect illusion of reality on stage, given circumstance, Stanislavski.

Physical. Making use of the body over the spoken word, the body being the primary communication with the audience. Dance, mime and body props.

Political. Theatre that comments on political and social issues.

Realism. Late 19th and 20th century. Everyday people and everyday problems. Believable dialogues spoken by believable characters in common settings. Stanislavski.

Stylised. The method of showing personality or mood by a character's movement onstage. There are specific techniques such as mime, dance, gesture and movement. Practitioners like Berkoff use stylised movement in their works, including robotic movement, slow motion with an ensemble, exaggerated movements/facial expressions and the use of asides. Elements of Greek theatre were also stylised.

Symbolism. In the theatre, symbolism may be achieved through costume, colour, props, character and even that character's movement. The symbol stands for or represents another thing. Props and set often have symbolic significance which audiences identify quickly.

T.I.E. Theatre in Education. Usually highly interactive, an aid to learning, uses forum techniques.

Tragedy. Terrible events, death/downfall of heroic characters, an individual's fate decided due to a moral weakness or flaw.

Verbatim. Documentary theatre (although documentary theatre is less about people's testimony and more about events). Using pre-existing documentary material as the source of a play about real people and events. Could be TV documentary, newspaper or even a diary. Voice, movement, interviewing and storytelling.

Practitioners

Artaud, Antonin. Early 20th century. Theatre of Cruelty, movement, gesture and dance, masks and puppets, shocking the audience, attack on the emotions, shocking action and images, striking costumes, minimal dialogue, symbolic objects.

Berkoff, Steven. Contemporary. Highly stylised movement (slow motion), exaggerated facial expressions, stylised mime, direct address, exaggerated vocal work, tableaux, mask, ensemble, minimalism, Lecoq.

Boal, Augusto. Late 20th century. Theatre of the Oppressed, social and political change, Interactive Theatre, Forum Theatre, Image Theatre, Invisible Theatre, short scenes with a strong image that the audience can easily understand and identify with.

Brecht, Bertolt. Early 20th century. Direct address, narration, episodic structure, political message, multi-role, 'gestus', placards, Spass/'Tickle and Slap', music and songs, alienation, montage, didactic, gestic, epic theatre, no fourth wall.

Elliot, Marianne. Contemporary. Directs using all aspects of theatre making, Brechtian techniques, physical theatre, puppetry, music and song.

Godber, John. Contemporary. Political comedy (Hull Truck Theatre), Action theatre, 'imagination, elliptical language, character and transitions', multirole, stylised realism, comedy.

Grotowski, Jerzy. Mid-20th century. Poor Theatre, not encumbered by lavish set or costume, little or no props, focus on the physical skills of the actor, the bare space, non-traditional space, paratheatre, non-commercial, Experimental Theatre.

Lecoq, Jacques. Mid-20th century. Physical Theatre, movement and mime, seven levels of tension, gesture, masks, uncomplicating, mimodynamics. See 7 levels of tension.

Meyerhold, Vsevolod. Early 20th century. Constructivism, anti-illusionistic, non-naturalistic, stylisation, use of rhythm and music, mask, the grotesque, robotics, biomechanics, symbolism movement.

Rice, Emma. Contemporary. Improvisation, music and song, ensemble, Shakespeare, storytelling, socially relevant, Kneehigh, no fear.

Rees, Marc. Contemporary. Performance, installations, sense of place, physical theatre, interdisciplinary, multi-media, work rooted in history, culture.

Stafford-Clark, Max. Contemporary. Political/ensemble theatre, improvisation, research, workshop process, flashcards, Out of Joint.

Stanislavski, Konstantin. 19th–20th century naturalism, the fourth wall, feeling of truth, the magic 'if', emotional memory, muscle memory, circles of attention, intonation and pauses, naturalistic movement, the three-dimensional character. Stanislavski's 'System/Method'.

Teal, Polly. Contemporary. Mix of physical theatre and text work, narrative very rarely linear, feminist theatre, adapts texts for Shared Experience.

Companies

Inspire your students by exposing them to the work of great companies out there like:

Complicité. Contemporary. Physical theatre, extreme movement, surreal imagery, Lecoq, storytelling, experimental approach to subject, space, form, sound and the actor.

Forkbeard Fantasy. Contemporary. Multimedia, projections and lighting, strong visual elements, elaborate and intricate sets.

Frantic Assembly. Contemporary. Physical Theatre, Theatre of the Absurd, cross-artform multimedia, humour, spatial awareness, focus and observation, non-naturalistic, music, 'Round by through' and 'Chair duets'. A leading contemporary practitioner/company.

Gecko. Contemporary. Stylised/physical theatre, epic, the complexity of human nature, 'athletic, honest and emotional'.

Imaginary Body. Contemporary. Visual style, magical realism, reality and fiction.

Kneehigh. Contemporary. Broad eclectic approach, storytelling and adaptation, honour the story, comedy, live music onstage, audience interaction, song and dance, multi-role, puppetry, inventive use of props.

Punchdrunk. Contemporary. Immersive, interactive theatre, promenade theatre, non-traditional, site sympathetic.

Shared Experience. Contemporary. Expressionism, 'inside out', the conflict between the inner and outer self, physicalisation of emotions, the hidden subtext, conveying meaning/feelings without words.

And in the USA

ERS. The Elevator Repair Service Theater NYC. Artistic Director John Collins. Original ensemble works. Using elements of slapstick comedy, hi-tech and lo-tech design, literary and found text. Very personal, highly choreographed style.

Lookingglass Theatre Company combines physical and improvisational rehearsal process centered on ensemble with training in theatre, dance, music, and the circus arts.

Pig Iron Theatre Company. Interdisciplinary ensemble dedicated to the creation of new and exuberant performance works. Expanding what is possible in performance by creating rigorous and unusual ensemble-devised works.

Waterwell. A group of artists, educators and producers dedicated to telling engrossing stories in unexpected ways.

8

Workshops and Games
(Referred to in Part 2)

Small children do it and most of us continue throughout our lives with flights of fancy, *what if*'s and day dreams. I'm a cop and you're a robber, I'm a soldier and you're dead. It all begins with a game. We accept it without question because, those are the rules: when you're playing, when you're 'making it up'. Improvising! Each version of the story is different, reinvented, fresh. If you ask students to form a circle and tell a story one line each, it often gets bogged down. But get up and play and there are no limits. So, it stands to reason that when making theatre we should start by playing. The unspoken rule of children's play is that we accept what is happening, we suspend disbelief. We are chivalrous with each other's ideas. Even the most serious of workshop can start with make-believe. Playing lowers our guard, it liberates imagination, allows us to risk failure, to take chances and gets everyone speaking the same language. With devising, much of the initial exploration takes place through improv and the physicalisation of a thought, emotion or concept. Games which encourage expression through movement are fantastic places to start, whatever the chosen theme.

Games also serve a purpose at the end of a lesson/workshop, either as a plenary to reinforce learning or simply grounding students before continuing their day.

I use the terms workshop/games throughout the book to describe that ever growing armoury of excellent games, warm-ups and workshops at our disposal. Games are fun, they focus the mind, teach discipline and develop skills. Below are suggestions to compliment your own favourites for use with the 200 topics in Part 2.

Alienation. Form a circle: exclude a member of the group, (perhaps with prior agreement), the circle moves to exclude, with the person now outside the circle, the 'outsider'. Through mime only try to re-enter the circle, not by force. Exclude by turning backs, whispering together or silence. At a given point allow/welcome the outsider back in. Describe how it felt to be the outsider and then an insider . . . Emotion/feelings.

Animal crackers. Place students in an improvised scenario. A doctor's waiting room with chairs, for example. Allow a few moments to establish themselves before asking them to open their folded paper. Each piece of paper contains a different animal. They should think about the animal and its characteristics. We are not asking them to become the animal, rather to allow their animal's traits to inform gesture, posture, movement and even vocal quality. (Physicalising some of the qualities.) So we don't want barking dogs or squawking parrots, rather, impatient pacing or bobbing up and down nervously on a seat.

Accusation! With prior arrangement, if necessary, one student is accused, either of taking something or making a hurtful remark. The rest of the group point and accuse. (Similar to the Alienation game.) Describe how it felt. Did it make students more or less sympathetic to others who may be falsely accused? Look at body language of both the accusers and the accused.

Body sculpture. Students facing each other in pairs. A sculpts B into everyday action shapes. Reading a newspaper, walking a dog, running etc. Use the backs of finger tips to gently move the other person and fine tune the finished sculpture. You can also try this without touching the 'statue' and speaking the commands instead. Ask a number of students to sculpt one statue. Works well with mirror imaging.

Brown Eyes/Blue Eyes. Look at *The Jane Elliot experiment*, where a group are excluded, made to feel inferior based on the colour of their eyes. (It could be the colour of their socks!) Variations of this can be sensitively used as a workshop with more mature students. Reverse this half way and see if those who suffered prejudice are less, or more likely to want to extract revenge. Should be thoroughly researched and explained before sensitive use with small groups as it was a highly controversial and thought-provoking social experiment with several flaws. However, as a workshop for students well versed in the suspense of disbelief I am of the opinion that it can be a valid stimulus.

Chinese Whispers. Two variations. Spoken and physical.
Spoken is the time-honoured game, where a whispered sentence is passed around a circle and the changes noted/discussed. The physical version is where you enact a mime (unseen by a selected 5 or 6 others) for one student who then re-creates it for one of the chosen 5/6, who then re-creates it for the next and so on until the final student shows what they have seen (or think they have seen). The class discusses what has changed and why. Good for reinforcing the need for strong obvious movements in mime, avoiding ambiguity and the use of muscle memory.

Circles of attention. Requires actors to consider a radius around them when they are speaking/performing on stage. Think of *three circles* around you. Stanislavski.

The *first circle* is up close and personal. The conversations we have with ourselves. Imagine being in a small, confined or crowded space but not interacting with anyone else. Keep yourself isolated in your own bubble. The contemplative state. Deep in thought, under stress, confused, a madness, perhaps muttering to oneself. All energy is focussed inward.

The *second circle* is the conversation you have with another person or at most two. The focus of your attention and energy is on that person only. Your task is to engage them in the circle, paying particular attention to them.

The *third circle* demands the most energy. A high status performance in which you engage everyone! Everything you think, say and do must be directly addressed to the whole audience.

The circles create an awareness of *how* you send your focus out into a space (your audience), and not simply what is said.

Confinement. Staying/performing in a confined/defined space, remove a sense, restrict movement, or ability to speak. How does it feel to be restricted? How do we compensate?

Control games. Ensemble moving as one without conversation. Ask the group to move around the space, stopping and starting on a clap.

Try clapping as one in a circle using only eye contact. Work toward the group being able to move as one, stopping and starting in leaderless unspoken agreement.

Try *Boal*'s **Columbian Hypnosis**: Working in pairs students lead each other around the space with one following the palm of the other's hand which should be placed around 6 inches (15 cm) from their partner's face. Those led should follow whilst maintaining the distance. Allow the pair to swap roles. Is it easier to lead or to follow?

Emotion memory. *Stanislavski.* A technique which asks us to forget about *acting* emotions but to *feel* them. It's not about faking it. As children we knew how to 'turn on the waterworks' use 'crocodile tears' because we are able to remember the feeling of sadness. Ask students to recall a sad moment and re-connect with the feelings, thoughts and emotions of the moment. (Use with caution.) The same can be done with anger, happiness, fear etc . . . Emotional or Affective Memory asks the actor to recall a memory similar in detail to one they are trying to portray and through empathy, live the moment instead of simply reciting it. Emotional memory is a particularly useful tool when using improv to explore a feeling/mood/tone for a devised piece.

Energy games. *Mr Hit* goes to tag. If being chased, call out name of someone still in the game. That person becomes Mr Hit. If caught you are Mr Hit for one go but then you are out.

Boots and Bats. Pairs back to back – half are boots, half bats. When your name (boot or bat) is called you turn and chase partner. If they reach the wall they're safe.

Splat! In a circle, one player in the middle is the shooter. Point at a player in the circle and shout 'Splat!' as loud as possible. The splatted player ducks down whilst the players either side shoots (splats) each other. The loser (slowest) sits down. If the splatted doesn't duck they are also out. Play until only two left and have a shoot-out draw! Reaction times and spatial awareness. *Zip, Zap Boing!* And many more.

Fear. Get the students to find a space of their own and stand in it. Get them moving about, keeping at arm's length from each other. Ask them each to decide upon the one person they fear and to keep as far away from them as much as possible whilst still moving about the space. Keep them in your sight at all times. Be wary, alert and protect yourself. Don't let the one you fear know you fear them! Now decide upon a protector. This person should always be between you and the one you fear.

Variations of this game are: Pick one victim, walk around the room feeling persecuted and feeling victimised. Try the opposite. You really like this person.

Gestus. *Brecht.* Students walk around the space neutrally, focussed and keeping to their own space. Teacher calls out stimulus words, for example *Hunger*, *Love*, *Fear*, *Homeless* etc. Students will form a *Gestus* in response to each stimuli. (The combination of a gesture and a social meaning/idea in a single movement.)

Get out of my way! Circle – one pupil is the 'victim'. Take it in turns to go up to them and say 'get out of my way'. If the 'victim' feels at all uncomfortable they step back and are replaced by the bully who then becomes the victim. No physical contact allowed.

Guide me! Exploring movement blindfolded. Being guided/helped by others around a space whilst blindfolded. Try a high kerb in a wheelchair. (See trust games.)

Grief. 3 Stages. In pairs students are given three simple scenarios. 1) A small child loses their teddy/doll. 2) A teenager's first heart break. 3) The death of a loved one. Each pair is allowed three words only. These are of their own choice and can be repeated as often or as little as needed in any order throughout three performances. The performances can be in any order but each must have an obvious ending. Only one chair is permitted, no props.

In the spotlight. Experiment with spot lights. Half in the light, lighting the face, creating tension in the darkness.

Levels of tension: 7 Levels of Tension Exercise (*Lecoq*).

1 Exhausted or catatonic. The Jellyfish.
2 Laid back. The Californian.
3 Neutral or the 'Economic'. No story
4 Alert or Curious.

(1–4 are everyday states).

5   Suspense or the Reactive. A perceived danger.

6   Passionate. A real danger

7   Tragic. The danger is realised. The body is solid tension.
Ask students to improvise a scenario with given levels

Lying (The burden of a lie). How does it make us feel, walk, talk? Three facts. All seem plausible, only one is the truth. Look me in the eyes and tell me, convince me. The group tries to guess which is true.

Memory games. Use a tray with 25 random objects. (Make them everyday objects like a rubber, a coin, a spoon, a stone, an empty jar etc . . . .) Place the tray in the space, either prominently or just to one side, depending on what you want to achieve. At some point take the tray away. Ask students to write down what was on the tray.

I went to market a bought a ***. Going through the alphabet for items.

Mirror image. In pairs, A and B. One is the person and one is their reflection. Begin with a simple copying exercise and build into a choreographed routine.

Muscle memory. Demonstrate the mimed doorbell. Keeping it always in the same place. Show how in mime, inaccuracy affects believability. Moving back to the same spot. Taking up exactly the same position at a table. Look at how we memorise moves in dance, console games, typing or playing the piano. (Works with mirror games/choreographed movement.)

Old man/woman walking. Training students to feel the immobility problems of the elderly. Using their arms to push themselves up out of chairs, Getting up from the floor. Pains in legs, knees and joints. Walk around with a friend on your back (Piggy-back). Empathy and the sympathetic study of how elderly people move, without parody.

Repetition exercises. To build focus. *Meisner*'s repetition exercise requires a performer to sit opposite a partner and make an observation about them. For example, 'You are looking at me'. The partner then repeats the observation back at them. The exercise creates a connection between the pair by requiring them to actively listen to each other. *Meisner* likened it to ping-pong. A foundation for emotional connection. After a while vary the connection by view point, for example 'You are looking at me', 'I am looking at you', 'I am sitting in front of you' and so on . . .

Repetition exercises for focus were also favoured by *Stanislavski* and *Mamet*.

Silent screams. Think of the things that make you scream. Terror, anger, frustration. Try to put all the feeling/emotion into that scream but without making a sound! Your face and body must convey all! Works well with tension exercises.

Soundscapes. With a group of students, ask them to close their eyes and imagine a place. For example, a busy train station or the seaside. Think of the sounds you hear there and list them. Using voice and body percussion only recreate the sounds of the place, sharing the various sounds among the group. Get one student to conduct the group, build and mix the sounds, experimenting with recreating the atmosphere of the chosen location.

Status. *Boal.* Using the levels 1–10 with 10 being the highest possible and 1 being the lowest of the low! I model them as a person coming on stage and giving their name and to say I am giving a talk on status! A bare stage with just a chair. From status 1 who hides in by the curtains to the guy who owns the stage. I use the chair at around status 3 being just able to sit on the edge. Status 9 using it backwards and 10 not needing it at all. I then ask students to improvise situations in pairs where one begins as status 1 and the other at 10, as the improv progresses there should be a smooth transition of each player slowly moving toward the opposite status. The rest of the group should clap when they believe the pair have become equal.

Using a table and three chairs. A performer should enter and take up a position (without moving the set). The challenge is for the next person to enter and take a position of greater status and so on until they reach a stalemate. All should be in silence and freeze frame. Lots of discussion about posture and gesture.

Once status numbers are established. Alter scenes by playing at different level 1–10. How does the piece change? What happens if everyone is the same status (10 or 1)? What if everyone is a 5?

Story circle. As the name suggests, students sit/stand in a circle and pass around in turn a sentence or word which builds into a story. In role as part of the circle you can change direction/focus if it is getting bogged down or there are long pauses, by adding, *fortunately* or *sadly*, etc. Can also be played using single words. Try introducing a theme or a starting point of high tension.

Super objective/pursuing a want. Explain super objective. Give students cards with an objective/want and ask them to cross the space. Can others guess what was on the card? How does pursuing a want inform a performance/action. Also **Walking the space** for physical theatre.

Sorry. In a circle each person says '*Sorry*'. The rule is, each time it must be given a different meaning. Try it with *insincerity, questioning, casually, wanting clarification, challenging, hurt, guilty, joking, embarrassed*, even *an apology*, Limit to just the word. Look at delivery/inflection and body language.

Stereotypes. Improvise simple stereotypes in mime only. This demonstrates how useful stereotypes can be in character work. Demonstrate simply to begin with 'gait', how a nosey person walks for example, leading from the nose. As a non-verbal exercise: choose a stereotype and reflect physically through movement, posture, gesture and facial expression, the characteristics of your chosen type. No physical contact at this stage, only eye contact. Once you establish characteristics, introduce a series of simple everyday improvisations.

That hurt. Work in pairs. **A** and **B**. Give **A** the line *'That hurt'*. and **B** the line *'I'm so sorry'*. Allow pairs to improv with their own situations before restarting and asking **A** to hold their face, as though slapped and see how this changes the improv. It can be more than a slap (knocked to the floor, which changes levels too).

The pointing game. Take a well-known monologue and demonstrate this game. The idea is you gesture (point at) what you refer to. Begin with a simple sentence like 'I love you', 3 gestures I, (self) touch heart, point at other person. Example Lord's prayer in Unit 026.

Trust games. Building on *Guide me*. Once there is trust, try guiding through called out instructions only using a calm voice, reassuring, authoritative etc. Build safely toward trust circles and falling and catching etc. Be safety conscious.

Third person narration. Students narrate the actions/intentions and thoughts of a performer on stage. For example: *She moves nervously around the room before sitting in an old arm chair. She wonders where everyone could be* ... It should be a commentary on the action and not instructions to the performers.

9

Lighting That Fire . . .

To ignite a passion, to set young minds off on a journey of research and experimentation, in which they explore a chosen topic, is a great responsibility. To then ask them to generate material through improvisation and other creative techniques, to fuel that fire, is devising. Your role is to ensure the fire never goes out, enabling them to refine the materials into a worthwhile and fulfilling piece of theatre. You must harness the power of collaboration and creativity, so that a story emerges which connects with audiences. You must be there to keep this on track, and yet not be in control, recognising that devising theatre is an ongoing and evolving process. There is no single 'right' way to devise a performance, every topic will present its own challenges and opportunities.

This is a book of recipes, feel free to experiment with a statement, a thought-provoking questionnaire, an image, language, a memory, a song, a poem, a painting or a book; a line from a play, a sculpture, a movie, a family photo, a headline, a trend, an injustice, or a ghost, not only as stimuli but also as integrated components of a theatrical work which will enhance impact and meaning.

Remember it doesn't always need bells, whistles and flashing lights, sometimes all it takes is a conversation, a controversial headline or quote. Followed by research and experimentation. Then lightly sprinkle with stimuli to keep the flame burning.

Enjoy experimenting with the 200 carefully selected topics, remembering to always consider the ethics involved in making art, such as representation, cultural sensitivity, and social responsibility.

PART TWO

Listing of 200 Topics

001   The suffragettes

		'Deeds not Words' (Emily Pankhurst – English suffragist).	
☙	11–15 years. Suits all-girl groups or mixed.		
⚑	**Workshops/games**: Role on wall. *Status games*, how it feels to be treated as inferior. **Look at**: Equal pay debate. Why is equality important? Mothers, daughters, rebels. Emily Davison, martyr or anarchist? Use film footage. *'Votes for women.'*		
🔅	Suffragettes on file. National archives educational resources. History of the Suffragette movement. **What the papers say**: Lots of newspaper archive material available. Horrible Histories. **Research**: The women's movement in the USA, Japan, Russia. Feminism. Misogyny, WWI, Victorian Britain.		
Stimulus	🐌	Banner, scarf, purple, white and green.	
	📕	*Unshackled: The Story of How We Won the Vote*: Christabel Pankhurst.	
	📝	*I Sit and Sew*: Alice Moore Dunbar-Nelson.	
	🎭	*Blue Stockings*: Jessica Swale. Scenes 2, 3 and 5. Great Monologues. S5 MRS WELSH's monologue. *Gut Girls*: Sarah Daniels. Act1, Scene 1 In the gutting sheds.	
	🎞	*Suffragette*: 2015 (12A). The soundtrack '*March of the Women*' by Smyth and Hamilton is a good piece to use to get groups moving and talking. *Enola Holmes*: 2020 (12).	
	🎵	*The March of Women*: Dame Ethel Smyth. *Sisters are doing it for themselves*: Eurythmics. *The Suffragette's Song*: Horrible Histories.	
	🎨	The Women's suffrage art project.	
🎭	Chorus work, dance and choral movement. Projections. Blank stage. Screens. Costume should be important but not complicated. Theatre of the Oppressed. Boal. Short scenes with strong images. Great opportunities for physical theatre/dance.		
⚠	A vast subject. Some students will need more teacher supervision.		
🔗	006, 018, 023, 066, 110, 115, 119, 130, 132, 146, 175, 200.		

002   Montgomery bus boycott

		'Each person should live their life as a model for others' (Rosa Parks – African-American civil rights activist).
⚥		13–16. Mixed abilities. Male and Female groups of 4 or more.
⚑		**Workshops/games:** *Status* and *super objective. Levels of tension.* **Look at:** The body language in Yoichi Okamoto's 1965 photo of President Lyndon B. Johnson meeting Martin Luther King.
☀		Birmingham Civil Rights Institute, BCRI (USA) has an excellent educational website. Library of Congress Rosa Parks classroom materials. **Research:** The Jim Crow Laws. Rosa Parks. Civil Rights campaign 1945–1965. **What the papers say:** *Montgomery Advertiser,* Sunday, 4th December 1955. *The Pittsburgh Courier,* Saturday, 4th January 1956.
Stimulus	🎟	A bus ticket and a police baton.
	📖	*My Story:* Rosa Parks.
	📝	*Rosa:* Rita Doves.
	🎭	*The Meeting at Mount Zion:* Charles Everett. *A Raisin in the Sun:* Lorraine Hansberry. Monologues: *For Coloured Girls Who Have Considered Suicide/When the Rainbow is Enuf:* Ntozake Shange.
	🎬	*Boycott:* 2001 (PG). *Hairspray:* 2007 (PG). *The Green Book:* 2018 (12A).
	🎵	*Sweet Home Alabama:* Lynyrd Skynyrd. *Southern Man:* Neil Young. *A Change is Gonna Come:* Sam Cooke.
	🎨	*The Struggle:* Jacob Lawrence. *Oh Freedom:* Barbara Jones. *Bus Boycott:* Scott Crockett.
🎭		DV8 or Frantic Assembly. Kneehigh (honour the story). Minimalist. Physical piece. Soundscapes, dance based. Immersive, punchdrunk.
⚠		There are movies which confront racism in the USA very forcibly. Age restrictions apply.
🔗		004, 016, 017, 061, 101, 128, 132, 133, 146, 174, 186, 189.

003 The disappeared (Argentina)

	'People spoke to foreigners with an averted gaze, and everybody seemed to know somebody who had just vanished' (Christopher Hitchens – English-born American journalist).
	16 upwards (able group).
	Workshops/games: *Status. Fear.* *'We want to know what happened to our children'. 'My Grandmother is still looking for me'.* Think about status and how and why it can rapidly change. Use levels of tension to explore. Master, servant.
	Mothers of the Disappeared. The dirty war. Teaching tolerance. Proyecto Desaparecidos. **Read:** Mario Bendetti's essay published in NACLA Report of November 1995. **Research:** The Abuelas. Argentine military junta. 1976 Jesuits. The guilt of the Catholic church
Stimulus	A Rosary, a photograph of a missing person/child.
	The disappeared: Gloria Whelan. *The Disappeared and the Mothers of the Plaza:* John Simpson. *Departing at Dawn:* Gloria Lise.
	The poetry of Roberto Santoro.
	Theatre against Dictatorship: Workshops/games of theatrical investigation. *The Disappeared:* David Holman. *The Madres:* Stephanie Alison Walker.
	The Two Popes: 2019 (12A). *Imagining Argentina:* 2003 (15). *The Mothers of the Plaza De Mayo:* 1985 (documentary narrated by Carmen Zapata).
	Mothers of the Disappeared: U2. *They Dance Alone:* Sting. Good tango pieces for physical work.
	Research the murals of Buenos Aires and the missing children. **Look at:** The photographic artwork of Marcelo Brodsky.
	Boal Theatre of the Oppressed. Lecoq. Grotowski. An ensemble piece. Black and white. Stark lighting/projections. Levels to depict oppression and light/absence of to represent disappearance. Stylised military uniform. Focus on fear and power over the weak/innocent. Physical work using tango.
⚠	Disturbing images and accounts.
	005, 043, 052, 063, 064, 079, 100, 115, 132, 133, 146, 174.

004   'I can't breathe'

		'Ignorance does not make you fireproof when the world is burning' (Nelou Keramati – Canadian author).
♟		Mixed ability/gender. Handled sensitively, all age groups.
⚑		**Workshops/games:** *Status. Control games. Confinement.* Hold your breath . . . How long before you had to . . .? Now imagine you couldn't . . .! **Look at:** The video evidence (if age appropriate). How did you feel after the death of George Floyd? Did you want to, or did you, do something?
☼		blacklivesmatter.com **What the papers say:** *The New York Times* has a set of teaching resources and ideas to help students make sense of the George Floyd protests, including lesson plans. Look around the world, at the victims of deadly systemic racism. **Research:** Adama Traoré, Paris 2016; Stephen Lawrence, London 1993; David Dungay Jr., Australia 2015.
Stimulus	💀	I can't breathe, hand held placard.
	📖	*Queenie:* Candice Carty-Williams. *The Bluest Eye:* Toni Morrison. *To Kill a Mockingbird:* Harper Lee.
	📝	*Instructions To The Jury:* (for George Floyd) Beau Beausoleil.
	🎭	*Gone Too Far:* Bola Agbaje. *Fences:* August Wilson. *A Raisin in the Sun:* Lorraine Hansberry.
	🎞	*When They See Us:* Netflix (4 part series), 2019 (15). *The Hate U Give:* 2018 (12A). *I am Not Your Negro:* 2016 documentary (12A).
	🎵	Watch/listen to (official video) H.E.R. 'I Can't Breathe'. *(Not suitable for younger students.)* *Mississippi Goddam:* Nina Simone. *Hurricane:* Bob Dylan.
	🎨	Look at: The BLM graffiti (33 powerful BLM murals – The Verg).
🎭		Verbatim theatre. Forum theatre. Theatre of the Oppressed. Boal. Ensemble. Using appropriate meaningful music and sound. Minimalist set. Black and white sheets/costume. Stark imagery. Placards of protest.
⚠		Teacher will need to be very aware of students and sensitive to group dynamics. Much of the media/film footage shows violence, profanity and racist behaviour. The slogan 'I can't breathe' is associated with George Floyd but they were the last words of Eric Garner, an unarmed man killed after being put in a 'choke hold' by a New York police officer in 2014.
🔗		002, 004, 017, 021, 025, 052, 057, 061, 063, 064, 066, 123, 128, 131, 138, 146, 149, 174, 175, 186, 197, 199.

005 Dictatorship

	'I don't care if they respect me so long as they fear me' (Caligula – Roman emperor).
⚑	14+ Mixed ability groups.
⚑	**Workshops/games**: *Status games. Confinement. Colombian hypnosis.* It is easier to lead than to follow. What do you think a dictatorship is? Can you name any? How do dictators achieve and maintain power? Define a dictatorship.
☼	The TES have a teaching resource democracy-dictatorships. (Available to purchase.) **Look at**: How freedom of the press is restricted in dictatorships. However, social media persists to challenge. **Research**: Modern day Afghanistan, North Korea. **What the papers say**: How the press is manipulated by dictatorships. Look also at public protest and graffiti. **More controversial**: What voice do the people of Russia have now?
Stimulus	Military uniforms. Jackboots.
	The Autumn of Patriarch: Gabriel Garcia Marquez. *The Feast of the Goat*: Mario Vargas Llosa. *In the Time of Butterflies*: Julia Alvarez.
	The Dictators: Pablo Neruda.
	Fear and Misery of the Third Reich and *The Resistible Rise of Arturo Ui*: Bertolt Brecht. *Andorra*: Max Frisch.
	Che: Part One: 2008 (15). *The Official Story*: 1985 (15). *The Great Dictator*: 1940 (U).
	Another Brick in the Wall: Pink Floyd. *Imagine*: John Lennon. *If You Tolerate this Your Children Will be Next*: The Manic Street Preachers.
	Los Cuatro Dictadores: Eduardo Arroyo. **Research** art which has been banned by dictators.
	Forum theatre. Theatre of the Oppressed. Invisible theatre. Boal. The use of satire. Brechtian theatre. Ensemble work. Lecoq/Berkoff.
⚠	Images within searches including the word '*dictatorships*' can be disturbing.
⚭	003, 008, 010, 061, 079, 100, 101, 107, 109, 110, 132, 133, 136, 138, 146, 147, 149, 174, 176.

006   WWI The Home Front

	'Two armies that fight each other is like one huge army that commits suicide' (Henri Barbusse – French novelist).	
🐝	11–15 Mixed groups. Encourage students to look at the family and how it was affected by war.	
🚩	**Workshops/games:** *Control games. Fear. Soundscapes.* Start with music/songs of the time. Saying goodbye to loved ones. Off to war. The great adventure. Role on wall. **Look at:** The propaganda of the time. Queuing for food. **Search for:** Language and imagery of WWI.	
💡	A large number of resources will be available through your Literature department and sites. War Poetry. The Imperial War Museum. The American Homefront. USHistory.org Voices of the First World War: life on the home front. A resource from the Imperial War Museum. **Look at the language:** For King and Country, For God, The enemy, Duty, Victory, Evil, Empire, British, Friends and Foe.	
Stimulus	☠	Letters from the trenches. Old photographs. Poppies. Rations tin. Gas mask.
	📖	*All Quiet on the Western Front:* Erich Remarque. *The Return of the Soldier:* Rebecca West. *Regeneration:* Pat Barker.
	📝	*Anthem for a Doomed Youth:* Wilfred Owen.
	🎭	*Journey's End:* R. C. Sherriff. *The Accrington Pals:* Peter Whelan.
	🎬	*War Horse:* 2011 (PG-13). *Private Peaceful:* 2012 (12) *Downton Abbey:* British period drama series, ITV.
	🎵	*Fighting for Strangers:* Steeleye Span. *Dance of Death:* Iron Maiden. *Long Way to Tipperary:* Irish music hall song.
	🎨	*Gassed:* John Singer Sargent. *The Menin Road:* Paul Nash.
🎭	Opportunities for naturalistic sets depicting home with stark contrast of the trenches. Monologues for letters home. Large ensemble pieces for war scenes. Stanislavski.	
⚠	Some war films, although PG-rated, can show graphic images.	
🔗	009, 014, 022, 025, 044, 052, 057, 064, 066, 071, 079, 085, 107, 115, 119, 132, 141, 148, 176, 178, 189.	

007 Hiroshima (A Case study unit, see Chapter 5)

	'The genius of Einstein leads to Hiroshima' (Pablo Picasso – Spanish Artist).
👥	15+ (but could be younger depending on focus). Mixed ability.
🚩	In the lesson before use the body sculpture exercise. (See Chapter 8.) See details in Case study, Unit 07, Chapter 5.
💡	National Archives Special topics pages (The Atomic Bombings of Hiroshima and Nagasaki, August 1945). Visit the many online sites. For example the website for the Hiroshima Peace Memorial Museum. *Hiroshima* by John Hersey, newyorker.com/magazine/1946/08/31/hiroshima **What the papers say:** Google images of newspaper archives of Hiroshima and Nagasaki. Look also at how the Japanese newspapers (*Japanese Times*) reported the bombings. **Research:** The second bomb dropped on the city of Nagasaki 3 days later which killed an estimated extra 74,000 men, women and children. **More controversial:** Did the bombings speed up the end of WWII and by so doing save lives?

Stimulus	💀	The ashes and dust were with an older group in mind as it represents the dead. We looked at the watches and clocks stopped at 8:15, the flattened city, the remaining dome, the shadow images on the walls.
	📖	*Hiroshima:* John Hersey. *Children of the Atomic Bomb:* Yamazaki and Fleming. *Death in Life: Survivors of Hiroshima:* Jay Lifton.
	📝	*Hiroshima Child:* Nazim Hikmet. *Hiroshima:* Gordon Whittaker.
	🎭	*After Apocalypse: Four Japanese Plays of Hiroshima and Nagasaki.* Translated by David Goodman. *Seven Streams of The River Ota:* Robert Lepage.
	🎞	*Empire of the Sun:* 1987 (PG) *Children of Hiroshima:* 1952 (Japanese film) *Silence Has No Wings:* 1966 (Japanese film). *Hiroshima:* 2005 (TV-12). *Oppenheimer* 2023 (15) *Hiroshima out of the Ashes.:* 1990 (PG). *Dropping the Bomb – Hiroshima:* A BBC Documentary.
	🎵	*Symphony No 5 'Hiroshima':* Masao Ohki (1953). *Threnody to the Victims of Hiroshima* Krzysztof Penderecki (1961). *Eve of Destruction:* Barry McGuire. *A Hard Rain A-Gonna Fall:* Bob Dylan. **Research** the sounds/music of the *Hibaku Piano*.
	🎨	**Look at:** The work of artists like Takashi Murakami and Seitaro Kuroda. The Ground Zero 1945 collection (paintings of the survivors). The bronze sculpture 'Wind of no Return' by Hisashi Akutagawa.

🏛	See details in Case study, Unit 07, Chapter 5.
⚠	Articles and accompanying images of Hiroshima and Nagasaki contain harrowing images and accounts.
🔗	008, 009, 014, 022, 052, 057, 079, 107, 119, 132, 157.

008   Refugees, evacuees and asylum seekers

		'No one leaves home unless home is the mouth of a shark' (Warsan Shire – British/Somali poet).
👥		11+ Mixed groups.
🚩		**Workshops/games:** *Fear. Control. Soundscapes.* What would make you leave everything you know and love? How do we treat those who seek shelter in our land? Refugees and asylum seekers are often dehumanised and portrayed as a threat to the host counties, try to portray both sides.
🔦		**Search for:** Gatwick Detainees Welfare Group. Amnesty International have created some excellent resources for a better understanding of the refugee crisis. See also UNHCR, the UN Refugee Agency. **Look at the language:** Is there a difference in the language used to describe refugees from the Continent of Africa and Ukrainian refugees? **Research:** Bibby Stockholm. How refugees contribute to our culture, our literature, art and film.
Stimulus	💀	Suitcases, passports. **Search for:** Images of refugees, evacuees and asylum seekers.
	📖	*Refugee Boy:* Benjamin Zephania. *Between Shades of Grey:* Ruta Sepetys. *Are You Happy with That?* An anthology complied by Hafan Books.
	✍️	*Immigrant Blues:* Li-Young Lee.
	🎭	*Hannah and Hanna:* John Retallack. *Refugee Boy:* Benjamin Zephania. *The Evacuees:* (Musical) Chris Adams and Michael Sullivan.
	🎞️	*When You Don't Exist:* 2012 (Amnesty International short film). *First They Killed My Father:* 2017 (15). *Malak and The Boat: Unfairy Tales* UNICEF (YouTube).
	🎵	*Émigré:* Alela Diane. *Bombs Turn into Roses:* Maya Youseff (Music). *Look into Their Eyes:* David Crosby.
	🎨	**Look at:** The works of Arabella Dorman, Ai Weiwei and Banksy who have all created artworks to raise awareness of the refugee crisis. *Kurdish Refugees* by MotionAge Designs.
🎪		The sounds of war, nightmare journeys, of discrimination and racism. Coming to a new country from places like Syria. Multi-role with simple modification of costume. Ensemble, choral movement.
⚠️		Be aware of the backgrounds/cultures of each class member and sensitive to audience experience.
🔗		010, 011, 013, 014, 015, 016, 023, 025, 052, 064, 065, 066, 072, 079, 084, 085, 088, 101, 106, 107, 108, 111, 112, 114, 122, 128, 139, 147, 149, 172, 174, 183, 186, 196.

009 PTSD (Post-traumatic stress disorder)

	'You wake up every morning to fight the same demons that left you so tired the night before, and that, my love, is bravery' (Unknown).
👥	15+ Mixed groups.
🚩	**Workshops/games:** *Levels of tension.* Explore the difference between sudden excitement and fear followed by solitude silence. Focus on the effects of PTSD on soldiers and their families. Once referred to and then generally ignored as 'Shellshock'.
🔅	Help for Heroes. Operation *We Are Here*. **Research:** NIHM. MIND. NAMI. National Centre for PTSD (US). PTSD UK. **What the papers say:** *Express* newspaper article dated 29/06/2020, 'Brave Army veteran who battled PTSD pens emotional poem on soldiers' struggles'. PTSD could be as a result of exposure to *any* traumatic event such as: domestic violence, sexual assault, child abuse, traffic/air accidents.

Stimulus		
	💀	I put together a PowerPoint presentation of returning soldiers from many conflicts set to Dylan's *Blowing in the Wind,* focussing not on their injuries but the expression on their and their family's faces.
	📖	*War and the Soul:* Edward Tick. *The Things They Carried:* Tim O'Brien. *The Invisible Injured:* Adam Montgomery.
	📝	*Mental Cases:* Wilfred Owen.
	🎭	*Pink Mist:* Owen Sheers. *Black Watch:* Gregory Burke. *Listen:* Matt Fox (Male monologue). *PTSD and Me:* Erika Renee Land (Female Monologues).
	🎬	*The Deer Hunter:* 1978 (X). *The Hurt Locker:* 2008 (15). *Thank You for Your Service:* 2017 (15).
	🎵	*Tears of a Warrior:* (Military PTSD song) YouTube. *Safe and Sound:* Taylor Swift. *Mars, the Bringer of War:* Holst.
	🎨	**Look at:** The work of Andy Farr, in particular his exhibition *Twisted Rose.* *War Trauma:* Krzysztof Grzondziel. *The Night:* Max Beckman. *Look Inside My Mind:* A UNSW Sculpture collaboration, Canberra, Australia.

🎭	Ensemble piece, lots of SFX cut to silence and darkness. Physical, strongly choreographed. DV8/Frantic. Homecoming parades for heroes with fanfares and flags superimposed with images of domestic violence and drug dependence.
⚠️	In particular if you work in a school/college which serves a military community, take great care and look at individual students. Although a valid piece of community theatre it is not always appropriate.
🔗	004, 006, 008, 010, 014, 022, 025, 027, 033, 048, 050, 055, 060, 061, 063, 064, 071, 073, 074, 077, 079, 096, 097, 107, 157, 174, 197.

010   Child soldiers

	'Child soldiers are forced to give violent expression to the hatreds of adults' (Olara Otunnu – Former President of the Uganda People's Congress).
	Small groups (mixed) 14+.
	Workshops/games: Play children's games (war) then watch the documentary: *Lost Children* 2005 (Ali Samadi Ahadi). Thousands of children are serving as soldiers in wars around the world. Boys and girls, some as young as eight! This isn't fighting for a country, this is exploitation.
	Research: Human Rights Watch. Child Soldiers: Childhood's end. United Nations International Labour Organisation (ILO). Amnesty International. As many as 250,000 boys under 18 years of age served in the British Army in WWI. Today chid soldiers are boys and girls who have been abducted and forced into military conflict. proof.org/child-soldiers Media for Social Justice,

Stimulus		
		A soldier's uniform. A teddy bear. Toy guns. Images of children playing happily/maybe playing soldiers contrasted with the horrifying images of child soldiers.
		First They Killed My Father: Loung Ung. *A Long Way Gone: Memoirs of a Boy Soldier:* Ishmael Beah. *To Zenzi:* Robert L. Shuster.
		Child Soldier: Richard Wlodarski.
		Far Gone: John Rwothomack. *Child Soldier:* J. Thalia Cunningham.
		Beasts of No Nation: 2015 (15). *Innocent Voices:* 2004 (R). *First They Killed My Father:* 2017 (15).
		Song for a Child Soldier: Ishmael. *Child Soldier:* FLBYZ featuring Paul Kelly. *Warchild:* Emmanuel Jal.
		Child Soldier: Banksy. *Child Soldier:* Yader Alejandro. *Child Soldier:* Derrick Colter.

	A group (7 students) filled the stage with children's toys and entered silently to sit and play as young children. They played alone and in silence, then slowly became vocal as they joined together. Their games became more physical until as an ensemble they fought each other and froze to blackout.
⚠	Some web images are upsetting. Teacher supervision.
🔗	005, 006, 009, 011, 014, 022, 064, 066, 069, 071, 079, 107, 109, 191.

011   The Rwandan Genocide

	'. . . and my eyes no longer gaze the same on the face of the earth' (Jean Hatzfeld – French journalist).
⚤⚥	13+ Mixed ability/gender.
🏁	**Workshops/games:** *Brown Eyes/Blue Eyes. Status games.* *'During 100 days in 1994 approximately one million Tutsi were murdered.'* Forgiveness and reconciliation. Having learned some of the history, discuss 'What would I have done if I had been there?' **More controversial,** The UN turned its back because Rwanda has no oil.
🔆	**United Nations.** un.org Africa renewal SURF (Survivors Fund) Solace Ministries. **What the papers say:** International Press Institute report (No. 1,2000). *'How the Media Missed Rwandan Genocide.'* **Look at:** The children of the Hutu perpetrators after the genocide. **Research:** How Belgium historically set Rwanda on a course of self-destruction.

Stimulus	☠	The skulls of Bisesero (photo) is a very powerful image.
	📖	*Machete Season:* Jean Hatzfield. *Christophe's Story:* Nicki Cornwell. *We Wish to Inform You That Tomorrow We will be Killed with Our Families:* Philip Gourevitch.
	✍	*Rwanda: Where Tears Have No Power:* Haki R. Madhubiti.
	🎭	*Children of Killers:* Katori Hall. *The Overwhelming:* J.T. Rogers.
	🎬	*Hotel Rwanda:* 2004 (12A). *Shooting Dogs:* 2005 (15). The documentary *'My Neighbour, My Killer'* (Gacaca Films).
	🎵	*Songs of Solace:* The Solace Gospel choir. *Do You Ever Wonder:* Lorne Clarke and Tom Flannery.
	🎨	The Kigali genocide memorial. Look at the work of Helen Wilson, Epaphrodite Binamungu and the fresco of Bruve Clarke (*Les Hommes Debout*) part of the Trail of Art in Brussels.

🎭	Historical event. Explore the tension of silence. Make characters and their intentions super objectives. Physical theatre/dance. Music of Solace Gospel (see Song/Music/SFX). Or Forum theatre. Boal. One group looked at how faith has helped the healing process.
⚠	There is a lot of information about the genocide. Young people's exposure to some of the information/pictures must be managed.
🔗	003, 008, 010, 012, 013, 016, 021, 044, 052, 061, 063, 064, 100, 107, 128, 141, 144, 174.

012   The Holocaust

<table>
<tr>
<td></td>
<td></td>
<td colspan="2">'The opposite of love is not hate, it's indifference'
(Ellie Wiesel Holocaust survivor).</td>
</tr>
<tr>
<td>👥</td>
<td colspan="3">11+ All students.</td>
</tr>
<tr>
<td>🚩</td>
<td colspan="3">Workshops/games: Status games. Confinement.
Take Edmund Burke's words, 'Evil triumphs when good men to do nothing.'
More controversial: Research The Jane Elliott Experiment: Blue Eyes and Brown Eyes.
Variations of which can be sensitively used as a workshops/games with more mature students.</td>
</tr>
<tr>
<td>🔆</td>
<td colspan="3">Search for: International Red Cross icrc.org for Holocaust WWII.
National Archives Timelines of WWII Anti-Semitic propaganda.
Imperial War Museums img.org.uk Teaching the holocaust to children.
The word 'genocide' was coined by a Polish Lawyer (Raphael Lemkin).
For teachers: https://holocausteducation.org.uk/</td>
</tr>
<tr>
<td rowspan="7">Stimulus</td>
<td>🐌</td>
<td colspan="2">Old shoes, suitcases, letters, dolls.
Yellow Star of David (to be worn on clothing).</td>
</tr>
<tr>
<td>📖</td>
<td colspan="2">The Diary of a Young Girl: Anne Frank.
The Dark Room: Rachel Seiffert.
The Boy in the Striped Pyjamas: Scott Boyne.</td>
</tr>
<tr>
<td>📝</td>
<td colspan="2">At Terezin 'Teddy' 1943.</td>
</tr>
<tr>
<td>📜</td>
<td colspan="2">Ghetto: Joshua Sobol.
Kindertransport: Diane Samuels.
Fear and Misery of the Third Reich: Bertolt Brecht.</td>
</tr>
<tr>
<td>🎞</td>
<td colspan="2">The Boy in the Striped Pyjamas: 2008 (12A).
Schindler's List: 1993 (15).
The Pianist: 2002 (15).</td>
</tr>
<tr>
<td>🎵</td>
<td colspan="2">Der Partizanerlid also known as Zog nit Keynmol: 1943 written in the Vilnius Ghetto and is widely regarded as the unofficial anthem of Holocaust survivors worldwide.
Tomorrow Belongs to Me: from the musical Cabaret.</td>
</tr>
<tr>
<td>🎨</td>
<td colspan="2">Drawings from Terezin Concentration camp (Children's).
Research: Yad Vashem Museum Jerusalem.</td>
</tr>
<tr>
<td>🎭</td>
<td colspan="3">Brecht as main practitioner and look at influences from 'Fear and Misery'. Placard. Strong lighting. Black and white.
Berkoff, mask, physical, exaggerated, ensemble.</td>
</tr>
<tr>
<td>⚠</td>
<td colspan="3">There is a lot of information about the Holocaust. Be careful to manage young people's exposure to some of the information/images.</td>
</tr>
<tr>
<td>🔗</td>
<td colspan="3">008, 011, 013, 015, 016, 048, 061, 063, 064, 066, 090, 106, 119, 122, 132, 144.</td>
</tr>
</table>

013   Ethnic cleansing

		'Forgetting extermination is part of extermination' (Jean Baudrillard – French author and philosopher).
⚥		16+ An able mixed gender group.
⚑		**Workshops/games:** *Status games. Circles of attention. Brown Eyes/Blue Eyes.* **Look at:** Culture/religion as a given circumstance. Personal accounts read by teacher.
☼		**Research:** Crimes against humanity, war crimes. The first forms of ethnic cleansing took place as early as the 9th and 7th centuries BC with the forced resettlement of millions by the Assyrians. More recently, six million European Jews during the Holocaust. Bosnia. Rwanda. Darfur. Chechnya. East Timor . . . **More controversial:** The Homestead Act in 1862, USA. Russia and The Ukraine. Israel and the Palestinians.
Stimulus	🎭	I use students' drawings only.
	📖	*Exterminate All The Brutes:* Sven Lindqvist. *Nana's Shoes:* Aisa Softic. *Ethnic Cleansing and the Indian: The Crime That Should Haunt America:* G. C. Anderson.
	🎭	*Hannah and Hanna:* John Retallack. *Scenes from 68* Years:* Hannah Khalil. *The Clearing:* Helen Edmundson.
	🎞	*Behind Enemy Lines:* 2001 (12). *As If I Am Not There:* 2010 (18). *Shrek:* 2001 (U). An evil man who exiles all the fairy tale creatures to a swamp. (Ghetto)
	🎵	*Living Darfur:* (Official Music Video) YouTube.
	🎨	*Guernica:* Pablo Picasso. *The Battle of Little Big Horn:* Edgar Samuel Paxson.
🎭		Projections and sound (multimedia). Katie Mitchell. Verbatim. Docudrama. Older students could use comedy (with care) to make points, 'Tickle and slap'. Songs and music. Brecht.
⚠		Be careful to manage young people's exposure to some of the information/images.
🔗		008, 011, 012, 015, 016, 048, 061, 063, 064, 066, 106, 119, 122, 132, 144, 186.

014   War games

	'But you know that if you cross your fingers, And if you count from one, You can get up off the ground again. It doesn't matter The whole thing's just a game' (Kid's Game from *Blood Brothers* by Willy Russell)
👥	11+ Group sizes could vary depending on artistic intention.
🚩	**Workshops/games:** *Soundscapes*. Try using the song *Kid's Game* from *Blood Brothers* fused with the adult reality. War, armed conflict, hostilities . . . Whatever name it's given, man has been doing it on a large scale since at least 2700 BC. Of the past 3,400 years, we have been at peace for only 268 of them. In the 20th century at least 108 million people were killed in wars. Yet when we are not engaged in war, we play war. From toy guns to *Medal of Honour*.
🔆	Imperial War Museum. www.iwm.org.uk The British Red Cross have produced a teaching resource, *Conflict and Its Consequences*. **Look at the language:** 'IT'S WAR!' Look at headlines. The sensationalising of war. Does mankind need war? **More controversial:** Who makes money from armed conflict? **Research:** The advancement of war simulation games. List the war games available. **Search for:** Images of children playing war games.

Stimulus		
	💀	Toy guns, Nerf guns, computer games.
	📖	*War Games:* David Bischoff.
	📝	*Dulce et Decorum Est:* Wilfred Owen.
	🎭	*Blood Bothers:* Willy Russell. *Sink The Belgrano:* Steven Berkoff.
	🎲	*Small Soldiers:* 1998 (12).
	🎵	*Games Without Frontiers:* Peter Gabriel. *Where Do The Children Play?:* Yusuf Cat Stevens. *War:* Edwin Starr.
	🎨	**Research** the photography of Léon Gimpel, *The rue Greneta army 1915*.

🎭	**Look at:** Children playing war, computer games and contrast with the horrors of the real thing. Ensemble, Berkoff/Lecoq.
⚠️	Many of the images of war/conflict are disturbing. Know your students.
🔗	006, 007, 008, 009, 010, 016, 021, 022, 023, 044, 066, 079, 097, 119, 132, 144, 165, 191, 197.

015 Colonial Genocide

		'Traveller, there are no paths. Paths are made by walking' (Australian Aboriginal saying).
👥		14+ Mixed groups.
🏳		**Workshops/games**: *Status games. Alienation.* Discuss the three words: Massacre, Genocide and Colonisation. **Look at:** Culture/religion as a given circumstance.
🔆		Australian Museum *australian.museum* resource; *Genocide in Australia.* List of massacres of indigenous Australians. Wikipedia. Historically 1700s up to the late 1920s. **Research:** National Sorry Day in Australia. The 'Stolen Generation'. The massacre of indigenous Australians.
Stimulus	🐌	Prints of Aboriginal art. Images of kangaroos and wallabies, boomerangs and didgeridoo, all the tourist stuff juxtapose with the horrifying facts and figures.
	📖	*Benevolence:* Julie Janson. *On Red Earth Walking:* Anne Scrimgeour. *The Little Red Yellow Black Book:* AIATSIS.
	✍	*Spiritual Song of The Aborigine:* Hyllus Maris.
	🎭	*Our Country's Good:* Timberlake Wertenbaker. (Look at the journal of the real Arthur Phillip). *Radiance:* Louise Nowra. *Stolen:* Jane Harrison.
	📽	*Rabbit-Proof Fence:* 2002 (PG). *Blackfellas:* 1993 (15). *Black Genocide in Australia EXPOSED:* YouTube video. John Pilger. Disturbing!
	🎵	*Treaty:* Yothu Yindi. *Black Fella, White Fella:* Warumpi Band. *They Took the Children Away:* Archie Roach. Look also at *Coroborees.* Mime and song re-telling.
	🎨	1888 drawing of a massacre at skull hole by Carl Lumholtz.
🎭		Ensemble work narrating the brutality and massacres which followed the First Fleet's arrival in 1788 to the present day. (Deaths in custody.)
⚠		Respect and honour the Aboriginal and Torres Strait Islander culture.
🔗		011, 012, 013, 015, 016, 017, 036, 052, 079, 100, 132, 133, 140, 161, 174, 190.

016   Xenophobia

<table>
<tr>
<td></td>
<td>'The world is full of people who think that different is synonymous with wrong' (David Levithan – American author).</td>
</tr>
<tr>
<td>👥</td>
<td>12+ Mixed groups of 4–5.</td>
</tr>
<tr>
<td>🚩</td>
<td>Workshops/games: Fear games. Gestus.
What are you afraid of? Do you hate it? Xenophobia, the fear of anything strange or foreign that turns into hatred.
Two main kinds of xenophobia – 1: Stranger/immigrant. 2: Cultural.
Look at: Those jokes people make. The one about the Irishman, Mexican, Frenchman, Welshman etc. . . .
Look at the Language: 'Enforce our borders.' 'Learn to speak English!' 'No, where are you really from?'</td>
</tr>
<tr>
<td>🔆</td>
<td>Look at: Xenophobia within Africa.
More controversial: 'Every life matters.' Stop xenophobia.
How were Asian people treated in your town during Covid?
Historically: In 2016 Dictionary.com selected 'Xenophobia' as the word of the year.
Research: The anti-immigrant rhetoric of Donald Trump.
How big a part did xenophobia play in the Brexit vote?</td>
</tr>
<tr>
<td rowspan="6">Stimulus</td>
<td>💀 A spider/bat/snakes/dogs/cats . . . Images of things we fear.
A pro-Brexit poster.</td>
</tr>
<tr>
<td>📖 Out of the Shadows: Jason Wallace.
Splithead: Julya Rabinowich.
The Lines We Cross: Randa Abdel-Fattah.</td>
</tr>
<tr>
<td>📝 Refugee Blues: W. H. Auden.</td>
</tr>
<tr>
<td>🎭 Hannah and Hanna: John Retallack.
Zero Tolerance and Other Plays: Disrupting Xenophobia, Racism and Homophobia in School: Tara Goldstein.</td>
</tr>
<tr>
<td>🎞 District 9: 2009 (15).
American History X: 1998 (18).
Gangs of New York: 2002 (18).
More controversial: Since 2019 Disney+ has included a message ahead of some of its classic movies which warns., 'May include outdated cultural depictions'.</td>
</tr>
<tr>
<td>🎵 A Change is Gonna Come: Sam Cooke.
People are People: Depeche Mode.
Enough is Enough: Chumbawamba.

🎨 Look at: Spirit of The Carnival: Tam Joseph (1982).
The poster art series 'I Still Believe in Our City': Amanda Phingbodhipakkiya. New York City Commission on Human Rights.</td>
</tr>
<tr>
<td>🎪</td>
<td>Ensemble work. Good opportunities for costume and lighting. Monologues.
Carnival dance pieces work well too.</td>
</tr>
<tr>
<td>⚠</td>
<td>Be aware of any potential issues within the group.</td>
</tr>
<tr>
<td>🔗</td>
<td>002, 004, 008, 011, 012, 017, 021, 061, 062, 063, 064, 079, 088, 092, 108, 132, 155, 160, 161, 186.</td>
</tr>
</table>

017   Racism

	'Racism is a white problem, constructed and created by white people' (Robin Di Angelo – American Academic).
👥	All ages and abilities.
🏁	**Workshops/games:** *Get out of my Way. Status games.* Use dictionary definitions. Watch the final courtroom scene (closing statement) from the 1996 Movie *A Time to Kill.* 'Now imagine she's white.' Rated (15). Racism is another Pandemic!
🔆	*The New York Times* produced some excellent resources for teaching about race and racism (March 2021). **Research:** NAACP. Black Youth Project. KIND. Stop Hate UK. The BLM movement. Dance/NYC has a racial Justice resource. **Look at:** Anti-racism work done by rugby and football around the world. 'Taking the knee.' **What the papers say:** Examine the coverage of George Floyd case in the US. **Look at:** Racism against Latinos, Aboriginals, Native American Indians, Asians. It's not as simple as skin colour.

Stimulus		
	💀	Images of the BLM protests after the killing of George Floyd. Photos of overt racism from the US, UK and Apartheid South Africa.
	📖 📝	*Out of The Shadows:* Jason Wallace. *The Bluest Eye:* Toni Morrison. *Roll of Thunder, Hear My Cry:* Mildred D. Taylor. Look at the collected poems of Maya Angelou.
	🎭	*Advice for the Young at Heart:* Roy Williams. *Shades:* Alia Bano. *Gone Too Far:* Bola Agbaje.
	🎬	*Green Book:* 2018 (12A). *BlacKkKLansman:* 2018 (15). *Race:* 2016 (PG). *When They See Us.* 2019 (Netflix).
	🎵	*Living for the City:* Stevie Wonder. *Accidental Racist:* Brad Paisley. *Southern Man:* Neil Young.
	🎨	*The Problem We All Live With:* Norman Rockwell (1964). **Look at:** The work of artists like Kerry James Marshall, Kara Walker, Faith Ringgold, Bill Traylor, Jacob Lawrence and Jean-Michel Basquiat.

🎭	Brechtian theatre with direct audience address – Tickle and Slap. Theatre of the Absurd and comedic devices (Commedia dell'arte). The language should always be vital and honest.
⚠	Some resources contain offensive, racist material/language.
🔗	002, 004, 008, 011, 012, 016, 021, 061, 062, 063, 064, 079, 088, 092, 108, 132, 155, 160, 161, 186.

018   Gender Equality

	'We've begun to raise daughters more like sons . . . but few have the courage to raise our sons more like our daughters' (Gloria Steinem – American feminist journalist).
👥	All ages. Mixed groups, unless they are making a specific point!
🚩	**Workshops/games:** *Status games.* Worldwide, women have less opportunities for economic participation than men. Less access to education, greater health and safety risks, and less political representation. Does this make you angry or sad. Use still image followed by thought tracking to develop these feelings.
💡	**Research:** Mary Wollstonecraft (1792), *Principles for the Emancipation of Women.* A great deal of progress has been made over the ensuing 200 years, however; look at persisting global inequalities. **More controversial:** Are some cultures/faiths more guilty of repressing women than others? **What the papers say:** Headline. Afghan Girls Contemplate a Future Without School.
Stimulus	**Search for** *Gender bias in 1950's advertising* (images). Also *Sexualisation of women/ men in advertising* (images).
	The First Woman: Jennifer Nansubuga Makumbi. *A Woman is No Man:* Etaf Rum. *If I Had Your Face:* Frances Cha. *The Penguin Book of Feminist Writing:* Anthology, Hannah Dawson. *A Doll's House:* Henrik Ibsen. *Shakers Re-Stirred:* Godber and Thornton. Shakespeare's *The Taming Of The Shrew.* Is it a misogynistic play or a play which questioned the values of society at the time?
	On the Basis of Sex: 2018 (12A). *Made in Dagenham:* 2010 (15). Documentary *Period. End of Sentence* 2018 (PG). *I Am Woman:* Helen Reddy. *Man I Feel Like a Woman:* Shania Twain. *Behind the Wall:* Tracy Chapman. **Look at** Picasso's *Tête de Femme.* Andy Warhol's *Marilyn Monroe.* **Research:** Guerrilla Girls (an anonymous artist activist group). 'The Art of Behaving Badly.'
🎭	All of the women had the same name 'Eve'. Male characters with loud hailers delivered a tirade of sexist jokes. The Eves went about domestic tasks silently, wearing masks over their mouths. There were references to violence against women and girls. Brechtian theatre. Another group used comedy to pose the question 'What if the shoe were on the other foot?'
⚠️	Searches in this area may result in disturbing/inappropriate images. Be aware of cultural/religious differences within the classroom.
🔗	001, 032, 054, 070, 077, 078, 108, 109, 110, 130, 135, 160, 174, 188, 191, 196, 197, 199, 200.

019   Ageism

	'Aging is an extraordinary process where you become the person you always should have been' (David Bowie – British singer).
👥	Any age! Try to go for mixed groups.
🚩	**Workshops/games:** *Old man/woman walking. Levels of tension. Guide me.* Think of examples, too old to work, too young to care! Sorry you're not old enough! You're too old. When does old stop meaning 'experienced' and become incapable? When does young stop meaning 'able' and become inexperienced? In this unit we are looking at discrimination against seniors.
💡	**Research:** World Health Organization global report on ageism. NCEA www.ageuk.org.uk Ageing in the 21st century resources from HelpAge International. Does the media perpetuate ageism? Look at ageism in advertising. Look at the age of Prime Ministers and Presidents. Wisdom or past their sell by date? **More controversial:** Was ageism obvious during the pandemic? Consider how different cultures treat the elderly.
Stimulus	💀 A walking stick. The warning 'Old people' road sign. An hour-glass/clock. A hearing aid. Images of elderly wrinkled faces.
	📖 *Reading in Bed:* Sue Gee. *Ending Up:* Kingsley Amis. *Senior Wonders:* K. L. Pepkin and W. C. Taylor.
	📝 *Ageism Poem:* Frank Duggan.
	🎭 *Playhouse Creatures:* April De Angelis. *The Duck Variations:* David Mamet. *Linda:* Penelope Skinner. 'Grandma's Song' from *Billy Elliot:* YouTube.
	🎞 *The Best Exotic Marigold Hotel:* 2011 (12A). *Driving Miss Daisy:* 1989 (U). *Last Tango in Halifax:* 2012 (BBC).
	🎵 *When I'm Sixty Four:* The Beatles. *When We Were Young:* Adele. *When You're Old and Grey:* Tom Lehrer.
	🎨 *Ageism:* Iratxe Lopez de Munain. Robbie Kaye's photo series *'Beauty and Wisdom'*.
🎪	A group of students used a very talented parkour runner dressed as an old man to literally fly around a theatre space, after standing in a queue of young job applicants. Theatre based on interviews with elderly relatives. Verbatim/docudrama.
⚠	Avoid personal stories with younger students.
🔗	018, 021, 025, 027, 046, 051, 052, 056, 057, 058, 067, 068, 069, 084, 101, 107, 110, 132, 143, 157, 160, 161, 174, 186, 192.

020   Homophobia

	'Being gay is not voluntary, hate is' (Gay Pride).
👥	15+ mixed small groups. Sensitive. Students need to really examine their honest attitude to the subject.
🚩	**Workshops/games:** *Fear. Trust games.* Read aloud the poem *First they came:* Martin Niemöller. **Questionnaires:** Take an (online) homophobia test. Examine your attitude! Do you bully/are you bullied because of your sexual orientation or that of others? The unit is not about being Gay, it's about people's prejudices against people who are identified or perceived as being lesbian, gay, bisexual or transgender.
🔆	**Research:** Affective, Cognitive and Behavioural Homophobia. Look at the Gay civil rights movement. Definition of LGBTQ+. How attitudes have changed and acceptance in different countries. Secondary school resource pack for teachers from Barnardos.org.uk on tackling homophobic, biphobic and transphobic (HBT) bullying. TES also have excellent resources on LGBT+ in their PSHE sections.

Stimulus	🖼️	Rainbows poster, images of the common perceptions/jokes in society.
	📖	*The Price of Salt:* Patricia Highsmith. *Middlesex:* Jeffrey Eugenides. *Rubyfruit Jungle:* Rita Mae Brown.
	📝	*Time for Love:* Sean Lionadh (YouTube BBC).
	🎭	*Tomorrow I'll be Happy:* Jonathan Harvey. *Bent:* Martin Sherman. *Angels in America:* Tony Kushner.
	🎞️	*Carol:* 2015 (15). *Go Fish:* 1994 (18). *Angels in America* 2003 (15) TV Mini-series.
	🎵	*You Make Me Feel Mighty Real:* Sylvester. *Don't Stop Me Now:* Queen. *Born This Way:* Lady Gaga.
	🎨	*Two Figures:* Francis Bacon. *Gay Liberation:* George Segal Sculpture. Look at Tate Britain exhibition 'Queer British Art 1861–1967' (Online).

🎭	Challenging Forum, or Verbatim theatre. Upper school T.I.E. projects. Highly rehearsed scenes presented as improvised. Strongly led by an MC who uses comedy to explore and uncover the levels of phobia within the audience. Lots of projections and SFX.
⚠️	A vast and sensitive subject, requires meticulous planning by the teacher. Mixed groups tend to be more reflective and grounded in this area.
🔗	016, 018, 021, 024, 025, 051, 053, 059, 064, 066, 070, 078, 107, 109, 128, 139, 160, 174, 182, 186, 196, 199, 200.

021 Bullying

	'You can't be against bullying without actually doing something about it' (Randi Weingarten – American labour leader).
♀♂	All ages but take care with the selection of research/stimulus materials. Groups of 4/5.
⚑	**Workshops/games:** *Columbian Hypnosis. Get out of my way! Levels of tension.* List the reason why a person might be bullied. Why would you be a bully or a bystander? When you say nothing, you say it's okay. Are you a bystander or an upstander? *'Strong people stand up for themselves but the strongest people stand up for others.'* *'Laugh at it and you're part of it.'* Use improv with Flashbacks and Flash-Forwards to create context. Freeze frame and ask questions. Do you agree or disagree with?
💡	**Look at.** The *body* **language,** hands on hips, taking up space, fists, staring, invading personal space, frowning, stillness. Taking belongings. **More controversial:** Bullies are victims. *School Bully*, Key and Peel YouTube.

Stimulus		
	☠	Diary extracts. Letters. Mobile phones. Masks. Sticks and stones.
	📖	*Some Girls Are:* Courtney Summers (Older students). *The Ugly One:* Leanne Statland Ellis (Younger students).
	✍	*Death by Bullying:* Francis Duggan.
	🎭	*A Memory of Lizzie:* David Foxton. *Girls Like That:* Evan Placey. *Sparkleshark:* Philip Ridley. *DNA:* Dennis Kelly. For younger students *Henry The Monster:* Holly Groome.
	🎞	*Elephant:* 2003 (15). *Speak:* 2004 (PG-13). *Wonder:* 2017 (PG). Anti-bullying week videos from www.anti-bullying-week
	🎵	National Bullying Prevention Month has a playlist of 12 songs with videos.
	🎨	Art-against-bullying.eu. Website contains works of art that challenge bullying plus short stories and articles/research into bully–victim relationships.

🎭	Lends itself well to physical theatre. Avoid long stories, look at the act of bullying and standing by while bullying takes place. Use music. Sound effects. Choreographed sequences for shock effect. A T.I.E. piece for younger students to watch.
⚠	Bullying always needs to be approached sensitively. Be aware of classroom dynamics and school policies.
🔗	005, 008, 016–020, 024, 025, 032, 034, 053, 054, 059–064, 070, 071, 073, 074, 075, 081, 088, 100, 106, 107, 110, 112, 115, 126, 127, 128, 130, 132, 135, 139, 160, 161, 174, 185, 186, 191.

022   Peace

	'All we are saying is give peace a chance' (John Lennon – English singer/songwriter).	
	12+ Mixed	
	Workshops/games: *Levels of tension. Stillness.* It is estimated that in only 8 percent of recorded history have humans been entirely free of conflict! We tend to think of peace as the opposite state to war but it can mean silence or a calmness of mind, a state of rest. 'She is at peace now.'	
	Search for: The Role of the Media in Peace Processes **Research:** Peace Studies. International Peace and Security. The United Nations. un.org International Peace Institute. https://www.ipinst.org/ Finding peace and quiet. Peace from madness.	
Stimulus		⊕ A dove, an olive branch, a white poppy, a broken rifle, Pax symbol, the V gesture. In other cultures it can be mistletoe, a boar, a bell, rain, a cubic stone, a palm branch, Yin Yang. Origami.
		Beyond War: Douglas Fry. *Confronting the Bomb:* Lawrence Wittner. *War and Peace:* Tolstoy.
		The Rock Cries Out to Us Today: Maya Angelou.
		The Madness of Esme and Shaz: Sarah Daniels. *Peace:* Aristophanes. *A Golden Peace of Mind:* Debra A. Cole.
		Gandhi: 1982 (A). *Grave of the Fireflies:* 1988 (12A). *Countdown to Zero:* 2010 documentary (PG).
		Imagine: John Lennon. *Blowin' in the Wind:* Bob Dylan. *Heal the World:* Michael Jackson. *Dove of Peace:* Pablo Picasso.
		Spin AKA 47: Damien Hirst. *Armoured Peace Dove:* Banksy.
	Use contrast to emphasise peace; sound effects (war) and frantic movements then silence and stillness. Dance piece. Lighting and music can also have a similar effect.	
	Get those artistic intentions written down and adhered to!	
	006, 007, 008, 014, 023, 025, 050, 058, 059, 071, 074, 106, 107, 123, 125, 149, 167, 174.	

023   Terrorism

	'Wanton killing of innocent civilians is terrorism, not a war against terrorism' (Noam Chomsky – American Linguist).
👥	15+ Groups of 4–5 mixed.
🚩	**Workshops/games:** *Stereotypes* and challenge them. What does a terrorist look like? **Look at the language:** Terrorist, Freedom Fighter, Guerrilla warfare, Rebels. Some sound better than others? The very word terror for example cannot sound positive, but freedom fighter? **More controversial:** If terrorism is against unarmed civilians, consider, alongside, the Manchester Arena attack or 9/11; the British 'Terror Bombings' of German cities during World War II aimed specifically at civilians.
💡	The names: IRA, ISIS, Al-Qaeda, Boko Haram, Hezbollah, Hamas, FARC. *Che Guevara:* Freedom fighter, murderer and terrorist or icon? **Research:** *Mahatma Gandhi* who fought against British rule in India. Freedom fighter, Father of the Nation or icon? **What the papers say:** Depending on where you go to fight, your country's media will brand you an unsung hero or a ruthless mercenary/terrorist. 'Not in my name.'

Stimulus	📷	Images of 9/11, newspaper headlines from any terror attack. The aftermath of the bombing of Dresden, Hiroshima, Nagasaki.
	📖	*'One man's terrorist is another man's freedom fighter.'* Gerald Seymour, in his book *Harry's Game.* *'The object of terrorism is terrorism.'* George Orwell's *1984.*
	📝	*The Secret Agent:* Joseph Conrad.
	🎭	*Girls:* Theresa Ikoko. *Black Watch:* Gregory Burke. *Accidental Death of an Anarchist:* Dario Fo.
	🎬	*Hotel Mumbai:* 2018 (15). *In the Name of the Father:* 1993 (15). *London River:* 2009 (12).
	🎵	*Zombie:* The Cranberries. *Spanish Bombs:* The Clash. *How Beautiful Are the Feet:* from Handel's *Messiah.* *9/11 Elegies:* Ejay Weiss
	🎨	*Trinity Root:* A bronze casting by sculptor Steve Tobin. *After 9/11,* by American artist Miya Ando (Sculpture). **Research:** *Art of the Troubles* exhibition Museums NI.

🎭	Epic. Didactic drama avoiding illusion. Using 'gestus', alienation effect, to distance the audience from emotional involvement. Brechtian, the absence of realism. Minimalist. Some good work also done with large ensemble stylised movement. Lecoq/Berkoff.
⚠️	Students can be overwhelmed by the amount of information available.
🔗	005, 014, 044, 052, 061, 066, 079, 088, 100, 101, 102, 106, 107, 132, 133, 141, 142, 144, 146–150, 160, 174, 175, 186, 187, 189, 197.

024   Cyber Bullying

		'Sticks and stones may break your bones but words can hurt like hell' (Chuck Palahniuk – American journalist and novelist).
👥		12+ Small mixed friendship groups
🚩		**Workshops/games:** *Alienation. Status games.* Through social media, the spreading of lies or posting of embarrassing photos. If you put your social life online, are you asking for trouble? Hurtful messages via messaging platforms, impersonation with intent to embarrass or worse.
💡		eubully.eu have produced a drama teacher's resource. Childnet international. unicef.org end violence how-to-stop-cyberbullying. **More controversial:** Facebook's CEO says it is difficult for his social media network to police cyberbullying content.
Stimulus	📱	A mobile phone, A laptop with messages on messaging platform. Make a poster using the language students communicate with online.
	📖	*Don't Read the Comments:* Eric Smith. *Boar Island:* Nevada Barr. *A Smart Kid's Guide to Cyberbullying:* David Jakubiak (USA).
	📝	*Cyberbully:* Francis Duggan.
	🎭	*Girls Like That:* Evan Placey. *Mobile Phone Show:* Jim Cartwright.
	🎬	*Cyberbully:* 2015 (15) British. *Unfriended:* 2014 (15) USA *Submit: The documentary.* The Virtual reality of Cyberbullying. 2013
	🎵	National Bullying Prevention Month has a playlist of 12 songs with videos.
	🎨	Freeart.com/art/prints/cyberbullying/all/ Art-against-bullying.eu. Website contains works of art that challenge bullying. Look at the many anti-bullying posters. Kristina Webb's anti-bullying drawings.
🎭		Forum theatre. A simple, uncluttered set using projections and other multimedia (Katie Mitchell). More ambitious work could involve the audience's mobile phones.
⚠️		Bullying always needs to be approached sensitively.
🔗		016, 017, 020, 021, 025, 054, 059, 061, 062, 063, 070, 071, 073, 075, 077, 080, 081, 092, 107, 109, 112, 128, 139, 152, 164, 182, 183, 185, 186,

025 Inner Conflict

		'Nobody can bring you peace but yourself' (Ralph Emerson – American philosopher, essayist and poet)
⚧		14+ age. Great for pair work.
🚩		**Workshops/games**: *Circles of attention. Levels of tension.* Begin with stream of consciousness monologues. The kinds of conversations we have with ourselves. 'Should I, shouldn't I?' Inner turmoil. Belief v. need. Improvise with an angel and devil on each shoulder. Recite a monologue or perform a simple task whilst hearing this conflict. How does it affect your actions, voice, facial expression?
💡		**Research**: Man v Self. Character conflict. Identity Crisis. Explore internal conflict in literature **More controversial**: Is it possible for a nation to have a conflict of self-perception. For example, we are a great and generous nation but we have no more room for refugees?
Stimulus	🎭	Use two different masks. A mirror to argue with yourself.
	📖	The inner struggle of Ebeneezer Scrooge in Dickens's *A Christmas Carol*. George's turmoil at the end of Steinbeck's *Of Mice and Men*.
	🎭	Drama is conflict; some of the best theatre is where the protagonists have some kind of internal conflict. These are the troubled characters, the really interesting ones! HAMLET's 'To be or not to be'. MACBETH's loyalty to DUNCAN and his own ambition. OTHELLO's love, jealousy and rage. Often revealed in Soliloquy.
	🎞	*Up*: 2009 (U). *Toy Story*: 1995 (PG). Buzz Lightyear, a toy who doesn't realise he's a toy. *The Lion King*: 1994 (U). Simba's duty versus his fear.
	🎵	*Don't Let Me Be Misunderstood*: The Animals. *Bloodstream*: Ed Sheeran. *Brain Damage*: Pink Floyd.
	🎨	*The Scream*: Edvard Munch. *Inner Conflict*: Martin Kammler. Look at the self-portraits of *Freda Kahlo*. *Inner Demon*: (Digital art) Sherry Holder Hunt.
🎭		Expressionist theatre to convey the conflict between the inner and outer self, physicalising emotions, using mirrors, showing the hidden subtext, conveying meaning/feelings without words. Shared experience
⚠		Be aware of mental health issues.
🔗		008.009, 016, 020, 021, 023, 026, 027, 033, 039, 044, 045, 055, 058, 059, 062, 063, 070, 071, 073, 074, 075, 076, 077, 079, 087, 097, 098, 104, 107, 109, 123, 135, 136, 137, 139, 142, 144, 163, 168, 176, 182.

026   Who is God?

		'Just a stranger on the bus' (Eric M. Bazilian – American musician, songwriter).
👥	All ages. Suits large mixed groups.	
🚩	**Workshops/games:** *The pointing game* to The Lord's prayer. *Status games.* How would you explain it to someone who didn't speak your language? Sign it. **Questionnaire:** What does the word/concept 'God' mean to you? Putting a face to a name. Ideas for an audience to consider. Something visual, something tangible. We considered Judaism, Christianity, Islam and Hinduism but you don't have to stop there.	
🔆	https://christianheadlines.com **Research:** How God has been portrayed throughout history. **Consider:** What are his thoughts on how we've done so far, as a species? **More controversial:** Does God look like Charlton Heston or Morgan Freeman? Why does he allow such terrible things to happen? Lenny Bruce once said, *'Every day people are straying away from the church and going back to God'*. What do you think he meant?	
Stimulus	👑	Any permitted/tasteful religious image/artifact.
	📖	*God and Other Minds:* Alvin Plantinga. Holy Books: *The Tipitaka* (Buddhism). *The Bible* (Christianity). *The Vedas* (Hinduism). *The Quran* and *The Hadiths* (Islam). *The Tanakh* and *The Talmud* (Judaism). *The Guru Granth Sahib* (Sikhism). *The Dao De Jing* (Taoism).
	🎭	*Coffee with God:* Kal Wagenheim. *Hand to God:* Robert Askins. *Waiting for Godot:* Samuel Beckett.
	📽	*Creation:* 2009 (PG). *The Story of God with Morgan Freeman:* TV documentary Series 2016–2019 (14). *Islam: Empire of Faith:* 2000, TV Series. *Naga the Eternal* Yogi: 2016.
	🎵	*Lord Give Me a Sign:* DMX. *Goodness of God:* Jenn Johnson. *My Hero:* Harris J. Salam. *One of Us:* Joan Osbourne. *The Messiah:* Handel.
	🎨	*The Last Judgement:* Michelangelo. *God The Father:* Pieter de Grebber. *The Ghent Altarpiece:* Van Eyck. **Search for:** The face of God in Art (images).
🎭	Forum theatre accompanied by dramatic music and projected images. Greek theatre/chorus. Ensemble physical work. Berkoff/Lecoq. Promenade theatre.	
⚠	Be sensitive with all faiths. Many Muslims consider it offensive to depict the Prophet Mohammed in any circumstances.	
🔗	027, 028, 041, 043, 046, 048, 050, 109, 169, 176, 192, 196, 197.	

027   The meaning of life

	'The meaning of life is to find your gift. The purpose of life is to give it away' (Pablo Picasso – Spanish artist).
♀♂	Any age, mixed. Sensitively try to mix groups to encourage debate.
🏳	**Workshops/games**: *Mirror images. Repetition exercises.* What is the meaning of life? Write one sentence to represent your answer. ('I don't know' is OK!). How would you draw, sculpt this? Make it a tableau. What does it say? How would you describe it to an alien visitor? If there is no meaning to life, perhaps it is our purpose to give it meaning . . . So what will you do?
💡	Why are we here? Does my life have a purpose? **Research:** how the different religions answer these two questions.

Stimulus		
	💀	A mirror. A selfie. A Holy Book. A large question mark.
	📖	*The Little Prince:* Antoine de Saint-Exupéry. *Man's Search for Meaning:* Viktor Frankl. *The Power of Now: A Guide to Spiritual Enlightenment:* Eckhart Tolle.
	📝	*The Road Not Taken:* Robert Frost.
	🎭	*Waiting for Godot:* Samuel Beckett. *The Duck Variations:* David Mamet. *Asking Strangers The Meaning of Life:* William Missouri Downs.
	🎬	*About Schmidt:* 2002 (15). *Soul:* 2020 (PG). *The Meaning of Life:* Monty Python 1983 (18).
	🎵	*Waiting on the World to Change:* John Mayer. *You Can't Always Get What You Want:* The Rolling Stones. *Here for a Reason:* Ashes Remain.
	🎨	*Where Do We Come From? What Are We? Where Are We Going?:* Gauguin.

🎭	Historical drama looking at people/characters who have given meaning to the world. Character work. Stanislavski. Monologues. Forum theatre (older students). Docudrama.
⚠	Respect different faith/cultures within groups.
🔗	025, 026, 033, 035, 044, 051, 057, 065, 071, 074, 076, 087, 107, 114, 119, 132, 149, 151, 158, 159, 179, 190, 192, 196, 198, 199, 200.

028   Jesus (Yeshua)

		'God had an only Son, and He was a missionary and a physician' (David Livingstone – Scottish explorer and missionary).
⚥		All ages, abilities and gender mixes. Differentiate by content.
🚩		**Workshops/games**: *Alienation. Accusation. Status games.* I played *How He Loves* by Kim Walker-Smith, whilst showing images of Man's cruelty to man. (War, genocide, murder, pollution etc.) This led to a very open discussion about the man and what he represents today.
🔆		Archaeology confirms 50 real people in the Bible. See baslibrary.orgrequest.org.uk/teachers is a space for RE teachers. **Search for**: Historical proof of the existence of Jesus of Nazareth. *The Historical Jesus*, YouTube. Yale University. **Research**: The shroud of Turin. **More controversial**: Why is Jesus so often portrayed as a white European?
Stimulus	☠	A crown of thorns. A crucifix. Prints of Great Masters and later images of Christ.
	📖	*The Gospel According to the Son*: Norman Mailer. *The Testament of Mary*: Colm Tóibín. *The Case for Christ*: Lee Strobel.
	✍	*Jesus Began to Weep*: Raymond Foss.
	🎭	*Messiah*: Steven Berkoff. *A Man Called Jesus*: J. B. Phillips. *Godspell*: Musical John-Michael Tebelak.
	📽	*The Passion of the Christ*: 2004 (R). *The Last Temptation of Christ*: 1988 (18). *Son of God*: 2014 (12).
	🎵	*Personal Jesus*: Jonny Cash cover. *How He Loves*: Kim Walker-Smith. *Jesus Was An Only Son*: Bruce Springsteen.
	🎨	*Christ cleansing the temple of Jerusalem*: Bernardino Mei. *Christ on the Mount of Olives*: Battistello. *Baptism of Christ*: Leonardo da Vinci.
🎭		'If Jesus came back today, would we treat him any better?' In the round or promenade. Ensemble piece Berkoff/Lecoq using Mask/Chorus, stark lighting.
⚠		Be sensitive to the cultural mix within your class.
🔗		026, 027, 029, 030, 044, 045, 046, 048, 076, 088, 101, 142, 161, 172, 182, 197, 199.

029   The seven deadly sins

	'Envy is Pride's infection on inspiration . . . while Angered then Eaten by the Greed of a Lazy Lust' (Criss Jami – American Author).
	All age groups/abilities. Could suit 7 small groups, pairs.
	Workshops/games: *Super objective. Gestus. Body sculpture.* **Questionnaire:** Begin by asking the students to name them and what they mean. How many think they are from the bible? Each sin carries a story. They are: Lust, Gluttony, Greed, Sloth, Envy, Wrath and Pride. Can they think of an object, image or tableau to represent each? Think of seven modern day sins!
	The seven deadly sins are also known as the capital vices or cardinal sins. **Research:** Medieval Morality. The origins. The Christian ascetic Evagrius Ponticus of the 4th century CE. The seven virtues are: Kindness, Charity, Temperance, Chastity, Humility, Diligence and Patience.

Stimulus		
		A red rose, a cross, a mirror, a box of chocolates, a lily, an apple, gold coins and treasure. Images of lust (age appropriate).
		One or more of the seven deadly sins feature somewhere in most movies and literature. *Canterbury Tales:* Geoffrey Chaucer.
		The Seven Deadly Sins: Richard Tarlton. An English Morality play c. 1585. *The Bacchae:* Euripides 405 BC In Shakespeare's *Othello* most, if not all, seven sins are shown in the characters.
		Just about every movie features at least one of the seven sins. Get students thinking about how to represent each sin on stage.
		The Lazy Song: Bruno Mars. *I'd Be Jealous Too:* Dustin Lynch. *Money for Nothing:* Dire Straits. *Money:* Pink Floyd. *I'm on Fire:* Bruce Springsteen. *Jealous Guy:* John Lennon. *Love the Way You Lie:* Eminem. *Seven Deadly Sins:* The Travelling Wilburys.
		The Seven Deadly Sins: Paul Cadmus. *The Seven Deadly Sins and the Four Last Things:* Hieronymus Bosch. Which colours would best represent the seven sins?

	Look at each sin and the cure the bible offers. Students made the sin natural and every day and gave the cure a supernatural, non-naturalistic/highly stylised flavour. Lecoq.
	Be conscious of the diversity of faiths/beliefs in your school.
	045, 048, 061, 062, 063, 064.075, 105, 109, 129, 169, 192.

030   It's Christmas!

		'Maybe Christmas, the Grinch thought, doesn't come from a store' (Doctor Seuss – American children's author).
⚭		Any age. Works well with groups of 4/5.
🚩		**Workshops/games:** *Soundscapes.* No matter the age of the students, I begin by reading/enacting to them *Jesus' Christmas Party* by Nicholas Allan (5 minutes). Then ask them for a Christmas list. Compare it to what was available 100 years ago. Talk about what Christmas means to them. Describe Christmas morning/day in your house. How many traditions? How much excitement and stress? So what about the baby Jesus?
💡		Christmas is an Anglo-Saxon word – Cristesmæsse, a word first recorded in 1038. Is Christmas over-commercialised? **Research:** Christmas TV adverts. How Christmas is celebrated (or not) around the world. The origins of Father Christmas/Santa . . .
Stimulus	🐌	Father Christmas costume. The tree and decorations. The songs, the food.
	📖	*A Child's Christmas in Wales:* Dylan Thomas. *Letters from Father Christmas:* J. R. R. Tolkien. *Christmas Around the World:* Mary D. Lankford.
	📝	*'Twas The Night Before Christmas:* Clement Clarke Moore.
	🎭	*Who's Holiday!:* Matthew Lombardo. *A Christmas Carol:* Charles Dickens, adapted by David Edgar. *Nativity Mysteries:* From the nativity cycle of the York Mysteries.
	🎞	What makes a Christmas movie? *The Christmas Chronicles:* 2018 (PG). *The Snowman:* (TV short) 1982 (U).
	🎵	*It's Beginning to Look a Lot Like Christmas:* Bing Crosby. *Happy Xmas (War Is Over):* John Lennon. Handel's Messiah, *For unto us a child is born.* (Dance to it!) *Fairy-tale of New York:* The Pogues and Kirsty MacColl.
	🎨	*The Census at Bethlehem:* Pieter Bruegel the Elder. *The Mystical Nativity:* Sandro Botticelli.
🎭		Juxtaposition. Looking at the day through different eyes. Different times. Artistic intent can be religious or irreligious. Storytelling. Waterwell. Dance to traditional Hymns. 'The Nativity play.'
⚠		Some families don't celebrate Christmas. For others it can be a tough time. Know your students!
🔗		028, 041, 046, 065, 084, 085, 095, 096, 099, 101, 104, 112, 120, 172, 183, 188, 191, 196, 197.

031   Superstition

		'One way or another, all humans are superstitious' (Abhijit Naskar – Indian Neuroscientist).
⚖		Older students will explore this in greater depth and look at the more sinister side. Younger groups will enjoy some of the simple well-known beliefs we find in nursery rhymes.
🏁		**Workshops/games**: *Levels of tension. Fear. Silent scream.* **Questionnaire**: What superstitions do people have and do they know the origins? Which superstitions (Old Wives' tales) are about good luck and how many more are ominous warnings? **Look at**: Ritual and the comfort it gives. Storytelling.
☀		**Watch**: *Where do superstitions come from?* – Stuart Vyse, YouTube. **Research**: The superstitious rituals of highly creative people. Artists, writers, actors etc. . . . Don't just look at your own local (national) superstitions. There are fascinating and very different superstitions all around the world, many of which share a common theme.
Stimulus	☠	A broken mirror. A horseshoe. Pictures of magpies, black cats. The number 13.
	📖	Most of Walter Scott's *Waverley Novels*. *Recipes for Good Luck:* Ellen Weinstein.
	✍	*Ode to Superstition:* Samuel Rogers.
	🎭	*Blood Brothers:* Willy Russell. Look at superstition in the theatre. (When you create magic/suspend disbelief, you invite trouble!) Shakespeare's *A Midsummer Night's Dream*. Act 2, Scene 1, PUCK 'Over hill, over dale'.
	🎞	*The Village:* 2004 (12A). *Fiddler on the Roof:* 1971 (G). Look at how superstition is exploited in horror movies. E.g. *Friday the 13th.* The Black Cat in *The Matrix.*
	🎵	*Knock on Wood:* Eddie Floyd. *Superstition:* Stevie Wonder. *Bad Luck:* Neko Case.
	🎨	Salvador Dali, surrealism and superstition. The Black Cat in French art. *Superstition Painting:* Milos Belja.
🎪		Mirrors and smartphones to create dark tales of stolen souls. Non-naturalistic, stylisation, use of rhythm and music, mask, the grotesque, robotics, biomechanics, symbolism movement. Meyerhold. Waterwell.
⚠		Some superstitions reflect outdated prejudices and practices.
🔗		031, 032, 033, 034, 038, 049, 055, 074, 153, 169, 190, 191, 196.

032   Witchcraft

	'What are these so withered and so wild in their attire, That look not like the inhabitants o' the earth, And yet are on't?' Macbeth. 1:3 (Shakespeare – English Playwright and poet)
	14+ Mixed small groups.
	Workshops/games: *Silent scream. Control games.* Consider differing interpretations from Roald Dahl to Shakespeare. The Salem Witch trials to modern day trials in The Democratic Republic of The Congo. What do we know about witches? **Look at the language:** Curse, hex, jinx, spell, white witch, dark magic, wicked!
	English Heritage: *A Journey into Witchcraft Beliefs.* Historic UK: *Witches in Britain.* Ask Smithsonian, '*A Brief History of the Salem Witch Trials*' **Research:** The history of witchcraft and witch trails. In many countries *today* women are hunted and persecuted, even executed as witches! **More controversial:** Having looked at the classical painting, now consider more 'modern' art and how it has tended to sexualise witches, often depicting them naked.

Stimulus		Broomsticks, pointed hats, familiars, a cauldron (traditional ideas). Images of witches from the middle ages. Compare with modern day witches.
		The Witches: Roald Dahl. The *Harry Potter* series J. K. Rowling.
		Witch Burning: Silvia Plath.
		The Crucible: Arthur Miller. *The Witch:* Thomas Middleton. *Vinegar Tom:* Caryl Churchill.
		Gretel and Hansel: 2020 (15). *The Witches:* 2020 (PG). *The Craft: Legacy:* 2020 (15).
		Black Magic Woman: Santana. *Witches' Song:* Marianne Faithfull. *Witch's Promise:* Jethro Tull.
		The Coven and *Witches Sabbath:* Goya. *An Assembly of Witches:* Frans Franken. *The Triple Hecate:* William Blake.

	Students can avoid the stereotypical witches on broomsticks and look instead at women who were different, how they were persecuted and still are. Physical theatre Berkoff/Lecoq.
	Try to avoid comedy. Many TV series seek to portray witches through sitcom. Popular on TV but less successful on stage!
	031, 033, 034, 035, 040, 048, 054, 055, 074, 082, 160, 190, 192, 196, 200.

033 Mirror, Mirror (A Case study unit, see Chapter 5)

	'If art reflects life, it does so with special mirrors' (Bertolt Brecht – German poet, playwright).
♣♦	12+ Small mixed groups.
🏁	See details in Case study, Unit 33, Chapter 5.
💡	There are a number of superstitions attached to mirrors. These days we have the selfie and our image is always near us. But for some reason a mirror is different. **Research**: Narcissus. Images of mirrors as portals. Do other cultures have different superstitions regarding mirrors?

Stimulus		
	💀	A mirror – full length or a small hand held one. A couple of quotes. *'The mirror is my best friend because when I cry it never laughs'* Charlie Chaplin. *'Life is like a mirror, we get the best results when we smile at it'* Unknown.
	📕	*Face:* Benjamin Zephaniah. *Snow White:* The Brothers Grimm. *Through the Looking Glass:* Lewis Carroll.
	✍	*The Lady of Shalott:* Tennyson.
	🎭	*Mirrors:* Jerome McDonough. We looked at plays which use a mirror as an important prop; Shelagh Stephenson's *The Memory of Water* or Ben Myers' *Walking with Shadows*.
	🎬	Look at moments/scenes in movies in which a mirror is focal. *Taxi Driver* (1976). *Black Swan* (2010). *Raging Bull* (1980). *Women* (1977). *Inception* (2010).
	🎵	*Man in the Mirror:* Michael Jackson. *Mirror in the Bathroom:* The Beat. *Shit Mirror:* Nine Inch Nails.
	🎨	Norman Rockwell's *Girl at Mirror*. Manet's *A Bar at the Folies-Bergere*. Picasso's *Girl Before a Mirror*. Rene Magritte's *Not to be Reproached*.

🎪	See details in Case study, Unit 33, Chapter 5.
⚠	Self-image issues. Ensure mirrors are safe and unlikely to break. If using broken mirrors they should be made safe (clear tape).
🔗	031, 034, 054, 055, 070, 075.

034   Fairy Tales (the darker side)

<table>
<tr>
<td></td>
<td colspan="2">'If You want your children to be intelligent, read them fairy tales'
(Albert Einstein – German-American physicist).</td>
</tr>
<tr>
<td>👥</td>
<td colspan="2">All ages/mixed groups.</td>
</tr>
<tr>
<td>🚩</td>
<td colspan="2">Workshops/games: Fear. Story circle. Soundscapes. Silent scream.
Focus on fear and superstition in fairy tales and nursery rhymes.
Try physicalising some of Collected Grimm's Tales: Carol Anne Duffy and Tim Supple.
Look at the rhyme/meter.</td>
</tr>
<tr>
<td>💡</td>
<td colspan="2">Watch, 10 disturbing secrets about nursery rhymes that will ruin your childhood. YouTube.
Where do superstitions come from? Stuart Vyse (YouTube).
What the papers say: BBC article. The dark side of nursery rhymes (Culture article).
US News.com published an article 13 Superstitions from around the world (2017).</td>
</tr>
<tr>
<td rowspan="8">Stimulus</td>
<td>💀</td>
<td>Copies of nursery rhymes/fairy tales. A musical box. A large mirror. Soft toys.</td>
</tr>
<tr>
<td>📖</td>
<td>Knock on Wood: Janet Wong.
Warts and All: The Origins and Meanings of Nursery Rhymes, Superstitions and Sayings: Sandy Leong.</td>
</tr>
<tr>
<td>📝</td>
<td>Revolting Rhymes: Roald Dahl.</td>
</tr>
<tr>
<td>🎭</td>
<td>Blood Brothers: Willy Russell.
Collected Grimm's Tales: Carol Anne Duffy and Tim Supple.
Peer Gynt: Ibsen.</td>
</tr>
<tr>
<td>🎞️</td>
<td>Shrek 1 and Shrek Forever After: 2001 and 2010 (U).
Mother Goose Goes to Hollywood: 1938 (8M short parody).
The Brothers Grimm: 2005 (12A).</td>
</tr>
<tr>
<td>🎵</td>
<td>Ring Around the Rosie: Unknown.
The Red Shoes: Kate Bush.
The Emperor's New Clothes: Sinead O'Connor.</td>
</tr>
<tr>
<td>🎨</td>
<td>Cinderella: Valentine Cameron Prinsep (1899).
Little Red Riding Hood: Henry Liverseege (1830).
David Hockney's Brothers Grimm Fairy Tales.</td>
</tr>
<tr>
<td>🎭</td>
<td>Shakespearian foreshadowing. Soundscapes.
Strong lighting/smoke machines and use of shadows. Gothic works!
Look at Gestus (older students).
Emma Rice. Storytelling/Polly Teal, Marianne Elliot. Waterwell. Narration. Pysicalisation.</td>
</tr>
<tr>
<td>⚠️</td>
<td colspan="2">Some nursery rhymes have particularly violent 'original meanings', whilst others contain outdated cultural notions and language.</td>
</tr>
<tr>
<td>🔗</td>
<td colspan="2">031, 032, 033, 035, 038, 044, 049, 082, 055, 088, 090, 101, 115, 134, 157, 160, 172, 178, 190, 191, 192.</td>
</tr>
</table>

035   The Soul

	'What is a soul? It's like electricity – we don't really know what it is, but it's a force that can light a room' (Ray Charles – American singer and pianist).
	14+ Mixed groups of 3–5.
	Workshops/games: *Circles of attention. Energy games. Levels of tension.* **Look at the language:** Think of expressions/idioms which use the word 'soul'. There are over 100 in everyday use. You can bless it, pour it out, sell it and swear upon it. The eyes are a window to it and everyone has one! But what is it? How would it move, does it dance? Look into a mirror. Is your soul visible to you?
	Research: How Plato divided the soul into three parts. The existence of the soul is an ancient belief in many cultures. The ancient Greeks believed your reflection was your soul. **Search for:** Robert Johnson who sold his soul to the devil at the crossroads. We also talk about 'The Spirit' which somehow seems more tangible.

Stimulus		
		Draw your soul. (Difficult?) **Search for** images of the soul (google).
		Soul Taken (The Life after Trilogy): Katlyn Duncan. *The Five People You Meet in Heaven:* Mitch Albom. *The Book Thief:* Markus Zusak.
		A Dialogue between the Soul and the Body: Andrew Marvell,
		Doctor Faustus: Christopher Marlowe. *Night of the Soul:* David Farr. *100:* Diene Petterle, Neil Monaghan and Christopher Heimann.
		Soul: 2020 (PG). *21 Grams:* 2003 (15). *Coco:* 2017 (PG).
		My Father's Eyes: Eric Clapton. *Devils and Dust:* Bruce Springsteen. *Awake my Soul:* Mumford and Son
		Hell: Eduard Wiiralt *Odysseus' Journey:* Adolf Hirémy-Hirschl. **Look at:** The works of Paul Gustave Doré

	A soul for sale or trade. Ensemble, tormented souls in hell. Grotesque masks, stylised movement. Lecoq/Berkoff. Pain and purgatory. Red up-lighting and projections coupled with some well written monologues.
	Be aware of cultural/faith issues, recent family bereavements.
	025–028, 033, 036, 037, 041, 046, 047, 055, 057, 087, 157, 158, 159, 169, 192.

036   Aboriginal Dreamtime

		'Those who stop dreaming are lost' (Australian Aboriginal proverb).
🧑‍🤝‍🧑		Works well with younger students.
🚩		**Workshops/games:** *Soundscapes.* The sounds of the didgeridoo in complete darkness. Close your eyes and imagine the beginning of time! With younger students I read them some of the dreamtime stories. Body sculpt some of the characters. **More controversial:** How far removed from the Dreaming has the white European taken them?
☼		**Search for:** Francis Firebrace, an Aboriginal storyteller who comes in to schools and gives performances along with music and art workshops. Dreamtime dates back 65,000 years. Essentially, parables passed on by word of mouth and song. **Research:** *The Stolen Generation.* Listen to the song *They Took the Children Away* by Archie Roach.
Stimulus	🪕	A Didgeridoo, Bullroarer, Monkey sticks, Clapsticks, Prints of Aboriginal art, A boomerang, Red sand, Dry sticks,
	📖	*Growing up Aboriginal in Australia:* Anita Heiss. *Mysteries of the Dreamtime:* James Cowan. *Gadi Mirrabooka:* Pauline E. McLeod, Francis Firebrace Jones and June E Barker.
	🎭	*The Seven Stages of Grieving:* Wesley Enoch and Deborah Mailman. *City of Gold:* Meyne Wyatt.
	🎞	*Warburton Range Expedition:* 1935 (Documentary film/Anthropological Research – non-Indigenous researchers and directors).
	🎵	The music of *Archie Roach, No Fixed Address* and *William Barton.* *The Spirit of Uluru:* YouTube. Investigate Songlines and Dreamtime.
	🎨	Traditional paintings on canvas, linen and board, sometimes referred to as 'dot art'. But also look at Awelye body paint, bark paintings, rock art, ochre paintings, wood carvings and sculptures. The colours of aboriginal art.
🎪		Be aware of the cultural significance of the stories. Keep it firmly rooted in the natural order of the land. Ensemble/dance pieces linked with music played on real instruments by the performers.
⚠		**Research:** and be sensitive to Aboriginal and Torres Strait communities beliefs. Public performances of Dreamtime stories need to be granted permission. (This is a courtesy/protocol.) Consult the Australia Council for the Arts.
🔗		013, 016, 017, 027, 039, 040, 046, 055, 056, 120, 140, 155, 174, 176, 190, 196.

037   Norse mythology

		'Loki makes the world more interesting but less safe' (Neil Gaiman – English fantasy writer).
🧒		11+ Works well with young students in mixed groups.
🚩		**Workshops/games:** *Status games.* Thor! Odin! Loki! Asgard! Students will be familiar with the names from the MCU movies, in particular the Thor movies. The 9 realms/worlds have great stories and characters. Older students can look at the similarities that exist with other religions/beliefs. Role playing, heroes and villains.
💡		There are plenty of teaching resources available on the Vikings and Norse Mythology. Godchecker.com The Viking Gods of Norse Mythology, norse-mythology.org **Research:** Hávamál. How popular culture has embraced characters like Thor and Odin, with TV shows/films and role playing games.
Stimulus	💀	An image of the tree (Yggdrasil) and the nine worlds. Viking images of the Norsemen and their ships. Thor's hammer.
	📖	*The Hammer of Thor:* Rick Riordan. *Norse Mythology:* Neil Gaiman. *The Lost Sun:* Tessa Gratton.
	📝	**Research:** Bragi, the god of poetry in Norse mythology.
	🎭	*The Norse Mythology Ragnasplosion:* Don Zolidis. *Valhalla:* Wade Bradford. Shakespeare; invoked Greek and Roman/Pagan gods in his plays.
	🎬	*Thor Ragnarok:* 2017 (12A). *Beowulf:* 2007 (12). *Vikings:* 2013–2020 TV series (12).
	🎵	*Immigrant Song:* Led Zeppelin. *Ride of The Valkyries:* Wagner.
	🎨	*Thor's Fight with the Giants:* Marten Eskil Winge. *Valkyries Riding into Battle:* Johan Gustaf Sandberg. The sculpture *Thor Resting His Hammer:* Herman Ernst Freund.
🎭		Younger students: The stories of the Norse gods through narration and dance. Emma Rice. Storytelling/Polly Teal, Marianne Elliot. Narration. Physicalisation. Older students: Theatre of Cruelty, highly choreographed, movement, gesture and dance. Masks and striking costume. Little dialogue, symbolic props. Artaud. The cruelty within some of the tales.
⚠		When researching be aware that some of the rituals involved animal and human sacrifice.
🔗		014, 026, 038, 035, 038, 046, 048, 066, 072, 079, 103, 114, 132, 134, 153, 190, 196.

038   Fate/chance

		'Chance is the fool's name for Fate' (Fred Astaire – American dancer, actor, singer).
♟	11+ Any size/mix groups.	
⚑	**Workshops/games:** *Body sculpture. Control games.* **Questionnaire:** What is your star sign and is it relevant? Is life just a game of chance, or a dance with fate? This can be the decision about artistic intent! **Look at the language:** A chance meeting. Fated to be so . . . 'Star crossed lovers'. He took a chance. God's will? What are the chances? Kismet. Fate seems dark and foreboding whilst chance offers hope. Is fate a power we cannot control?	
☀	**Research:** Star signs. Horoscopes and astrology. Ideas of fate and destiny in other cultures. Fortune tellers. Omens and signs. Tea leaves and tarot. Superstition v. belief.	
Stimulus	🎲	A Horoscope. Your star sign. What's the story behind that image?
	📖	*Life and Fate:* Vasily Grossman. *Cloud Atlas:* David Mitchell (also a film). *The Alchemist:* Paulo Coelho.
	📝	*It Might Have Been:* Ella Wheeler Wilcox.
	🎭	Consider fate over chance in *Romeo and Juliet, Hamlet* and *Macbeth* . . . Look at fate and destiny in *Blood Brothers.* Foreshadowing!
	🎞	*Blind Chance:* 1987 (15). *Serendipity:* 2001 (PG). *Amélie:* 2001 (15).
	🎵	*Invisible String:* Taylor Swift. *Simple Twist of Fate:* Bob Dylan. *Que Sera Sera:* Sly and the Family Stone.
	🎨	Look at images of *The Three Fates* in Art.
🎭	Fate, chance and choice. Physical theatre/dance Ensemble. A piece based on star signs using projections. Forum theatre involving the audience in choices about the outcome.	
⚠	Beware of some online sites.	
🔗	027, 031, 032, 034, 037, 051, 057, 076, 098, 101, 119, 151, 163, 168, 169.	

039   Aesop's Fables

	Αἴσωπος (*Aisōpos*) 'Once a wolf, always a wolf' (Aesop – Greek Fabulist).
🏺	Works very well with younger students.
🚩	**Workshops/games**: *Animal crackers.* Can you write a modern fable of your own? What is the moral you want to convey? How many of Aesop's fables could you adapt for the modern age?
💡	**Research**: The most popular of the 725 fables. A way of teaching a moral lesson. A fiction that points to the truth. Unicorn Theatre have published an excellent teachers' resource pack on Aesop's Fables. Compare to nursery rhymes and fairy tales. **Look at the language**: Aesop has enriched our language with phrases like: 'Sour grapes', 'Crying wolf', 'Honesty is the best policy', 'Actions speak louder than words', 'Look before you leap' .
Stimulus	🎞️ Pictures of animals (the characters are normally animals with human traits). List animals and their human traits.
	📖 *Aesop's Fables: Complete Collection (Illustrated and Annotated)*: Literary Classics collection. Book 6. *The Grasshopper's Song: An Aesop's Fable Revisited*: Nikki Giovanni. *The Complete Fables*: Penguin Classics.
	🎭 *Aesop's Fables: on Stage: A Collection of Children's Plays (Onstage Books, Book 1)*: Julie Meighan. *The Moon and Her Mother*: Linda Kohler. *Short Plays Based on Aesop's Fables*: Albert Callum.
	📽️ *The Million Dollar Duck*: 1971 (U). *The Tortoise and The Hare*: 1935 (U). *Aesop: Biography of a Great Thinker*: YouTube.
	🎵 *Life on the Wicked Stage*: Judy Garland. *The Boy Who Cried Wolf*: John Stegman. *Aesop's Fables in Song*: Ralph Martell.
	🎨 **Research**: Illustrators of Aesop's Fables, such as: Arthur Rackham, Tim Hayward and Walter Crane.
🎭	Playing the parts as humans but possessed of animal qualities/characteristics. Physicalising of animal-like qualities/movements. Berkoff. Younger students look at modern equivalents/narration-led pieces.
⚠️	Try not to simply re-tell the story. Look for the child and the humour in each.
🔗	031, 034, 040, 044, 045, 056, 068, 081, 082, 101, 109, 135, 160, 161, 175, 178, 186, 190, 192, 196, 197.

040   Urban Legends

	'There are more things in heaven and earth, Horatio, than are dreamt of in your philosophy' Hamlet: (William Shakespeare – English Playwright and poet).
⚎	Depends on the chosen urban myth but I tend to introduce this to students in the upper school/college. 15+ Mixed groups.
⚑	**Workshops/games:** *Chinese whispers* with a rumour! Start your own modern myth. **Questionnaire:** Are you aware of any local urban legends? Can you name any? From Area 51, Bigfoot and Chupacabra to the vanishing hitchhiker. Decide on a focus; happenings, hauntings, sightings or legends.
💡	Wikipedia.org list of urban Legends. *Teachers Pay Teachers* have some excellent resources on Urban Legends. **What the papers say:** Urban legends are nothing new but look at how quickly legends/rumours and fake news spread now due to media and in particular the internet. Do today's urban legends demonstrate modern society's fears and anxieties?

Stimulus	💀	Focus of the photographic evidence of sightings. Images of famous urban myths.
	📖	*King Rat:* China Miéville. *The Girl from the Well:* Rin Chupeco. *Be Afraid. Be Very Afraid: The Book of Scary Urban Legends:* Jan Harold Brunvand.
	📝	*Urban Myths and Legends: Poems about Transformations:* Rachel Piercey and Emma Wright.
	🎭	*The Survivor and Other Urban Legends:* Brian Starchman. *Death by Drama and Other Medieval Urban Legends:* Jody Enders.
	🎬	*The Blair Witch Project:* 1999 (15). *Urban Legend:* 1998 (18). *Chernobyl Diaries:* 2012 (15). *Urban Legends:* 2007 (TV series).
	🎵	*Stairway to Heaven:* Led Zeppelin. *Crossroads:* Robert Johnson. **In the Air Tonight:** Phil Collins. **Research:** The 21 Club. 'The Devil's interval' (tritone or augmented 4th).
	🎨	**Search for:** Urban myths. A Collaborative Project of Artists Drawing Popular Urban Legends. Urban Legends of Art – The Museum of Hoaxes.

🎪	Look for humour more than the horror. Theatre of the Absurd and highly choreographed physical work, Frantic Assembly, to tell/expose some of the crazier urban myths.
⚠	Some searches may lead to unsavoury material.
🔗	031–035, 041, 047, 076, 088, 102, 103, 109, 114, 119, 123, 129, 144, 145, 153, 156, 162, 171, 172, 173, 177, 178, 179, 181, 187, 190, 192, 195.

041   Angels

	'All God's angels come to us disguised' (J. R. Lowell – American poet).
⚸	11+ Small groups mixed.
🏴	**Workshops/games:** *Guide me. Trust games.* **Questionnaire:** Do you believe in angels? What do they look like. Draw an angel. Are they superhuman servants of God or a wishful mews? Are angels strictly a Christian thing? Can you feel the existence of an angel?
�	Genesis 1:26 **Search for:** Live Science article 'Are Angels Real?' Also Captured images of angel. **Look at the language:** Angel of death. Avenging angel. She's an angel. Angels of Mercy. Hell's Angels. Why did the brightest and best of them fall? Angels and gender. Superheroes and Angels. Angels exist in multiple religions.

Stimulus	☠	Angel costumes/wings. Images of angels abound! **Search for:** Images of *Heavenly Angels* and compare with the results of a search for *Earthly Angels.*
	📖	*Skellig:* David Almond. *Hush, Hush:* Becca Fitzpatrick. *Daughter of Smoke and Bone:* Laini Taylor.
	📝	*The Angel:* William Blake.
	🎭	*The Mysteries:* Tony Harrison. *Dr Faustus:* Christopher Marlowe. *Language of Angels:* Naomi Iizuka.
	🎞	*City of Angels:* 1998 (12). *It's a Wonderful Life:* 1946 (U). *Constantine:* 2005 (15). 'Lisa The Skeptic': Season 9, episode 8 of *The Simpsons.*
	🎵	*Angels:* Robbie Williams. *There Must be an Angel:* Eurythmics. *Angels Cry:* Mariah Carey. *Panis Angelicus:* Franck/Wager.
	🎨	*The Sistine Madonna:* Raphael. *The Angel Standing in the Sun:* William Turner. *Angel of the North:* Antony Gormley's modern sculpture

🎭	Great dance pieces. Promenade (mystery plays). Angel Gabriel and Angel Lucifer dance/physical duet.
⚠	Respect other faiths/cultures.
🔗	022, 026, 033, 035, 040, 044, 048, 049, 051, 055, 058, 076, 088, 116, 117, 141, 157, 158, 159, 169, 176, 184, 192, 197.

042   The Devil

	'Sometimes Satan Comes as a Man of Peace' (William Blake - English Poet and Bob Dylan - American singer/songwriter).
♣♀	15+ Mixed.
▷	**Workshops/games:** *Status.* Look at the list of sayings/phrases concerning the Devil. For example, *'Speak of the Devil'*. Look at the different names he is known by. Fallen Angel? Something to fear? **Research:** The downfall of Angel Lucifer in the opening scene of *The Mysteries:* Tony Harrison. Make masks to show Devils from different cultures/faiths.
☼	BBC Bitesize GCSE CCEA Religious Studies, '*The problem with evil and suffering*'. Look at the Bible, Islam and other major religions. Sikhism does not have a concept of Satan but that demons and devils are the product of our ego. Look at the history of Satan, Lucifer, Beelzebub (The Lord of the Flies). **Look at the language:** How the popular press use the word 'devil(s)'.

Stimulus		
	☠	There are many symbols and images of the Devil, 'evil'.
	📖	*I Lucifer:* Glen Duncan. *The Devil You Know:* Tom Holt. *The Sorrows of Satan:* Marie Corelli. *The History of the Devil:* Gerald Messadié.
	✍	*The Devil – Had He Fidelity:* Emily Dickinson.
	🎭	*The Devils:* John Whiting. *The Messiah:* Berkoff. *Dr Faustus:* Cristopher Marlowe. 'The Devil can cite scripture for his purpose', ANTONIO in *The Merchant Of Venice*. Shakespeare.
	🎬	*The Devil's Advocate:* 1997 (18). *The Witches of Eastwick:* 1987 (18). *Lucifer:* 2016 (TV series Netflix).
	🎵	*Sympathy for the Devil:* The Rolling Stones. *Man of Peace:* Bob Dylan. *The Damnation of Faust:* Berlioz.
	🎨	The works of Hieronymus Bosch. *Saint Michael Vanquishing Satan:* Raphael. *Witches' Sabbath:* Goya. Watch the 2015 documentary *Hieronymus Bosch, Touched by The Devil*.

🎭	The Rolling Stones' *Sympathy for the Devil* as a dance/physical piece. Ensemble influenced by Satan's monologue in Berkoff's *Messiah, Scenes from A Crucifixion*. Choral movement based on 'Get thee behind me, Satan'.
⚠	Any web-based research should be supervised. Images and content may not be suitable. Be audience aware.
🔗	26, 28, 29, 31, 32, 34, 35, 40, 45, 46, 48, 50, 55, 129, 179.

043   Abuse in the church

	'We have realised that these wounds never disappear' (Pope Francis – Argentine).
(symbol)	16+ Mature, mixed small friendship groups.
(symbol)	**Workshops/games:** *Trust. Status games.* Vulnerability. Lack of control/power over your own life. Look at the abuse of having your culture torn from you. The sexual/physical abuse is highly sensitive, but this does not mean it shouldn't be addressed.
(symbol)	**Research:** The mass graves at the children's home in Canada. 'Remove the Indian from the child.' Over a century of abuses at residential schools that stripped children of their Indigenous cultures and languages. **Look at:** The rest of the quote by Pope Francis. **What the papers say:** The reporting of church cover ups of sexual abuse by the clergy. Historically, look at witch trials, missions, The Inquisition, The Crusades . . . The disappeared Irish children/babies.

Stimulus		
	(symbol)	A cross, a bible, prison bars on a window, a stained glass window.
	(symbol)	*Crimes of the Father:* Tom Keneally. *Beyond Belief:* David Yallop. *For the Love of God:* Natasha Moore.
	(symbol)	*Be my Baby:* Amanda Whittington. *The Magdalen Whitewash:* Valerie Goodwin. *Doubt:* John Patrick Shanley.
	(symbol)	*Doubt:* 2008 (15). *Twist of Faith:* 2004 (TV-MA) 18+ *The Mission:* 1986 (PG). *'The woman in The Wall'* BBC TV series.
	(symbol)	*Slow Train Coming:* Bob Dylan. *Jesus Doesn't Want Me for a Sunbeam:* Nirvana. *The Mission Theme:* Ennio Morricone.
	(symbol)	The sculpture *Cardinal Sin:* Banksy.

(symbol)	Sensitive Verbatim theatre. Symbolism or 'In yer Face' but be very cautious. Duologues, Frantic Assembly. Theatre of the Absurd.
(symbol)	This has to be sensitive and never personal. Check school policies. I recommend permission from home/letters of explanation (artistic intent).
(symbol)	003, 013, 015, 020, 026, 029, 044, 045, 048, 059, 063, 064, 071, 100, 107, 132, 157, 160.

044   Good v Evil

<table>
<tr>
<td></td>
<td></td>
<td colspan="2">'The battleline between good and evil runs through the heart of every man'
(Aleksandr Solzhenitsyn – Russian writer).</td>
</tr>
<tr>
<td></td>
<td colspan="3">All ages. Small groups.</td>
</tr>
<tr>
<td></td>
<td colspan="3">Workshops/games: Control games. Status.
Have two students represent good/evil and whisper advice to a third in a given scenario. How did it feel?
From history, select 2 really good/bad people.
Improvisations based on good deeds and bad deeds
Look at the language: Black and white, right and wrong, good and bad, the dark side. Yin Yang. Heroes and villains.</td>
</tr>
<tr>
<td></td>
<td colspan="3">TES have produced some excellent teaching resources on Good Versus Evil.
Research: The Philosophy/ethics of Good and Evil. Nietzsche.
Watch: Nike's famous advert 'Good vs Evil' on YouTube.
The battle between good and evil is ancient. Today both good and evil have a platform on social media.</td>
</tr>
<tr>
<td rowspan="7">Stimulus</td>
<td></td>
<td colspan="2">Select images of extreme opposites; people from history and some less obvious. Place them on the floor and ask students to put them in a right to left order from the most evil/terrible to the most saintly/good and discuss.</td>
</tr>
<tr>
<td></td>
<td colspan="2">The School for Good and Evil: Soman Chainani.
The Great Divorce: C. S. Lewis.
Midnight in the Garden of Good and Evil: John Berendt.</td>
</tr>
<tr>
<td></td>
<td colspan="2">Lemon Tree: Landis Everson.</td>
</tr>
<tr>
<td></td>
<td colspan="2">Doctor Faustus: Christopher Marlowe.
Nat Turner's Last Struggle: P. A. Wray.
The Crucible: Arthur Miller.
Research: The Morality Plays.</td>
</tr>
<tr>
<td></td>
<td colspan="2">The Harry Potter films.
The Passion of the Christ: 2004 (R).
The Lion King: 1994 (U).</td>
</tr>
<tr>
<td></td>
<td colspan="2">The Devil Went Down to Georgia: Charlie Daniels.
Onward Christian Soldiers: A Hymn by Sabine Baring-Gould.
Sympathy for the Devil: The Rolling Stones.</td>
</tr>
<tr>
<td></td>
<td colspan="2">The Good and the Evil Angels: William Blake.
David and Goliath: Courtois.
The Third of May 1808: Goya.</td>
</tr>
<tr>
<td></td>
<td colspan="3">Simple costume, using light, levels and mask. Modern comparisons.
Noh theatre and shadow puppets both work well.
Sound can be important.</td>
</tr>
<tr>
<td></td>
<td colspan="3">Some images may be disturbing.</td>
</tr>
<tr>
<td></td>
<td colspan="3">005, 007, 014, 025–029, 034, 035, 039, 041, 042, 043, 045, 048, 079, 109, 133, 142, 144, 160, 174, 187, 197.</td>
</tr>
</table>

045   Temptation

	'I generally avoid temptation unless I can't resist it' (Mae West – American actress).
⚑	15+ Suits mixed groups.
🚩	**Workshops/games**: *Control games.* The temptation to have an extra slice of cake, to smoke, to drink, to lie, to cheat, to kill . . . Put students in pairs. Use tempting language to get partner to do what you want. Giving in and the guilt. Emotions and feelings. **Questionnaire**: Have you ever been tempted to . . .? **Look at the language**: Tempting offers. You know you want to. Can I tempt you? Resist temptation. Tempting fate . . .
☼	**Research**: The three sources of temptation according to the bible. How Eve tempted Adam with an apple and what this has meant for womenkind ever since. **Look at**: 'Tempting offers' in advertising. Even the naming of some products. **What the papers say**: BBC news magazine article 'Why people give in to temptation when no-one's watching', Sept 2013.

Stimulus		
	🐌	Images of a snake/serpent. An apple. A doughnut.
	📖	*The Bible*: Genesis, Mathew and Luke. *Temptation*: Douglas Kennedy. *The Last Temptation*: Nikos Kazantzakis.
	📝	*Goblin Market*: Christina Rossetti.
	🎭	*Dr Faustus*: Christopher Marlowe. *Temptation*: Václav Havel. *Macbeth*: Shakespeare.
	🎞	*Dangerous Liaisons*: 1988 (15). *The Last Temptation of Christ*: 1988 (18). *The Simpsons – The Last Temptation of Homer*: Season 5, Episode 9.
	🎵	*Me and Mrs Jones*: Billy Paul. *Jolene*: Dolly Parton. *Don't Stand so Close to Me*: The Police.
	🎨	*The Temptation of Saint Anthony*: Various interpretations. The works of Hieronymus Bosch and Salvador Dali.

🎭	Good and bad. Sin or redemption. Physical theatre. Masks and costume. Puppets. Artaud.
⚠	Searches containing the word 'temptation' require a safe search filter and/or supervision!
🔗	021, 029, 031, 034, 039, 045, 062, 063, 075, 077, 086, 087, 096–099, 104, 105, 123, 135, 136, 188, 192.

046   Reincarnation and afterlife

	'I believe in reincarnation, and I believe I've lived quite a few lives' (Dr. Dre – American rapper).	
🎭	15+ Able students mixed groups of 3 or 4.	
🚩	**Workshops/games:** *Body sculpture. Emotion memory.* Start with a clear idea of what the group feels. Challenge students to improvise around a 'what if' scenario . . . If I came back would I remember? Ever had that feeling of Déjà vu? Create an image by talking about/remembering a relative who has passed away. Are they still alive because we remember them? Their deeds, a turn of phrase, their love for us . . .	
🔆	In Christianity, Judaism and Islam afterlife is promised by God. **Research:** The differing faiths and how they treat life after death. **What the papers say:** The Salvation Army magazine *Others* has some interesting articles, 'Ten reasons to believe in life after death'.	
Stimulus	🐌	Old photographs. An hourglass/a clock. A candle (torch). A mirror. Dead flowers. A bell. A ladder. A butterfly.
	📖	*The Brief History of the Dead:* Kevin Brockmeier. *What Dreams May Come:* Richard Matherson. *Sum: Forty Tales from the Afterlives:* David Eagleman.
	📝	*Fairy-Land:* Edgar Allan Poe.
	🎭	*100:* Diene Petterle, Neil Monaghan and Christopher Heimann. *After Life:* Jack Thorne.
	🎬	*Coco:* 2017 (PG). *What Dreams May Come:* 1998 (15). *Truly, Madly, Deeply:* 1990 (PG). *Surviving Death:* A Netflix docuseries.
	🎵	*Tears in Heaven:* Eric Clapton. *Death is not the End:* Bob Dylan. *He that Dwelleth in Heaven:* Handel's *Messiah.*
	🎨	*The Garden of Earthly Delights:* Hieronymus Bosch. *For the Love of God:* (Sculpture) Damien Hirst. Look at the image of passengers for heaven boarding Concorde in the movie '*Heaven Can Wait*'.
🎭	Berkoff, Lecoq. Ensemble piece. Black and white set. Light and dark/shadows. Soundscapes, choral. Dance to a Handel's *Messiah* fusion with disco lights and levels.	
⚠️	Be sensitive to other people's faiths.	
🔗	048, 049, 050, 055, 057.076, 123, 169, 192,	

047   Ghosts

		'*The Supernatural is the Natural, just not yet understood*' (Elbert Hubbard – American writer/philosopher).
⚉		Any age and group size (differentiate by maturity).
⚑		**Workshops/games:** *Levels of tension. Silent scream.* I sat everyone down and plunged the studio into darkness (the usual screams!). Why did you scream? Do you believe in ghosts? What does Halloween mean to you? Have you seen a ghost? Dreamed about a ghost?
☼		**Look at:** nationaltrust.org.uk and look for 'Our most haunted places'. **Search for:** 'Local ghosts', 'Global Ghost Stories' **Research** 'Famous hauntings'. Live Science article *Are Ghosts Real?* Ghosts were very real to people centuries ago and even today's more cynical generation is still driven to seek out stories of the dead returning. **What the papers say:** Newspapers like to follow ghost sightings/hauntings as stories. Often as the lighter side of life . . .
Stimulus	☺	The usual Halloween stuff.
	📖	*The Woman in Black:* Susan Hill. *The Amityville Horror:* Jay Anson. *The Turn of the Screw:* Henry James.
	✍	*The Kind Ghost:* Wilfred Owen.
	🎭	*The Woman in Black:* Susan Hill adapted by Stephen Mallatrat. *The Train Driver:* Athol Fugard. *Black Harvest:* Nigel Gray.
	🎬	*Ghost:* 1990 (15). *Coco:* 2017 (PG). *Truly, Madly, Deeply:* 1990 (PG).
	🎵	*Ghosts that We Knew:* Mumford and Sons. *Ghostbusters:* Ray Parker Jr. *Tubular Bells Part 1:* Mike Oldfield.
	🎨	*The Nightmare:* Henry Fuseli. **Search for:** 'Angela Deane's playful ghosts'.
🎦		A child's music box. The rocking chair from *The Woman in Black!* The unseen is more frightening than the 'thing' itself. Simple sound effects and rising tension. The white mask!
⚠		Think of health and safety! The objective is not to frighten the performers!
🔗		031–037, 040, 041, 042, 046, 049, 050, 057, 064, 074, 088, 107, 123, 144, 157, 169, 190.

048   Heaven and Hell

		'Heaven and hell are within us . . .' (Joseph Campbell – American writer).
🎭🧍		All ages. Mixed
🚩		**Workshops/games**: *Emotion memory. Circles of attention.* Describe the best place you can imagine. Now the worst. How does it feel to be there? Look at deeds leading to heaven or hell.
💡		BBC Bitesize GCSE Religious, WJEC, The afterlife/heaven and hell. **Search for**: The case for heaven and hell. **Look at the language**: Explore how the press uses the words 'Heaven' and 'Hell'. One man's heaven is another man's hell. A matter of juxtaposition.
Stimulus	💀	Heaven and Hell stock photos.
	📖	*Hell*: Robert Olen Butler. *The Five People You Meet in Heaven*: Mitch Albom. *Heaven and Hell*: Bart D Ehrman.
	✍️	*Heaven and Hell*: Francis Thompson.
	🎭	*100*: Diene Petterle, Neil Monaghan and Christopher Heimann. *The Mysteries*: Tony Harrison. 'I'll follow thee and make a heaven of hell', HELENA in *A Midsummer Night's Dream*.
	🎞️	*The Shack*: 2017 (12A). *Legend*: 1985 (PG). *What Dreams May Come*: 1998 (15).
	🎵	*Heaven and Hell*: Black Sabbath. *Knocking on Heaven's Door*: Guns N' Roses. *Highway to Hell*: AC/DC.
	🎨	Hieronymus Bosch. In particular the triptych, *The Garden of Earthly Delights*. *The Abyss of Hell*: Botticelli.
🎪		Show heaven and hell on earth, both geographically and historically. A metaphor for change. Physical/dance based performance to one piece of music. Use lighting, levels and ladders/poles. DV8.
⚠️		Be sure of artistic intentions from an early stage.
🔗		026, 035, 041, 042, 045, 046, 050, 055, 144.169, 182, 192

049   Fairies

		'Those who don't believe in magic will never find it' (Roald Dahl – British writer).
🐝		Everyone! Depending on the age of your students this can be as light or dark as they wish.
🏁		**Workshops/games**: *Body sculpture. Circles of attention.* Light up your drama space with colours and mirrors (for the younger students). *Light up thumbs*, are magical and available through the usual online retailers. If you have woodlands nearby, suspend disbelief and take your class for a look. Use music/dance in rehearsals.
💡		The study of fairies is known as Fairyology **Search for:** The science of fairies. Up until the mid-1800s most people believed in magical creatures. **What the papers say:** Newspaper articles from the 1917 Cottingley Fairies scam. **More controversial**: Not all fairies were nice! Often, lustful, vindictive and even murderous! Compare this with the Disney image! **Research:** The murder case of Bridget Cleary in 1895 Ireland.
Stimulus	💀	A toadstool. Shiny objects, buttons, badges, paperclips, glitter and fairy dust. Silks and gossamer. Spider's webs . . .
	📖	*The Girl Who Circumnavigated Fairyland in a Ship of Her Own Making:* C. M. Valente. *The Night Fairy:* Laura A Schlitz. *Artemis Fowl:* Eoin Colfer.
	📝	*The Stolen Child:* W. B. Yates.
	🎭	*At the Black Pig's Dyke:* Vincent Woods. *Collected Grimm's Tales:* Carol Anne Duffy and Tim Supple. Look at PUCK's monologue 'I am that Merry Wanderer of the Night', Act 2, Scene 1, *A Midsummer Night's Dream.*
	🎬	*Maleficent:* 2014 (PG). *Pan:* 2015 (PG). *Strange Magic:* 2015 (U). *Fairies:* BBC 2014 Documentary. YouTube.
	🎵	Fairy Song to TITANIA in Shakespeare's *A Midsummer Night's Dream*, Act 2, Scene 2. *April Come She Will:* Simon and Garfunkel. *Stolen Child:* Loreena McKennitt.
	🎨	Look at the art/literature of the Pre-Raphaelites. Also 'Fairy Painting' as a genre. Fairy painting of the Victorian era.
🎪		J. M. Barrie's idea that 'Wherever there are fairies, there are children'. Sinister gothic piece about children being stolen (changelings) and swopped for fairies. Take the Disney/Tinker Bell fairy idea and enchant/convince your audience with mirrors, light and trickery.
⚠		Some fairies are just not nice!
🔗		031–035, 040, 041, 047, 054, 055, 076, 120, 157, 158, 172, 176, 192.

050   NDE (Near death experience)

		'Life is a dream walking. Death is going home' (Chinese proverb).
♨		15+ Sensitive/mature, small mixed groups. Research based.
⚑		**Workshops/games:** *Emotion memory. Body sculpture. Mirror images.* An unexplained bright white light in a darkened space. Do the students walk toward it or away from it. Whether they believe or not, share some statements, quotes about NDEs. **Look at the language:** 'My life flashed before me.' Visions of the afterlife?
💡		**What the papers say:** See article by ABC News 6th January 2006, *'Scientists Validate Near-Death Experiences'.* First recorded medical report of a NDE was by an 18th-century military doctor, Pierre-Jean du Monchaux. Where do our minds wander to when we daydream? Consider the more scientific research/journals.
Stimulus	🕯	A lit candle. An hour-glass/timer. A bright light. A river to cross, a set of gates. An olive branch, a red rose, old photos of relatives, a mirror.
	📖	*Passage:* Connie Willis. *Wenny Has Wings:* Janet Lee Carey. *After:* Bruce Greyson M.D. *Dance through It:* C. E. Renfrow.
	📝	*The Rime of The Ancient Mariner:* Samuel Taylor Coleridge.
	🎭	*Hamlet:* William Shakespeare. *Notes to Future Self:* Lucy Caldwell.
	🎞	*Dragonfly:* 2002 (12). *Flatliners:* 1990 (15). *Surviving Death:* 2021 (Netflix) (13+).
	🎵	*Your Near-Death Experience:* Lola's Pocket PC. Listen to/watch: *Anathema* from *Internal Landscapes.* *Oh Death:* Handel's Messiah.
	🎨	**Look at:** The paintings of David Ditchfield, the works of Hieronymus Bosch and Gustav Doré.
🎭		Dance without music. Images flashed across screens, narration. Play with light and shadows. Physical Theatre, collaboration of art forms using physical/dance, dialogue, soundscape and music building an emotional story for a character, DV8.
⚠		Trust and sensitivity is very important.
🔗		033, 046, 048, 055, 057, 123, 151, 182,

051 Love

		'Love is just a four-letter word' (Bob Dylan – American singer/songwriter).
		12+ All abilities. Mixed groups work well.
		Workshops/games: *Gestus. Body sculpture.* List the types of Love: of country, money, self, parents, our children, wife, life and good food! Unrequited, at first sight and selfless. The movies, the songs, the literature. What does love mean to you?
		Search for: How love is used in advertising. Make a list of the people you love, people who are loving, who define love. Great love affairs like: Richard Burton and Elizabeth Taylor, Charles and Di, Edward and Mrs Simpson. **What the papers say:** High profile love affairs. How are they treated? **Look at the language:** I'd love to. Love that idea. Love it! Love you. In love. For love. Loving couple. . . How many more?
Stimulus		All those hearts and emojis!
		Jane Eyre: Charlotte Brontë. *Wuthering Heights:* Emily Bronte. *The Notebook:* Nicholas Sparks.
		If You Forget Me: Pablo Neruda. *Sonnet 116:* Shakespeare.
		Romeo and Juliet: Shakespeare. *Blood Wedding:* Lorca. *Lovesong:* Abi Morgan.
		An endless list to which you and your students can add or remove. *Five Feet Apart:* 2019 (12A). *City of Angels:* 1998 (12). *Like Water for Chocolate:* 1992 (15). *Romeo and Juliet:* Zeffirelli's and Baz Luhrmann's make good comparisons.
		The First Time Ever I Saw Your Face: Roberta Flack. *I Want to Know What Love Is:* Foreigner. *The Power of Love:* Frankie Goes to Hollywood.
		The Kiss: Gustav Klimt. *The Lovers:* René Magritte. *The Kiss:* Rodin. New York's famous 'LOVE' sculpture by Robert Indiana.
		Tongue in cheek, full blown musical style, perhaps with a Brechtian slap. Break Neck speed falling in love physical theatre. Frantic Assembly (duets). Mime/dance. Have fun with the visual side of the fool love makes of us all.
		Some search results may be explicit!
		033, 034, 038, 053, 058, 065, 069, 077, 078, 079, 086, 087, 078, 141, 181, 183.

052   Grief

<table>
<tr>
<td colspan="2"></td>
<td>'You never know how strong you are until being strong is the only option.
(Bob Marley – Jamaican Reggae musician).</td>
</tr>
<tr>
<td colspan="2">⚭♀</td>
<td>15+ mixed. Small friendship groups.</td>
</tr>
<tr>
<td colspan="2">🏁</td>
<td>Workshops/games: 3 Stages of grief. Silent screams. Emotion memory.
Discussion. (In a safe place.) When you hear the expression, 'My heart is broken' what does it mean to you?
A long term sadness, which doesn't have an easy solution. When drying your eyes and smiling doesn't help. Grief without a voice. Look for facial/physical expression of sorrow.</td>
</tr>
<tr>
<td colspan="2">🔆</td>
<td>Research: The New York Life Foundation.
Cruse bereavement support.
National Grief Awareness Week. (Childhood bereavement.)
Look at: How nations grieve. For example Princess Diana. The Queen. 9/11. Remembrance day.
Look at the language: 'Sorry for your loss.' Grief stricken. Mourning. Profound sorrow. RIP.</td>
</tr>
<tr>
<td rowspan="7">Stimulus</td>
<td>🐌</td>
<td>The flowers, the funeral and afterwards when the shared sorrow becomes only yours. A box of tissues.</td>
</tr>
<tr>
<td>📖</td>
<td>The Phone Box at the Edge of the World: Laura Imai Messina.
A Grief Observed: C. S. Lewis.
Beginner's Goodbye: Anne Tyler.</td>
</tr>
<tr>
<td>📝</td>
<td>Funeral Blues: W. H. Auden.</td>
</tr>
<tr>
<td>🎭</td>
<td>Pink Mist: Owen Sheers.
The Long Road: Shelagh Stephenson.
Hymns: Chris O'Connell. Frantic Assembly.</td>
</tr>
<tr>
<td>🎬</td>
<td>Truly, Madly, Deeply: 1991 (PG).
P.S. I Love You: 2007 (PG).
Afterlife: 2019–2022 (TV series) (15).</td>
</tr>
<tr>
<td>🎵</td>
<td>Supermarket Flowers: Ed Sheeran.
I'll be Missing You: Puff Daddy and Faith Evans.
I Grieve: Peter Gabriel.</td>
</tr>
<tr>
<td>🎨</td>
<td>Inconsolable Grief: Ivan Kramskoy (1884).
Death in the Sickroom: Edvard Munch (1893).</td>
</tr>
<tr>
<td colspan="2">🎪</td>
<td>Soundscape of the things people say at funerals. Small groups to show the isolation of grief.
Frantic Assembly duets.
Character work. Stanislavski. Emotion memory.</td>
</tr>
<tr>
<td colspan="2">⚠️</td>
<td>Know your students.</td>
</tr>
<tr>
<td colspan="2">🔗</td>
<td>003–015, 051, 057, 059, 068, 071, 080, 087, 117, 118, 127, 128, 156.</td>
</tr>
</table>

053   LGBTQ+

	'Love him and let him love you. Do you think anything else under heaven really matters?' (James Baldwin – American writer).
🎭	With small groups of friends, this unit can go in many positive ways. Age as you feel appropriate.
▱	**Workshops/games:** *Alienation. Body sculpture. Columbian hypnosis.* Start with Pride, a time for celebration. Celebrate historic LGBTQ+ figures who have made changes in the world. **Research:** The following people: Sylvia Rivera. Freda Kahlo. Josephine Baker. Michael Dillon. Virginia Woolf. Eleanor Roosevelt. Simon Nkoli. Nancy Cárdenas. Bayard Rustin. Each of their inspiring stories are well worth looking at and can be the seeds of an idea.
☼	TES have excellent resources on LGBT+ in their PSHE sections. **Research:** The history of LGBTQ+. Build a timeline of important events. February is LGBTQ+ History Month. Museum of London: LGBTQ+ and history. A downloadable resource from TATE. Tate teaching resource: Thinking about gender and bodies. Tate Kids: 5 LGBTQ+ Art Stories.

Stimulus		
	💀	Pride posters. The rainbow. A heart.
	📖	*On Earth We're Briefly Gorgeous:* Ocean Vuong. *All This Could Be Different:* Sarah Thankam Mathews. *Symptoms of Being Human:* Jeff Garvin.
	✒	*Until We Could:* Richard Blanco.
	🎭	*Death and Dancing:* Claire Dowie. *Bent:* Martin Sherman. *Neaptide:* Sarah Daniels.
	🎬	*The Death and Life of Martha P. Johnson:* 2017 (Documentary) (15). *Beautiful Thing:* 1996 (15). *Boys Don't Cry:* 1999 (18).
	🎵	*Dancing on My Own:* Robyn. *Raise Your Glass:* P!nk. *True Colours:* Cyndi Lauper.
	🎨	Research the works of: Robert Rauschenberg, Catherine Opie, Beauford Delaney and Mickalene Thomas.

🎭	Storytelling. Verbatim. Forum. Theatre for social change. Boal. Eddie Ladd. Kneehigh. Or, Movement, gesture and dance, masks and puppets. Artaud.
⚠	Know your students.
🔗	018, 020, 021, 025, 027, 033, 051, 054, 059, 063–066, 070, 071, 073, 076, 078, 080, 081, 135, 149, 160, 161, 174, 182–186, 192, 196, 199, 200.

054   Beauty

		'Everything has beauty but not everyone sees it' (Confucius – Chinese philosopher).
👥		14+ Mixed groups of 2–4.
🚩		**Workshops/games:** *Body sculpture. Mirror images. Stereotypes.* Think about, clothes, art and architecture which can be described as beautiful or ugly. Mozart or Slipknot? Beauty in the eye of the beholder . . . Juxtaposition of time, place and culture.
🔆		**Research:** Metaperception. The Media is obsessed with beauty. **Look at the language:** Adorable, cute, aesthetically pleasing, stunning, beautiful, gorgeous . . . **More controversial:** Some victims in the news are just more appealing than others! Question whether attractiveness and gender influence the value of the news we read and watch. Beauty is only skin deep?
Stimulus	💀	Famous poses by Marilyn Monroe or Brigitte Bardot and Olga Sherer or Sarah Jessica Parker. James Dean or Warren Beaty and Jonny Depp or Heath Ledger. A mirror, a selfie.
	📖	*On Beauty:* Zadie Smith. *Stronger, Faster and More Beautiful:* Arwen Elys Dayton. *North of Beautiful:* Justina Chen.
	📝	*Beauty Is Brief and Violent:* Snehal Vadher. *Sonnet 54:* Shakespeare.
	🎭	*The Beauty Manifesto:* Nell Leyshon. *Beauty and The Beast:* from Carol Ann Duffy's *Beasts and Beauties*.
	🎬	*Coco Before Chanel:* 2009 (PG-13). *America Beauty:* 1999 (18). *Collateral Beauty:* 2016 (12A). *The Social Media Beauty Cult:* (German) Documentary; YouTube.
	🎵	*Beautiful Girls:* INXS. *You're Beautiful:* James Blunt. *Girl Can't Be Herself:* Alicia Keys.
	🎨	*The Mona Lisa:* da Vinci. *Beautiful Monster:* Francis Picabia. *Twisted Beauty:* Zdzisław Beksiński. *Beauty on Beauty:* Photograph: Dirty Hans.
🎦		How social media affects trends in what is considered beautiful/acceptable. Using selfies taken before and during the show. Project onto screens whilst the characters on stage enact a story steered by how popular their selfie images is. Ensemble. Choreographed physical theatre/unison and coordinated movement.
⚠️		Be aware of body image issues.
🔗		53, 60, 70, 86, 87, 88, 110, 176, 182, 196.

055   Dreams and Nightmares

	'A dream itself is but a shadow' (Shakespeare – English playwright and poet).
	11+ Mixed groups.
	Workshops/games: *Fear. Repetition exercises. Silent scream.* **Questionnaire:** Who has dreams? Do you have a recurring dream? What about nightmares? The most common dreams: Losing teeth, falling, being chased, flying. **Look at the language:** The job was a nightmare! It was a dream job. He was dreamy. She was a nightmare! Do our dreams have meaning? Does the group share similar dreams? Are dreams a kind of improvisation?
	Research: Articles in science magazines and medical journals. In ancient times people believed our dreams were messages sent directly from relatives or deities as predictions/warnings of future events. Some civilisations believe their stories are re-told through dreams. Aboriginal Dreamtime (Unit 036).

Stimulus		What objects frequently appear in your dreams?
		Dreamfall: Amy Plum. *Some Dreams Are Nightmares:* James E. Gunn. *Dreamwork for Actors:* Janet Sonenberg.
		The Dream: John Donne.
		Four Nights in Knaresborough: Paul Webb. *Billy Liar:* Waterhouse and Hall. *Black Harvest:* Nigel Gray.
		Before I Wake: 2016 (15). *Extinction:* 2018 (15). *Mulholland Drive:* 2001 (15). Do Films influence our dreams/nightmares?
		Sweet Dreams (Are Made of This): Eurythmics. *All I Have To Do Is Dream:* The Everly Brothers. *Dream:* John Lennon.
		The Sleeping Gypsy: Henri Rousseau. *Jacob's Dream:* Raphael. *The Sleep of Reason:* Goya. *The Dream:* Picasso. *The Key to Dreams:* Magritte.

	Taking the idea that dreams are recurring, repeat a scene over and over but from a different perspective, time, angle, person. The dreamer being ever present sometimes as an observer. Real characters in a non-naturalistic environment. Slow motion and dance. Strobe (with care).
	Some sites on dreams should be looked at by the teacher first.
	033, 036, 037, 074, 123, 151, 176, 195.

056   The circle of life

	'It's the circle of life, and it moves us all, through despair and hope, through faith and love, 'till we find our place, on the path unwinding' (Elton John – English singer/songwriter).
👥	Suits large groups, Ensemble. All ages
🚩	**Workshops/games:** *Repetition exercises.* Draw a circle (clockface). Mark where you were born. Where are you now? A way of looking at life which can be comforting, in that life is a circle, a never-ending cycle: however, this could also be a negative . . . The end of one journey is the beginning of the next but do some circles go the other way? Try to physicalise these notions . . .
💡	Think about the way that events can come back around to their original starting point. Also used as a metaphor for someone or something coming back to their roots. The saying can be traced back to ancient philosophy and religions, but has come back in to popular culture. **Research:** Others cultures and the great circle of life.

Stimulus		
	💀	There are specific symbols/images associated with the circle of life. Circles and Celtic knots.
	📖	*The Circle of Life:* Dr Bruess. *Heron River:* Hugh Cook. *Before I Saw You:* Amy K. Sorrells.
	📝	*The Seven Ages of Man:* from Shakespeare's *As You Like It.*
	🎭	*The Lion King:* The Musical (Disney). *Circles:* Rachel De-lahay. *Lovesong:* Abi Morgan.
	🎲	*Life of Pi:* 2012 (PG). *Circle of Life:* 2015 (short) (PG). *Bodysong:* 2003 (Documentary) (18).
	🎵	*The Circle of Life:* from *The Lion King,* Elton John and Tim Rice.
	🎨	*Circle of Life:* Angelique Beauvence. Look at the *Life Cycles* paintings and sculptures of Martin Hill and Philippa Jones.

🎭	Physical theatre, ensemble/dance. Music, rhythms/beat. Musical instruments on stage with performers. Ensemble, mime. Lecoq.
⚠️	Open to vast possibilities, literal or metaphorical, students should make it their own.
🔗	013, 021, 025, 027, 033, 044, 055, 057, 074, 076, 101, 114, 119, 126, 151.

057   Death

		'The undiscovered country . . .' (Shakespeare – English playwright and poet).
⚰		15+ Mixed groups of 2–4
🚩		**Workshops/games:** *Emotion memory. Fear.* If we consider the images/artifacts it can become a negative and fearful. However, look at inspirational quotes about death and it can become more positive. We should try to encourage positive artistic intentions.
💡		MarieCurie.org.uk have produced a valuable resource on talking to children about death. Look at how death is reported by the press. **Look at language:** 'Peacefully' and 'passed away' to 'slaughtered' and 'perished'. Why are there so many comedy films/TV series about death and dying? **Look at:** How different cultures deal with death and dying and the process of mourning
Stimulus	💀	A snuffed candle, a skull, an hourglass, dead flowers. The Grim Reaper. A graveyard. A sickle/scythe. A coffin.
	📖	*White Noise:* Don Delillo. *One Hundred Years of Solitude:* Gabriel García Márquez. *My Sister's Keeper:* Jodi Picoult.
	✍	*Do Not Go Gentle:* Dylan Thomas.
	🎭	*Dr Faustus:* Christopher Marlowe. *Notes to Future Self:* Lucy Caldwell. *Hymns:* Chris O'Connell.
	🎞	*Coco:* 2017 (PG). *The Book of Life:* 2014 (U). *The Bucket List:* 2007 (PG).
	🎵	*I'll Be Missing You:* Diddy, Faith Evans, 112. *Supermarket Flowers:* Ed Sheeran. Chopin's *Funeral March.* 'The Last Post.'
	🎨	*The Wake:* Stephen Newton. *Thinking about Death:* Freda Kahlo. *Ophelia:* John Everett Millais.
🎭		Mask and puppet. Shock with movement and imagery Minimal words. Artaud. Melodrama. Dance and artwork based on *Dia de Los Muertos.*
⚠		Be aware of family bereavement. Investment of emotion/empathy will need special care.
🔗		46, 48, 50, 52, 58, 59, 69, 142, 166.

058   Assisted suicide

<table>
<tr>
<td></td>
<td colspan="2">'It's like telling God, You can fire me, I quit'
(Bill Maher – American stand-up comedian).</td>
</tr>
<tr>
<td></td>
<td colspan="2">16+ Small mixed groups.</td>
</tr>
<tr>
<td></td>
<td colspan="2">Workshops/games: Body sculpture. Guide me.
Life should be preserved: but what if you're terminally ill?
Questionnaire: If you were in such pain, would you choose dignity? 'Put me out of my misery!'
Is it more cruel to suffer? Should there be a legal right to die?</td>
</tr>
<tr>
<td></td>
<td colspan="2">The right for terminally ill patients to end their lives with dignity is a very topical issue (end of life issues). In the UK suicide has been decriminalised but not assisting suicide. Physician assisted suicide is legal in some countries under some circumstances.
Research: Which countries permit assisted suicide. Who are Dignitas?
What the papers say: Various newspaper articles about the Swiss assisted suicide centre Dignitas.</td>
</tr>
<tr>
<td rowspan="7">Stimulus</td>
<td></td>
<td>Images of a hospital bed, life support.
A goodbye letter.</td>
</tr>
<tr>
<td></td>
<td>Last Wish: Betty Rollin.
Shaking Hands with Death: Terry Pratchett.
When I Killed My Father: John B. Barry.</td>
</tr>
<tr>
<td></td>
<td>The Life That Is Not Life: R. L. Hodges.</td>
</tr>
<tr>
<td></td>
<td>Whose Life Is It Anyway: Brian Clarke.
Breathless: Lurlene McDonald.
An Instinct for Kindness: Chris Larner.
'To suffer the slings and arrows of outrageous fortune', Hamlet. Shakespeare.</td>
</tr>
<tr>
<td></td>
<td>You Don't Know Jack: 2010 (TV Movie) (15).
Me Before You: 2016 (PG-13).
Suicide Tourist: 2019 (15).</td>
</tr>
<tr>
<td></td>
<td>Canción Para Mi Muerte: Sui Generis.
Euthanasia – Idiot Prayer: Nick Cave.
Lazarus: David Bowie.</td>
</tr>
<tr>
<td></td>
<td>Look at the paintings of Doctor Jack Kevorkian which depict the human suffering he sought to alleviate through euthanasia of his patients.</td>
</tr>
<tr>
<td></td>
<td colspan="2">Naturalism, heightened realism.
Dialogue based. Stanislavski.
A simple-covered bed on a black stage (studio performance).
Would also work as a dance/physical piece.</td>
</tr>
<tr>
<td></td>
<td colspan="2">Consider all students involved and their audience.</td>
</tr>
<tr>
<td></td>
<td colspan="2">46, 48, 57, 59, 63, 67, 68, 80.</td>
</tr>
</table>

059 Suicide

	'People commit suicide for only one reason – to escape torment' (Li Ang – Chinese writer).
♣♥	16+ able group (mature, sensitive small friendship groups).
⚑	**Workshops/games:** *Emotion memory.* I didn't make an installation or presentation. Students chose 'Youth Suicide' from a short list of ideas and we gently explored. A sensitive teacher-led discussion in a small group within a safe environment.
☼	Washington University study of *Teenage thoughts and plans around suicide.* 2021. Meghan Romanelli. The Samaritans have produced a help site for educational professionals. DEAL. **What the papers say:** *Guardian* newspaper article on teen suicide during the pandemic, 22 November 2021. Famous people who have ended their own lives from Van Gogh to Robin Williams.

Stimulus		
	☠	Avoid the obvious. Projected images of the sad statistics involved.
	📖	*Thirteen Reasons Why:* Jane Asher (also a TV series). *Hold Still:* Nina LaCour. *All the Bright Places:* Jennifer Niven (see also 2020 movie). *My Heart and Other Black Holes:* Jasmine Warga.
	✍	*I Shall Not Care:* Sara Teasdale.
	🎭	*Leaves:* Lucy Caldwell. *Hymns:* Chris O'Connell. *4.48 Psychosis:* Sarah Kane.
	🎬	*The Virgin Suicides:* 1999 (15). *It's Kind of a Funny Story:* 2010 (12A). *Dead Poet's Society:* 1989 (PG).
	🎵	*Adam's Song:* Blink-182. *Everybody Hurts:* R.E.M. *Vincent:* Don Maclean. *Joining You:* Alanis Morissette.
	🎨	*Silent Shout:* Eva Charkiewicz (photographic art). *Le Suicide:* Edouard Manet. *The Suicide of Dorothy Hale:* Freda Kahlo.

🎭	Verbatim letters. Minimalist. The distance between suicidal thoughts and actions. Physical with little or no dialogue. Frantic Assembly.
⚠	Consider all students involved and their audience. Don't make it a personal story. Check school policies.
🔗	021–025, 071, 073, 084, 123, 135, 151, 182.

060   Living with disability

	'Aerodynamically the bumblebee shouldn't be able to fly. But the bumblebee doesn't know that so it goes on flying anyway' (Mary Kay Ash – American businesswoman).
	12+ Small groups.
	Workshops/games: *Guide me! Stereotypes.* Watch wheelchair dance sequences (YouTube). Stereotyping people. Acting and reacting. Character work.
	Think about the different types of disability. Is disability even the right word? *'I choose not to place "DIS", in my ability'* (Robert M. Hensel). **Look at** how Stephen Hawking challenged views on disability. **Search for:** National Disability Theatre. Does he take sugar? Disability is not the opposite of ability!

Stimulus		A disabled sign. A wheelchair. Steps.
		Pages I Never Wrote: Marco Donati. *Not If I See You First:* Eric Lindstrom. *Me Before You:* Jojo Moyes.
		Blindness: Charles Lamb.
		The Curious Incident of the Dog in the Night-Time: Mark Haddon. *Those Legs:* Noel Clarke. *Burning Bridges:* Amy Schindler.
		My Left Foot: 1989 (15). *Children of a Lesser God:* 1986 (15). *The Theory of Everything:* 2014 (12A).
		Wheelchair Waltz (Version 2): Jonny Crescendo. *Who You Are:* Jessie J. *Don't Laugh at Me:* Baby Jay.
		Art of disabled artists like: Maria Iliou, Peter Longstaff, Alice Schonfield and Keith Salmon.

	Verbatim theatre. TIE. Minimalist. Dance. DV8. Monologues. Combinations of realism and non-realism.
	Be sensitive to any disabilities within the group, their friends and family.
	006, 009, 014, 025, 033, 056, 058, 061–071, 076, 084, 090, 107, 113, 114, 122, 125, 151, 154, 160, 174, 175, 177, 186.

061 Anger

		'He who angers you conquers you' (Elizabeth Kenny – Australian nurse).
♣♟	Works with all ages. Small groups of 3 or 4.	
⚑	**Workshops/games:** *Levels of tension. Silent scream.* Releasing tension. Screaming/shouting together! **Questionnaire:** What makes you angry? What do you do when you get angry? How do you control/manage your anger? **Look at the language:** Rage, blood boiling, mad, pissed (off), temperature rising, about to blow, tantrum, righteous anger.	
☀	Anger can be a mental health issue. There are therapies, even drugs (antidepressants) to help people manage their anger. **Research:** Celebs with anger issues.	
Stimulus	☠	What does anger look like: Red? Smashed glass, lightning, broken furniture, bruises? What does it sound like: thunder, shouting, screaming, breaking glass, crying, sobs, silence?
	📖	*Anger Is a Gift:* Mark Oshiro. *Anger:* May Sarton. *Rage Becomes Her: The Power of Women's Anger:* Soraya Chemaly.
	✍	*A Poison Tree:* William Blake.
	🎭	*Medea:* Euripides. *People, Places and Things:* Duncan Macmillan. *Look Back in Anger:* John Osborne.
	🎬	*Inside Out:* 2015 (U). *Anger Management:* 2003 (15). *Falling Down:* 1993 (18).
	🎵	*Angry dance* from Billy Elliot (watch it on YouTube). *The Way I Am:* Eminem. *Threnody to the Victims of Hiroshima:* Krzysztof Penderecki.
	🎨	Freda Kahlo's *Little Deer.* Pablo Picasso's *Guernica.* *Rage the Flower Thrower:* Banksy.
🎦	From our *tension* workshops came a piece based on how anger can build up inside. The artistic intention was to see anger as another emotion, just as valid as any other. Or how anger can turn something beautiful into something ugly. A body, a face, a nation or a deed. Good duet work. Frantic Assembly.	
⚠	When using anger workshops be sure to warm down/calm students at the end of the session. Be aware of students with anger issues.	
🔗	004, 009, 014, 016, 017, 020, 021, 023, 024, 025, 029, 033, 042, 043, 044, 051, 052, 060, 063, 071, 074, 075, 077, 080, 096–101, 104, 107, 109, 126–151, 156, 157, 175, 177.	

062   Jealousy

		'The jealous are troublesome to others, but a torment to themselves' (William Penn – English writer and religious thinker).
		All ages. Groups of 2–5
		Workshops/games: *Levels of tension. Gestus.* **Questionnaire:** What makes you jealous? What does jealousy feel like? What does it make us look like? How do we act? Feelings of desire for what another person has. This could also be envy but jealousy is more negative. Look at the feelings of insecurity and fear that might cause jealousy.
		Search for: *6 Healthy Ways to Deal with Jealousy:* PsychCentral. Jealousy is a first-person emotion. The ancient Greeks believed that jealousy was the result of an overproduction of bile, which turns skin a slight shade of green. **Look at:** How social media creates jealousy. Envy is one of the seven deadly sins (Unit 029).
Stimulus		The colour green. Yellow roses. A broken mirror. A diary, a letter. A torn photograph of someone.
		Passing: Nella Larsen. *The Jealousy Man and Other Stories:* Jo Nesbo. *Wuthering Heights:* Emily Brontë.
		Jealousy: Rupert Brooke.
		A View from the Bridge: Arthur Miller. *Othello:* William Shakespeare, 'The green-eyed monster'. *Abigail's Party:* Mike Leigh.
		Atonement: 2007 (15). *Snow White and the Seven Dwarfs:* 1937 (A). *Seven Deadly Sins: Envy:* 2021 (TV Movie).
		Jealous Guy: John Lennon. *Green Is The Colour:* Pink Floyd. *Jealousy, Jealousy:* Olivia Rodrigo.
		Athena Visiting Envy: Karel Dujardin. The etching *'Envy' (Invidia):* Pieter van der Heyden.
		The destructive power of jealousy in love. Dark humour and realism to uncover the turmoil in a person's mind. Works well in a small intimate studio space. Dance: *Jealousy Tango,* as used in the movie *Moulin Rouge* to the song *Roxanne.*
		It should not be personal!
		025, 029, 034, 039, 045, 054, 081, 099, 107, 109, 115, 135, 136, 144, 175.

063   Guilt

		'Every man is guilty of all the good he did not do' (Voltaire – French writer and philosopher).
👥		All age groups. Mixed.
🏳		**Workshops/games:** *Accusation*! *That hurt. Sorry. Lying (The burden of a lie).* Start with defining the word. This is about 'feeling'. What is it like to *feel* guilty. Share experiences. How does guilt make you to respond to people? Explore body language.
💡		**Research:** Survivor's guilt. The guilt of a nation. Slavery, The Holocaust, Hiroshima, The Rwandan Genocide. Guilt and the church. Isaiah 6:1–4 Old Testament. Guilt and forgiveness. *Signs of Guilt.* A very useful article for older students by WebMD Guilty by association. Look also at other self-conscious emotions: embarrassment, shame, pride. **Look at the language:** Guilty as charged, as hell, as sin, the guilty party, riddled with guilt.
Stimulus	☠	**Look at:** The causes of guilt. From taking the last biscuit, to taking a life. Images of guilty faces, posture.
	📖	*Beloved:* Toni Morrison. *A Girl is a Half-Formed Thing:* Eimear McBride. *The Trial:* Franz Kafka.
	✒	*Guilt:* Robert Frost.
	🎭	*An Inspector Calls:* J. B. Priestley. *Too Much Punch for Judy:* Mark Wheeller. *The Train Driver:* Athol Fugard.
	🎬	*Flight:* 2012 (15). *Don't Go:* 2018 (15). *Manchester by the Sea:* 2016 (15).
	🎵	*Please Forgive Me:* Bryan Adams. *Sorry:* Justin Bieber. *I'm On Fire:* Bruce Springsteen.
	🎨	*Separation:* Edvard Munch. *Innocent or Guilty:* Katerina Apostolakou. **Look at:** Rodin's *Eve after the Fall*. Consider how she lowers her head and covers herself, shame, guilt?
	🎭	Look at the other feelings that accompany guilt, like regret. Use guilt and regret to create a piece which cast the audience in the role of accusers. Dramatic irony. Ensemble work based Catholicism and guilt with performers attempting to escape the physical restraints of feeling guilty. Cheek by jowl.
⚠		Complex issues. Know your students and group dynamics.
🔗		009, 052, 059, 071, 073, 075, 100, 104, 109, 117, 123, 126–137, 144, 175.

064   Fear

<table>
<tr><td></td><td colspan="2">'We have nothing to fear but fear itself'
(Franklin D. Roosevelt – American president).</td></tr>
<tr><td>👥</td><td colspan="2">10+ Mixed groups of 3–4.</td></tr>
<tr><td>🏴</td><td colspan="2">Workshops/games: Fear. Emotion memory. Colombian hypnosis.
'An instinct beyond our control.' Use a small, intimate place to rehearse tension, fear and confinement.
Questionnaire: What are you most afraid of? Is it rational? Can you control it?
Even the bravest of us have fears. It's not the same as cowardice. A coward is someone who lacks the courage to face those fears.
The joy of fear. Our relationship with fear. We pay to watch horror films, read horror, go on the scariest rides. As long as we are in control, it isn't fear. Fear is lack of control.</td></tr>
<tr><td>🔅</td><td colspan="2">Look at the language: Compare the use of words like coward, chicken, wimp, gutless. Or anxiety, dread, panic. Does the word 'Fearless' imply bravery or stupidity?
What the papers say: Is the media guilty of spreading fear sometimes? Slaughter, carnage, massacre, widespread, nightmare!
Research: The biology of fear. The Smithsonian Institute has done some excellent well-recorded research.
More controversial: Are we more prone to fear and anxiety because we live in a 'Nanny State?'</td></tr>
<tr><td rowspan="8">Stimulus</td><td>🐌</td><td>A white feather, skull and crossbones.</td></tr>
<tr><td>📖</td><td>To Kill A Mocking Bird: Harper Lee.
Lord of the Flies: William Golding.
Native Son: Richard Wright.</td></tr>
<tr><td>📝</td><td>Life Doesn't Frighten Me: Maya Angelou.</td></tr>
<tr><td>🎭</td><td>Fear and Misery of the Third Reich: Brecht.
Bazaar and Rummage: Sue Townsend.
Kvetch: Steven Berkoff.</td></tr>
<tr><td>🎬</td><td>Scream: 2022 (18).
Don't Look Up: 2021 (15).
Ghostbusters: Afterlife: 2021 (12A).</td></tr>
<tr><td>🎵</td><td>The Age of Anxiety: Jamie Cullen.
Don't Fear the Reaper: Blue Oyster Cult.
Fearless: Pink Floyd.
Tango fusion pieces. Bajofondo Mardulce.</td></tr>
<tr><td>🎨</td><td>The Face of War: Salvador Dali.</td></tr>
<tr><td>🎪</td><td>'The face of fear' Masks (Trestle) and dance. Grand Guignol, Berkoff/Le Coq.
Works well in a studio space. SFX/lighting.</td></tr>
<tr><td>⚠️</td><td colspan="2">Students may be prone to take this theme to dark places! Check artistic intentions.</td></tr>
<tr><td>🔗</td><td colspan="2">21, 32, 35, 54, 55, 57, 72, 97, 104, 126, 173, 175, 183, 184.</td></tr>
</table>

065 Happiness

	'Happiness comes in waves. It'll find you again' (Unknown).
♣♀	Any age. Larger groups.
🏴	**Workshops/games.** *Gestus. Stereotyping.* **Questionnaire:** What makes you happy. Make a list. Smile! Laughter/happiness is catching. Watch it spread around the room. Experiment with *Levels of happiness* and *Emotion memory*
🔆	Is there a secret to happiness? **Research:** How many other words are there for happiness? Is it the opposite of sadness? Everyone seeks happiness but it is difficult to describe. Try . . . **Look at:** How happiness is often associated with feelings of love . . . **Look at the language:** As happy as Larry? Smile and the world smiles . . . I'm not happy about . . . Don't worry be . . . .

Stimulus		
	🐌	Recorded sounds of laughter/happiness. List the objects that make us smile. A Birthday cake. Sunshine.
	📕	*The Happiness Advantage:* Shawn Achor. *14,000 Things to Be Happy About:* Barbara Ann Kipfer. *Eat, Pray, Love:* Elizabeth Gilbert.
	📝	*My Mind to Me a Kingdom Is:* Edward Dyer.
	🎭	For younger students, *The Happiness Shop:* Lindsay Price. For older students, *The Usual Auntijies:* Paven Virk.
	🎞	*Forrest Gump:* 1994 (12). *It's A Wonderful Life:* 1946 (U). *Happy Feet:* 2006 (U).
	🎵	*Walking on Sunshine:* Katrina and The Waves. *Hooked on a Feeling:* Blue Swede. *Celebration:* Kool and The Gang.
	🎨	Colours and happiness The bright yellows of Sunflowers (Van Gogh).

🎭	Contrast. A bright/vibrant, physical piece. Character based. Ensemble. Punchdrunk. Off Balance. Gecko work with mime and exaggerated movement. Stories . . . Simple set, mirrors.
⚠	It's not about comedy. Happiness is a feeling more than laughter, a smile more than a roaring laugh.
🔗	022, 025, 026, 027, 028, 030, 035, 036, 051–056, 058, 068, 071, 076–085, 087, 089, 090, 095–099, 105, 107, 114, 116, 120, 122, 123, 149, 151, 154, 177, 181, 185, 191, 192, 195, 198.

066   Bravery (Courage)

	'Fortune favours the brave' (Terentius Lucanus Roman senator).
👥	Any age. Groups of 4–6.
🚩	**Workshops/games:** *Fear. Soundscapes.* **Questionnaire:** Think of a brave act. What is your definition of courage? Form a tableau to depict bravery. In wars, people die for their country but is that the only kind of bravery? Perhaps the definition of bravery is changing. Having the courage to stand up for what you believe in. Bravery is not being without fear, it's about controlling that fear. To be true to yourself is to be brave.
🔆	**Research:** What Socrates said about courage. **Look at:** The courage of War Journalists. www.bcri.org Creative bravery and people who inspire change. The bravery of the medics around the world during the pandemic. **Look at the language:** Brave as a lion, be brave, brave the storm, a brave stance.

Stimulus		
	💀	Medals, Soldier's uniform. Images of strong animals (even mythical ones): lions, bears, dragons, griffins, eagles.
	📖	*I am Malala:* Christina Lamb and Malala Yousafzai. *The Alchemist:* Paulo Coelho. *Tuesdays with Morrie:* Mitch Albom.
	📝	*To Fight Aloud is Very Brave:* Emily Dickinson.
	🎭	*Private Peaceful:* Morpurgo and Reade. *Journey's End:* R. C. Sherriff. *Mother Courage and Her Children:* Brecht.
	🎬	*Hacksaw Ridge:* 2016 (15). *Darkest Hour:* 2017 (PG). *Brave:* 2012 (PG).
	🎵	*I Will Survive:* Gloria Gaynor. *So Strong:* Labi Siffre. *No Bravery:* James Blunt.
	🎨	The paintings of New York artist Tim Okamura. (Frontlines nurses during the pandemic.) The sculptures in *Kelly Ingram Park* Birmingham Alabama USA.

🎭	From the epic to the small silent protest. Freeze frame statues which come to life and tell their story. Audience interaction. Projections. Katie Mitchell.
⚠️	Don't only focus on the big epic acts.
🔗	001, 002, 006, 010, 021, 023, 025, 037, 044, 052, 053, 056–060, 064, 069, 071, 073, 075, 079, 080, 100, 106, 107, 109, 112, 114, 123, 126, 131, 137, 141, 142, 146, 150, 155, 156, 160, 174, 182, 183, 197.

067   Alzheimer's and dementia (A Case study unit, see Chapter 5)

	'Alzheimer's disease locks all the doors and exits. There is no reprieve, no escape' (Patti Davis – American author, daughter of Ronald Regan).	
♟ ♟	14+ Able (Mixed). Our best results were from paired work.	
🏳	See details in Case study, Unit 67, Chapter 5.	
☀	Named after Dr Alois Alzheimer. As far back as 1906 he recorded changes in brain tissue through mental illness. Alzheimer's Society. The 'Forget Me Not' Project. US Against Alzheimer's. Alzheimer's Association. alz.org Watch video by NIH *'How Alzheimer's changes the brain'* (YouTube).	
Stimulus	☠	An hour glass. A wedding ring. A dead rose/flowers. Old family photographs. A mirror. A wallet/purse. A hat. A wristwatch. A pen and paper. A pair of glasses.
	📖	*We Are Not Ourselves:* Matthew Thomas. *Still Alice:* Lisa Genova. *The Man Who Mistook His Wife for a Hat:* Oliver Sacks. *Now I Remember I Love You:* Janet Aird.
	✍	*Where Have You Gone?:* Phil Sharman.
	🎭	*Stage Seven:* Ruth Stevens. *The Father:* Florian Zeller. *Norah's Lost:* Alan Haehnel.
	🎞	*Away from Her:* 2006 (12A). *Still Alice:* 2014 (12A). *The Father:* 2020 (12A). *Elizabeth is Missing:* 2019 (TV movie) (12).
	🎵	*Helpless:* Neil Young. *I'm Not Gonna Miss You:* Glenn Campbell. *Every Grain of Sand:* Bob Dylan. *Forget Me Not:* A choral composition by composer Marc Yeats.
	🎨	**Look at:** The MOMA Alzheimer's project. Investigate the work and life of artist and Alzheimer's sufferer William Utermohlen.
🎦	See details in Case study, Unit 67, Chapter 5.	
⚠	Sensitivity is needed when guiding young people through the many stereotypes the topic unearths. Also consider family situations.	
🔗	019, 057, 058, 060, 068, 069, 071, 084, 088, 107, 123, 151, 157, 182.	

068   Old Age

		'Wisdom comes with winters' (Oscar Wilde – Irish writer and poet).
👥	All ages. Mixed groups	
🚩	**Workshops/games:** *Old man/woman walking. Memory games.* Think of the oldest person in your family, their traits, endearing and otherwise. Do we see old age as a positive or negative? Look at how different cultures revere the elderly and others are less sympathetic.	
💡	**Research:** Gerontology. www.ageuk.org.uk **Look at:** Age progression apps like AgingBooth and FaceApp. Why are we fascinated? Growing ageing populations, a worldwide phenomenon. **Look at:** Care for the elderly (Care homes). Cultural differences. Oldest people in history. The elderly and technology. Loneliness. Ageism (Unit 019).	
Stimulus	💀	A walking stick. A hearing aid. Slippers. Photographs.
	📖	*Live a Little:* Howard Jacobson. *These Foolish Things:* Deborah Moggach. *Still Life with Breadcrumbs:* Anna Quindlen.
	📝	*Sonnet 73:* Shakespeare.
	🎭	*Lovesong:* Abi Morgan (Frantic Assembly). *Death of a Salesman:* Arthur Miller. *The Duck Variations:* David Mamet.
	🎬	*The Bucket List:* 2007 (12A). *The Best Exotic Marigold Hotel.* 2011 (12A). *Last Tango in Halifax:* 2012–2020 (BBC) (12) . A Two Ronnie's Sketch called *The Hearing Aid Centre.*
	🎵	*Grandma's Hands:* Bill Withers. *When We Were Young:* Adele.
	🎨	*Old Age:* Robert Lenkiewicz. Robbie Kaye's photo series 'Beauty and Wisdom'.
🎭	Challenging the stereotypes. Highly physical, but slow and very graceful. Ballet/dance montage. Ensemble stylised realism.	
⚠️	Be mindful that much of the movie/TV industry's take on old age is through the eyes of comedy. Students need to be sensitive to how this genre is used and why.	
🔗	019, 027, 057, 058, 067, 069, 071, 078, 084, 160, 170, 182, 196.	

069   Young carers

		'It is not the load that breaks you down. It's the way you carry it' (Lena Horne – American singer, and Civil Rights Activist).
♣♀	11+ Small mixed groups.	
⚑	**Workshops/games**: *Trust games. Guide me.* Who looks after you? Sometimes it's the other way round. Mime some of the practical tasks: like cooking, housework and shopping. Physical care, such as helping someone out of bed. Emotional support, talking to someone who is distressed. Personal care, such as helping someone dress. Administering medicines. Helping someone communicate. Looking after younger siblings. Now imagine doing some or all of these things every day.	
☼	Young carers are people aged 25 and under who care for a family member who, for a variety of reasons, cannot cope without their support. Often without pay, without help or understanding. **Research**: The Children's Society UK. Carers Trust. The NHS (UK) has a site for young carers. Barnardo's. www.youngminds.org.uk www.carers.org	
Stimulus	☠	A wheelchair, a jar of pills, a bed.
	📖	*Guidebook for Young Carers:* Mike Raynor. *Me and My Sister:* Rose Robbins. *The Boy Whose Wishes Came True:* Helen Rutter.
	✍	**Search for:** 'Poetry written by young carers.'
	🎭	*That Face:* Polly Stenham. *Who Cares:* Matt Woodward.
	🎞	*What's Eating Gilbert Grape:* 1993 (PG-13). *My Sister's Keeper:* 2019 (PG-13). *Supporting Young Carers:* 2018 (Documentary).
	🎵	*Carers Song:* Care for the Carers (YouTube). *Count on Me:* Bruno Mars. *If Everyone Cared:* Nickelback.
	🎨	*Silent Shout:* Eva Charkiewicz (photographic art).
⛩	Verbatim: Testimony, monologues. **Look at:** How isolating an experience caring can be. Minimalist set. Duologues, physical theatre between carer and cared for. Frantic Assembly.	
⚠	Be very aware of each student's home situation.	
🔗	010, 019, 025, 051, 052, 058, 060–068, 071, 084, 087, 107, 109, 115, 139, 149, 156, 174, 175, 191, 197.	

070   Body image

<table>
<tr><td></td><td colspan="2">'Feeling Beautiful has nothing to do with what you look like'
(Emma Watson – British actress).</td></tr>
<tr><td>👥</td><td colspan="2">11+ Small groups. Allow, but don't encourage single sex groups.</td></tr>
<tr><td>🚩</td><td colspan="2">Workshops/games: Mirror images. Trust games. Body sculpture.
Poor body image is not just a female issue. For both men and women it can lead to dieting, over-exercising, eating disorders and steroid abuse.
Questionnaire: Look at your favourite selfie. What is it you like about it? Has it been altered and if so why? Who/what informs/influences your image of yourself?
Most of us don't like to watch videos of ourselves, even hating the sound of our own voice. Why?</td></tr>
<tr><td>💡</td><td colspan="2">Search for: mirror-mirror.org/body-image/perfect-body-image
Research: Ed Sheeran's struggle with body image. Body dysmorphic disorder (BDD).
Look at: https://thebodypositive.org
Globalised culture and the 'Westernised' Image of the perfect body.
Is body image a new thing? Was it as important in the 50s?</td></tr>
<tr><td rowspan="7">Stimulus</td><td>💀</td><td>A mirror, weighing scales, your smartphone, those selfies (what are you trying to say in them?). Your profile. Your clothes, your CV.</td></tr>
<tr><td>📖</td><td>Wonder: R. J. Palacio.
Hole in the Middle: Kendra Fortmeyer.
Beautiful You: Rosie Molinary.</td></tr>
<tr><td>📝</td><td>This Body: Joyce Sutphen.</td></tr>
<tr><td>🎭</td><td>Girls Like That: Evan Placey.
Shapeless: Sean Carthew.
The Beauty Manifesto: Nell Leyshon.</td></tr>
<tr><td>🎬</td><td>I Feel Pretty: 2018 (12A).
Little Miss Sunshine: 2006 (15).
The Illusionist: A documentary about Body Image (YouTube).</td></tr>
<tr><td>🎵</td><td>I Feel Pretty: from Bernstein's West Side Story.
Beautiful: Christina Aguilera.
New Man: Ed Sheeran.</td></tr>
<tr><td>🎨</td><td>Japanese Manga images.
Look at: MoMA Learning, The Body in Art.
The work of Jody Steel, 'Body Image'.</td></tr>
<tr><td>🎭</td><td colspan="2">Physical theatre, stylised with good rhythm. Frames to suggest mirrors with reflection work.
Make up rituals, masks and dance.
Projections of media perfection, cat walks and red carpet excesses.
Projected selfie images being, distorted, through physical theatre.</td></tr>
<tr><td>⚠️</td><td colspan="2">Mutual trust within the groups is vital. Set rules from the start. Know your students.</td></tr>
<tr><td>🔗</td><td colspan="2">018, 021, 024, 025, 033, 053, 054, 060, 062, 063, 068, 071, 073, 075, 086, 097, 130, 160, 184, 185, 186, 188.</td></tr>
</table>

071   Mental Health

	'If depression can kill Robin Williams, it can get any of us at any time' (Jason Manford – English comedian).
👥	15+ Small friendship groups.
🚩	**Workshops/games**: *Emotion memory. Gestus. Levels of tension.* Promote an awareness of mental health issues in general but with such a vast field, try to limit to one specific condition based on students' own research. mind.org.uk provides an A–Z of Mental Health. What are the symptoms? How can we help? Encourage students to select one area to work with for a final piece.
💡	There are many different mental health problems, some of them have similar symptoms. **Research:** Famous historical characters who suffered with their mental health. Are prescription drugs effective?
Stimulus	💀 There are some excellent, easy to understand posters available.
	📖 *The Illustrated Mum:* Jacqueline Wilson. *Every Last Word:* Tamara Ireland Stone. *Eleanor Oliphant Is Completely Fine:* Gail Honeyman.
	✍ *Fifteen, Maybe Sixteen Things to Worry About:* Judith Viorst.
	🎭 *The Madness of Esme and Shaz:* Sarah Daniels. *This'll Only Take A Second:* Zach Davis. *Every Brilliant Thing:* Duncan Macmillan. **More controversial**: *4.48 Psychosis:* Sarah Kane.
	🎬 *A Beautiful Mind:* 2001 (12). *Sylvia:* 2003 (15). *As Good as it Gets:* 1997 (15).
	🎵 *In My Blood:* Shawn Mendes. *Disturbia:* Rihanna. *Vincent:* Don McLean.
	🎨 *'Henry Ford Hospital' (1932):* Frida Kahlo.
🎪	A Verbatim approach works well but dance/physical/stylised theatre can be a sensitive way of exploring issues. Some areas could be monologues with strong character work. Stanislavski.
⚠	Know your students!
🔗	009, 021, 024, 025, 030, 052, 053, 055, 059–070, 073, 074, 075, 077, 083, 096–101, 104, 107, 109, 126, 130, 134, 135, 151, 156, 157, 163, 176, 182, 186, 195, 198.

072   Languages

<table>
<tr>
<td></td>
<td colspan="2">'To have another language is to possess a second soul'
(Charlemagne – Medieval European Emperor).</td>
</tr>
<tr>
<td>👥</td>
<td colspan="2">All ages. Small groups of 2 to 4</td>
</tr>
<tr>
<td>🚩</td>
<td colspan="2">Workshops/games: Soundscapes.
Divide class into A and B Write a simple task on a piece of paper and hand it to the As. They cannot speak, but may use numbers or sounds instead of English and get the Bs to carry out the task. Explore the frustration. Free them to explain the task . . . Discuss the liberation.
Write a simple sentence using only the emojis on your phone.
What is your mother tongue? List languages spoken in the group.
Use all the languages in the group to create a sound-scape/vocal chorus.</td>
</tr>
<tr>
<td>🔅</td>
<td colspan="2">There are 7,099 distinct languages spoken around the world.
Research: Top 10 Languages by Number of Native Speakers, and Top 10 Languages by Total Number of Speakers. . Growing up bi-lingual. How language and culture are connected.
Look at: Dialect and accent. What are endangered languages?
Words borrowed by English from other languages . . .
Try singing the same song in different languages.
Language/communication is our humanity's achievement.
More controversial: If you take away a people's language, you wipe out their culture and identity. Invaders and colonists always impose their language on the defeated.</td>
</tr>
<tr>
<td rowspan="7">Stimulus</td>
<td>💀</td>
<td>Flags of many nations.</td>
</tr>
<tr>
<td>📕</td>
<td>Lingo: Gaston Dorren.
Is that a Fish in Your Ear? David Bellos.
How We Are Translated: Jessica Gaitan Johannesson.</td>
</tr>
<tr>
<td>📝</td>
<td>Languages: Carl Sandburg.</td>
</tr>
<tr>
<td>🎭</td>
<td>Translations: Brian Friel.
Barber Shop Chronicles: Inua Ellams.</td>
</tr>
<tr>
<td>📽</td>
<td>Lost in Translation: 2003 (15).
Arrival: 2016 (12A).
The Interpreter: 2005 (12A).</td>
</tr>
<tr>
<td>🎵</td>
<td>Michelle: The Beatles.
Stand By Me: Prince Royce.
David Bowie's Helden.
Chimes of Freedom: Youssou Ndour.
Devil's Spoke: Mumford and Sons, Laura Marling and Dharohar Project.</td>
</tr>
<tr>
<td>🎨</td>
<td>Research: Early cave painting and the evolution of human language.</td>
</tr>
<tr>
<td>🎭</td>
<td colspan="2">Cheek by jowl (Declan Donnellan). Performances in other languages. Original and translations. Mime and mask, sign language. Vocal work, Cicely Berry. Character work. Stanislavski. Dance/movement pieces. Lorca. Surrealism and Spanish folk culture. Flamenco music of Andalucía.</td>
</tr>
<tr>
<td>⚠</td>
<td colspan="2">Not really about learning a language. More of a celebration of the languages spoken at your school/college, some will have many, others only one or two.</td>
</tr>
<tr>
<td>🔗</td>
<td colspan="2">016, 021, 025, 076, 079, 085, 088, 089, 095, 106, 114, 125, 152, 160, 161, 172, 178, 183, 184, 186.</td>
</tr>
</table>

073   Self-Harm

	'I Hurt myself today to see if I still feel' (Nine Inch Nails – American industrial rock band).
👥	Applies to all age groups but be wary. Small groups.
🚩	**Workshops/games;***Repetition exercises. Mirror work.* **Look at:** The statistics in a sensitive conversation (small groups). Who is more likely to self-harm? When might this happen? Starting secondary school. New stresses/pressures. Self-esteem. Look at expressing something not easily put into words. Isolation, being trapped, being vulnerable and attacked, conflict and pain, escape, relief, through movement and dance.
🔆	independent.co.uk/topic/self-harm The Charity *MIND* has produced a PDF help document on Self-harm.

Stimulus		
	💀	Leave images/artifacts to a later stage and only then through the students' own thoughts and feelings/research.
	📖	*Girl in Pieces:* Kathleen Glasgow. *Cut:* Patricia McCormick. *Break:* Hannah Moskowitz. *Bleed Like Me:* Christa Desir. *Cutters Don't Cry:* Christine Dzidrums.
	📝	*Resumé:* Dorothy Parker.
	🎭	*Scratching The Surface:* Mark Wheeller. *Hidden:* Nina Lemon. *Under My Skin:* A T.I.E. piece produced by Pegasus Theatre and Oxfordshire County Council (CAMHS).
	🎞	*Thirteen:* 2003 (18). *Spencer:* 2021 (12A). *Sharp Objects:* 2018 (18). *Self-Harm and Me:* Gemma Collins (TV Documentary).
	🎵	*Tell Tale Signs:* Frank Turner. *Because of You:* Nickelback. *Self-Inflicted:* Smile Empty Soul. *On Earth As It Is In Heaven (The Mission):* Ennio Morricone (a dance idea).
	🎨	Links between art and self-harm. Tattoo/piercings. Popular culture. *'I paint sunflowers on my self-harm scars'* BBC news article 5/11/2017. **Look at:** The SAATCHI ART site under 'self-harm'. Teacher discretion.

🎭	A physical piece in which students explore changing emotional pain in to physical pain. Music is very effective. Puppets to show control and disassociation.
⚠	Self-harm often fails to show up on a student's record, don't assume. Beware of movie clips acting as triggers for self-harm. Know your students!
🔗	059, 071, 075, 097, 107, 135, 151, 182.

074   Madness

	'There is no great genius without a mixture of madness' (Aristotle – Greek philosopher).
	14+ Small mixed groups.
	Workshops games: *Levels of tension. Soundscapes.* **Questionnaire:** What madness means to them . . . Physical theatre, the energy of madness. Mime.
	Look at the language: She got really mad with him. He's mad about her. You must be mad. Truly, madly, deeply. Mad professor. A mad idea. Go mad! The madness of the world. A moment of madness. Mad laughter. Mad as a March hare. I drove like mad. Mad cool. Looney, nutter, whacko, crazy, deranged . . . Raving, ranting, seething and crazy for you!

Stimulus		A strait jacket. A photograph of Albert Einstein. *The Scream*: Edvard Munch.
		Alice's Adventures in Wonderland: Lewis Carroll. *The Shining*: Stephen King. *The Metamorphosis*: Franz Kafka.
		Howl: Allen Ginsberg.
		Moments of Madness: Jack J. Berry. *Woyzeck*: Georg Büchner. *The Madness of Esme and Shaz*: Sarah Daniels. Madness in *Hamlet, Macbeth, King Lear* and *Twelfth Night*.
		The Madness of King George: 1994 (PG). *Amadeus*: 1984 (PG). *Dr Strange in the Multiverse of Madness*: 2022 (12A).
		Crazy: Patsy Cline. *The Way I Am*: Eminem. *Brain Damage/Eclipse*: Pink Floyd.
		Research: Links between creativity and madness.

	Dance/physical. DV8/Frantic. Madness and energy. Berkoff ideas of exaggerated movement/characteristics for the stereotype/charicature. Brechtian techniques to highlight suffering.
	Know your students.
	009, 025, 027, 033, 045, 055, 056, 061, 067, 071, 076, 097, 107, 113, 116, 129, 134, 143, 151, 156–160, 162, 163, 165, 176, 182, 184, 195, 198.

075 Eating disorders

	'I am forever engaged in a silent battle in my head over whether or not to lift the fork to my mouth' (Jena Morrow – American activist).
	14+ Small friendship groups.
	Workshops/games: *Mirror imaging. Body sculpture.* **Look at:** What different cultures, societies consider beautiful. Examine how the Western idea of what is attractive is becoming more globalised. Consider the historical evidence.
	beatingdisorders.org.uk Free downloads and resources. eatingdisorderhope.com/information **Look at:** Celebrities with eating disorders. **What the papers say:** *Daily Mail* (online) article on Anneka Reay (June 2016). **Watch** *Our Minds Distort Our Mirrors*, YouTube. Choreographed by Paulina Narożnik.

Stimulus		Weighing scales. Photographs, diary entries. Photographs of models over the past 60 years.
		Wintergirls: Laurie Halse Anderson. *Just Listen:* Sarah Dessen. *Hunger:* Roxanne Gay.
		Ana (Anorexia): Samantha White.
		Hard to Swallow: Mark Wheeller. The script is a fantastic resource full of research and helpful information. Adaptation of the book/film *Catherine*, the life story of an anorexic.
		Hunger Point: 2003 (PG-13). *To the Bone:* 2017 (15). *My Skinny Sister:* 2015 (15). *Anorexia: A Boy in a Girl's World:* YouTube.
		Eyesore: Maria Mena. *Invisible:* Skylar Grey. *Tied Together With a Smile:* Taylor Swift.
		Look at: The drawings of Jenna Simon (sketches of what it's like to have an eating disorder). Also the drawings of Christine Begnell.

	Using a narrator can be very powerful. Verbatim. Frantic Assembly, fast moving, highly choreographed physical work. Music can play an important part. Character work with monologues and audience address. Mirrors and projections add another dimension.
	Eating disorders are not exclusively a feminine issue, boys exhibit different symptoms, are less likely to access mental health services and participate in groups, in particular mixed groups. Know your students.
	025, 021, 054, 059, 070, 071, 073, 092, 109, 111, 135, 182.

076   What if?

		'Following the light of the sun, we left the Old World' (Christopher Columbus – Italian explorer and colonizer). *'But what if we hadn't?'*
		Suits all ages. Large or small groups.
		Workshops/games; *Story circle* Historical drama with a twist! Alternative history. What if the Roman Empire still ruled Europe? What if Germany had won WWII? What if the South had won the Civil War? What if the Plague had wiped out all of Europe?
		A good example is the Marvel series 'What If?'. **Research** Alternative histories. Considering alternate histories helps us appreciate the world we have, to understand how history unfolds. Reverse slavery with an Africa which had become the dominant force.
Stimulus		Photoshop Roman passport. German road signs in London. Horse and carriage in a modern New York. If fossil fuels where never discovered.
		The Versions of Us: Laura Barnett. *The Years of Rice and Salt:* Kim Stanley Robinson. *Noughts and Crosses:* Malorie Blackman.
		What If: Benjamin Zephaniah.
		Alternative, unconventional theatre. What if MACBETH hadn't met the witches? FRIAR LAWRENCE'd letter got to ROMEO? The Johnston twins had not been separated? INSPECTOR GOOLE hadn't called? *Lord of the Flies* with only Girls?
		Red Dawn: 1984 (15). *Anonymous:* 2011 (12A). *What If?* 2021 (Marvel/Disney) animated series. *Yesterday:* 2019 (12A).
		Marvel's *Dr Strange* soundtrack. *What If?:* Coldplay.
		Look at: The work of Max Ernst. Surrealist art.
		Highly choreographed physical theatre. Large groups. DV8. Frantic. Also suits small groups/pairs duologues. Historical theatre. Character work.
		This unit is a lot of fun and offers many possibilities. Encourage a strong artistic intent early on in the process.
		Quite literally links with everything!

077 Divorce

	'A divorce is like an amputation: you survive it, but there's less of you' (Margaret Atwood – Canadian writer).	
⚥	15+ Small mixed groups (5 max).	
🏳	**Workshops/games:** *That hurt! Levels of tension.* *The Wedding March* followed by *Everybody Hurts*; REM. Form a wedding photo tableau. Add children to a Family photo. Then split the tableau and ask each person to speak a thought/feeling in character. Sensitive emotion memory work with students who know and trust you.	
💡	42% of marriages in the UK and almost 50% in the USA end in divorce. https://relate.org.uk Three most reported reasons for divorce: Basic incompatibility, infidelity and financial. **What the papers say:** High profile divorces/separations, celebrities, etc., why are we interested? Where do the children fit in? **More controversial:** Men are more than twice as likely to suffer from post-divorce depression than women (US stat).	
Stimulus	💀	Wedding photo, family photo, torn to separate mum from dad, brothers, sisters.
	📖	*The Secret Life of Lincoln Jones:* Wendelin Van Draanen. *Don't Make Me Smile:* Barbara Park. *What's Going to Happen to Me:* Barbara Berson.
	📝	*The Sick Equation:* Brian Pattern.
	🎭	*That Face:* Polly Stenham. *My Brilliant Divorce:* Geraldine Aron. *Like A Virgin:* Gordon Steele.
	🎬	*Boyhood:* 2014 (15). *Marriage Story:* 2019 (15). *Us:* BBC Drama (15).
	🎵	*Breakfast at Our House:* Gretchen Peters. *DIVORCE:* Tammy Wynette. *The Man:* Ed Sheeran.
	🎨	**Research** the paintings of Freda Kahlo and her husband (painter) Diego Rivera. *'Separation'.* Edvard Munch. Look at the sorrow on the young man's face. What is happening? Think of a story.
🎭	A narrated piece with three juxtaposed commentaries. Set on three levels in a house; Mother, Father and a child/children. Spot lit. Vocal work and proxemics. Declan Donnellan/Cheek by jowl. Dance work and singing.	
⚠	Be sensitive with family dynamics in your group. However students are often inspired by personal experience.	
🔗	009, 018, 045, 051, 062, 076, 078, 080, 084, 085, 086, 096–100, 107, 109, 111, 126, 130, 139, 181, 182, 199, 200.	

078   Marriage

		'All tragedies are finished by a death, all comedies by a marriage' (Lord Byron – English romantic poet).
⚥		15+ Small groups (pairs).
🏁		**Workshops/games:** *Control games. Body sculpture.* Start with Mendelssohn's Wedding March from *A Midsummer Night's Dream.* **Questionnaire:** What does this mean to you? What does marriage mean to you? Will you get married? Look at the ceremony and customs. Younger students look at the ceremony, Older ones tend to look at what comes in the years to follow.
☀		**Research** the whole industry; dating, engagement, stag/hen nights, wedding day, honeymoon, advice, on staying together and advice on divorce. Look at the advertising for each of these. Pre-nuptial agreements and what do they say about love? The status of marriage in other cultures and faiths.
Stimulus	🐌	Images/photos. Wedding dresses and suits (Charity shops). Watch how many want to dress up . . . Why?
	📖	*Middlemarch:* George Elliot. *Gone Girl:* Gillian Flynn. *Big Little Lies:* Liane Moriarty.
	📝	*Marriage:* Marianne Moore.
	🎭	*Blood Wedding:* Lorca. *Perfect Wedding:* Robin Hawdon. *A Doll's House:* Ibsen.
	🎞	*My Best Friend's Wedding:* 1997 (PG-13). *My Big Fat Greek Wedding:* 2002 (PG). *Revolutionary Road:* 2008 (15).
	🎵	*The Wedding Song:* Kenny G. *The Wedding March:* Mendelssohn. *Thinking Out Loud:* Ed Sheeran.
	🎨	*The Wedding Party:* Henri Rousseau. *Wedding Dress:* Alex Katz.
🎭		A wedding ceremony with a twist is a popular theme. Good ensemble opportunities. Great pair work, duologues on levels. Character work. Stanislavski.
⚠		Know your students and their family situations.
🔗		001, 006, 018, 029, 034, 045, 051, 053, 056, 057, 062, 065, 067, 068, 077, 081, 084–087, 104, 105, 123, 125, 126, 163, 179, 196, 199, 200.

079   Patriotism

Patriotism	*'They say that patriotism is the last refuge to which a scoundrel clings'* (Samuel Johnson-English writer).	
⚇	14+ Mixed groups (suits large casts).	
⚑	**Workshops/games**: *Filling the space. Stereotypes. Super objective.* Play your country's anthem. How do you feel when you hear this (say at a sports fixture)? **Questionnaire**: What is patriotism? What qualities define it? Are you patriotic? Describe that feeling. Artistic intent; to flesh out and question the simple definition 'love of one's country'.	
☼	America's first patriots were the Founding Fathers who had risked their lives to create a nation. **Research**: The Declaration of Independence. https://www.nationaltrust.org.uk/features/what-is-patriotism **More controversial**: Does patriotism make a country stronger or can it cause division through nationalism.	
Stimulus	💀	Your Nation's flag. Play your national anthem. What represents your nation? An Eagle, a Lion, a Dragon? National foods, costumes, music, dances, art. Customs, traditions, folk-law.
	📖	*Rule Britannia:* Daphne du Maurier. *The Pocket Book of British Patriotism:* George Courtauld. *Blue Sky White Stars:* Sarvinder Naberhaus.
	📝	*The British:* Benjamin Zephaniah. *Florida:* Elizabeth Bishop.
	🎭	*Biloxi Blues:* Neil Simon. *Sink the Belgrano:* Steven Berkoff. *Henry V,* the scenes before Agincourt. 'Once more unto the breach . . .' 3:1 and Saint Crispin's Day speech 4:3.
	🎞	*Saving Private Ryan:* 1998 (15). *The Patriot:* 2000 (15). *How Green Was My Valley:* 1941 (A).
	🎵	*America the Beautiful:* sung by Ray Charles. *Between the Wars:* Billy Bragg. *And the Band Played Waltzing Matilda:* Eric Bogle.
	🎨	*Saving Liberty:* Howard King. *Homecoming Marine:* Norman Rockwell. **Look at**: The British patriotic art of John Palliser. (controversial).
🎦	Theatre of Conflict. Patriotism is conflict based. Great ensemble pieces, epic works with fusions of Mother Courage and Henry V. The blurred lines between nationalism and patriotism. Projected images. Opportunities for great work with costumes and anthems/dance.	
⚠	Be aware of cultural mixes.	
🔗	006–011, 014–017, 023, 025, 061, 064, 066, 081, 085, 106, 107, 114, 119, 125, 132, 140, 150, 155, 160, 161, 174, 184, 189, 191, 196.	

080   Tears

<table>
<tr><td></td><td colspan="2">'We need never be ashamed of our tears'
(Charles Dickens – English writer and social critic).</td></tr>
<tr><td>👥</td><td colspan="2">All ages. Small groups.</td></tr>
<tr><td>🏳</td><td colspan="2">Workshops/games: Emotion memory.
Questionnaire: What makes you cry? Do you cry? Can you cry ? Sometimes the saddest thing doesn't make us shed a tear, then someone hugs us and we fall apart! Tears are often silent, private and painful. My culture, my tears. Men and tears, a sign of strength or weakness?</td></tr>
<tr><td>🔆</td><td colspan="2">Research: The release of endorphins and oxytocin when we cry. Basal/Irritant/Psychic.
More controversial: Crying on social media. A cry for help or just sharing an emotion.
Why does it feel good to cry?
Look at the language: Tears of a clown. Crocodile tears. Big boys don't cry. Find out how many.
It will all end in tears. Tears of joy. A tearful reunion.</td></tr>
<tr><td rowspan="7">Stimulus</td><td>💀</td><td>A box of tissues, a handkerchief. Tears on a face (image).
A lone magpie. A clown/Harlequin.</td></tr>
<tr><td>📖</td><td>The Fault in Our Stars: John Green.
My Sister's Keeper: Jodi Picoult.
The Kite Runner: Khaled Hosseini.</td></tr>
<tr><td>📝</td><td>Tears, Idle Tears: Alfred, Lord Tennyson.</td></tr>
<tr><td>🎭</td><td>Dialogues between the LANDLORD and the LANDLADY in Jim Cartwright's Two.
EVELYN and the unseen EVE confront the father, in Sarah Daniels' Beside Herself, Scene 9, and EVELYN's Monologue also in Scene 9.
DONALD in Scene 8 of Dennis Potter's Blue Remembered Hills. 'Come back dad'.</td></tr>
<tr><td>🎬</td><td>Look at: The act of crying in films like Truly, Madly, Deeply: 1990 (PG).
Robert De Niro in The Deer Hunter: 1978 (X).
David the Robot in A.I.: 2001 (12).
Inside Out: 2005 (U). When Sadness talks about why we should cry.</td></tr>
<tr><td>🎵</td><td>Tears of Rage: Bob Dylan.
I'm Not In Love: 10cc.
Tears and Rain: James Blunt.</td></tr>
<tr><td>🎨</td><td>Hero and Leandro: Cy Twombly.
Look at: Roy Lichtenstein's series of Crying Girl, Girl with Tear etc.</td></tr>
<tr><td>🎭</td><td colspan="2">Improvised work based on how it feels to cry. The intoxicating/contagious effect of tears. Mask work.
Dance/duets. Stanislavski, emotion memory.</td></tr>
<tr><td>⚠️</td><td colspan="2">Be careful with emotion memory work. Know your students.</td></tr>
<tr><td>🔗</td><td colspan="2">Too many to list!</td></tr>
</table>

081   Friendship

	'No person is your friend who demands your silence, or denies your right to grow' (Alice Walker – American author and activist).
	All age groups. Works in pairs to large ensemble.
	Workshops/games: *Fear. Trust games.* In a circle; point to a friend. **Questionnaire**: Write one sentence that defines a friend. How many of your Facebook friends really fit your definition? How many real friends do you have? Would you do anything for a friend? *'Friends are the family you choose.'* Discuss . . . **More controversial**: Can you marry a friend and stay friends? What breaks a friendship?
	Philia is another name for love between friends. We are social animals . . . We need friends, or do we? Plato thought that people from different social classes could never be friends. Do you think this is true? **Look at**: How friendship has changed. We are more able/willing to share emotions now. Cultural differences, even gender definitions of friendship differ. Pen pals v Facebook.

Stimulus		
		Let the students make a list of the objects/images that best describe friendship to them.
		The Kite Runner: Khaled Hosseini. *A Little Life:* Hanya Yanagihara. *Of Mice and Men:* Steinbeck.
		Us Two: A. A. Milne.
		Girls Like That: Evan Placey. *Those Legs:* Noel Clarke. *Di and Viv and Rose:* Amelia Bullmore.
		US TV Series *Friends:* 1994–2004 (15). *Toy Story:* 1995 (PG). *Stand by Me:* 1986 (15).
		You Got a Friend in Me: Randy Newman. *You're My Best Friend:* Queen. *With a Little Help from My Friends:* The Beatles
		Research: Famous friendships between artists. Vincent van Gogh and Paul Gauguin: Lucian Freud and Francis Bacon: Norman Rockwell and Grandma Moses: Pablo Picasso and Henri Matisse: Andy Warhol and Jean-Michel Basquiat. Compare their art, did they influence or challenge each other?

	Character work. For small group/pairs. Frantic Assembly. Larger groups, ensemble with the focus on a group of friends, dance, physical work. Costume/conformity.
	With young students don't ask 'Who is your best friend?' Try not to let it become personal.
	021, 025, 039, 051, 062, 065, 066, 079, 083, 096, 107, 135, 182, 183, 185, 186, 191, 192.

082   Animals

	'Animals are such agreeable friends – they ask no questions; they pass no criticisms' (George Eliot – English novelist).
♣♀♂	11+ Groups of 3–5.
🏁	**Workshops/games:** *Animal crackers.* Talk about your pets. We use animals for emotional support, to see and hear for us, for companionship and protection and yet we send them to war, to space, and the laboratory! Do animals exist solely for our sakes?
💡	**Research:** The symbolic meaning of different animals. Animal Rights Movements. rspca.org Animal Liberation Front. Consider how other cultures treat animals. **More controversial;** They feature in our fairy tales, superstitions and songs. We bet on them, sit on them, experiment on them and eat them. Animal lovers?

Stimulus	💀	Images. Guide/therapy dogs. The family cat, fish tank, our pets. Then look at sheep dogs, airport security dogs, Police dogs. Farm animals, the slaughter house. Vivisection.
	📖	We give animal traits to humans and human traits to animals when telling stories, especially to children. *Aesop's Fables* for example. *Watership Down:* Richard Adams. *Animal Farm:* George Orwell.
	✍️	**Look at:** Ted Hughes' use of animal imagery.
	🎭	**Look at:** How we use animal qualities in human characters. Ben Jonson's *Volpone* or David Campton's *Cagebirds.* Or where animals have human qualities: Ian Wooldridge's adaptation of Orwell's *Animal Farm.* Berkoff's adaptation of *Metamorphosis.*
	🎬	*The Jungle Book:* 2016 (PG). *Dolittle:* 2020 (PG). *Life of Pi:* 2012 (PG).
	🎵	Pink Floyd's album *Animals.* *The Animal Song:* Savage Garden. *Peter and the Wolf:* Prokofiev.
	🎨	*The Entry of the Animals into Noah's Ark:* Brueghel the Elder. *A Friend in Need:* C. M. Coolidge. The bronze statue *Charging Bull (The Bull of Wall Street)* – Arturo Di Modica.

🎭	Physical qualities of the animals, both movement and vocally. Use animal traits which inform characters. Very physical performances. Pieces influenced by animal cruelty. Movement is crucial and benefits from a choreographed approach. Expressionism/physical theatre. Lecoq/Artaud.
⚠️	Images of animal cruelty/anti-vivisection publicity can be upsetting.
🔗	006, 034, 036, 037, 039, 055, 081, 103, 121, 124, 191.

083 Laughter

		'There's a thin line between to laugh with and to laugh at' (Richard Pryor – American stand-up comedian).
👥		Any age. Pairs work well or Small groups of 3 or 4.
🏁		**Workshops/games:** *Soundscapes. Mirror images.* Lie in a circle with each person's head on the next one's tummy. Begin the laughter! Challenge students to 'make you laugh'. What do they resort to? Physical or spoken? Who can tell a joke?
💡		**Look at the language:** Belly laugh, cackle, chortle, chuckle, giggle, guffaw, horselaugh, laugh, snicker, snigger, titter, roar. Laughed like a drain, laughed myself silly, wet myself, you're having a laugh. Laughed my head off!! **Research:** Mischief Theatre. Try laughing in the mirror. Describe how your face transforms.
Stimulus	🎞	Film the group and play infectious laughter (Little children laughing). Watch how many of you smiled.
	📖	*Good Omens: The Nice and Accurate Prophecies of Agnes Nutter, Witch* Terry Pratchett and Neil Gaiman. *Catch–22:* Joseph Heller. *Why is That So Funny: A Practical Exploration of Physical Comedy:* John Wright.
	📝	*Solitude:* Ella Wheeler Wilcox
	🎭	Tragi Comedy *Girls:* Theresa Ikoko. Naturalistic comedy/parody, *Abigail's Party:* Mike Leigh. Dark comedy, *The Dumb Waiter:* Harold Pinter. Stylised social comedy, *Bouncers:* John Godber.
	🎦	*Dying Laughing:* 2016 (15). *Stan and Ollie:* 2018 (PG). *Jimmy Carr and The Science Of Laughter:* 2016 (BBC, Horizon Special).
	🎵	*Laughter in the Rain:* Neil Sedaka. *The Laughing Gnome:* David Bowie. *The Laughing Policeman:* Charles Jolly.
	🎨	**Search for:** 'The Art of Laughter: Humour in the Golden Age' on the Frans Hals Museum web site.
🎭		Using comedy to make an audience laugh before shocking them. Brecht's Tickle and Slap (Spass). How laughter is used to relieve tension. Younger students look at what makes us laugh. Slapstick, Commedia dell'arte, etc. ERS and Melodrama.
⚠		Comedy is cultural. Tasteless is never funny.
🔗		025, 033, 065, 074, 080, 081, 107, 120, 168, 176, 181, 195.

084   The Family Photo

<table>
<tr>
<td></td>
<td></td>
<td colspan="2">'A moment in time which can never slip away'
(Unknown).</td>
</tr>
<tr>
<td>👥👤</td>
<td colspan="3">Suits all age ranges</td>
</tr>
<tr>
<td>🏳</td>
<td colspan="3">Workshops/games: Emotion memory. Body sculpture.
Start by asking students to photocopy a family photo and place it on an A4 plain sheet. Then using stream of consciousness, to write, draw thoughts, feelings about that photo. Try not to influence.
Now remove the photo. Put one short sentence in the blank space to sum up what has been written. This will be the title of their piece.</td>
</tr>
<tr>
<td>🔆</td>
<td colspan="3">The family portrait dates back long before photography. Most families can look back on at least 100 years of family snaps . . . Now much of it is recorded on Facebook and other platforms.
How far can you go back? Can you name the people in the photo? What are their stories?</td>
</tr>
<tr>
<td rowspan="7">Stimulus</td>
<td>💀</td>
<td colspan="2">A family photograph. An old frame. An old SLR Camera. I made a montage of random family photographs (not anyone known).
If you Search for: Old Family Photographs-images, you will find all you need.</td>
</tr>
<tr>
<td>📖</td>
<td colspan="2">Family Pictures: Sue Miller.
The Only True Genius In the Family: Jennie Nash.
Forever Young: Bob Dylan, illustrated by Paul Rogers.</td>
</tr>
<tr>
<td>📝</td>
<td colspan="2">Family Picture: Mary Nagy.</td>
</tr>
<tr>
<td>🎭</td>
<td colspan="2">Dancing at Lughnasa: Brian Friel.
Find Me: Olwen Wymark.
My Mother Said I Never Should: Charlotte Keatley.</td>
</tr>
<tr>
<td>🎬</td>
<td colspan="2">Up: 2009 (U).
Encanto: 2021 (PG).
Eulogy: 2004 (15).</td>
</tr>
<tr>
<td>🎵</td>
<td colspan="2">Photograph: Ed Sheeran.
Photographs and Memories: Jim Croce.
Photographs can Lie: Elvis Costello</td>
</tr>
<tr>
<td>🎨</td>
<td colspan="2">Look at: MoMA's 1955 exhibition The Family of Man.</td>
</tr>
<tr>
<td>🎭</td>
<td colspan="3">Projections of family photos. Performers create an exact tableau of the pictures. Each performer steps out of the piece and tells a very different version of the events and family history from their point of view.</td>
</tr>
<tr>
<td>⚠</td>
<td colspan="3">Take care with old family photographs. Do not accept originals! Students should bring in photocopies with permission.</td>
</tr>
<tr>
<td>🔗</td>
<td colspan="3">006, 112, 030, 051, 052, 056, 057, 065, 068, 069, 078, 083, 085, 095, 106, 107, 109, 123, 126, 151, 176, 180, 185, 196.</td>
</tr>
</table>

085   Home

	'Home is where the heart is' (Proverb).
♟	Younger students enjoy this stimulus. Small groups.
⚑	**Workshops/games**: *Emotion memory, Gestus.* Improvising around the expression 'Home is where the heart is'. Or 'Comfort Zone'. Explore feelings like; happiness, safety, secure, loved, comfortable. **Questionnaire**: What does home mean to you? Being homesick. For one's country, town, home. What does home mean to you? What does home mean to different people across the world?
💡	**Look at the language**: House prices and Homelessness: Housing crisis. The Big Brother. Household. Homesick. Home from home. Home sweet home. **Watch**: *The History of Home* on Curiosity Stream. A home can mean many things. What about being confined to our home, either through illness/pandemic or even a fear of leaving it. **More controversial**: How wars are destroying homes and lives.

Stimulus	🐌	A Home Sweet Home doormat. A For Sale sign. Net curtains!
	📖	*Refugee Boy*: Benjamin Zephaniah. *Housekeeping*: Marilynne Robinson. *Home*: Julie Meyerson.
	📝	*Home*: Edward Thomas.
	🎭	*Bruised*: Matthew Trevannion. *The Homecoming*: Harold Pinter. *Dancing at Lughnasa*: Brian Friel.
	🎬	*Home Alone*: 1990 (PG). *Away We Go*: 2009 (15). *Home*: 2015 (U).
	🎵	*Homeward Bound*: Simon and Garfunkel. *Castle on the Hill*: Ed Sheeran. *Our House*: Madness.
	🎨	*The Yellow House* and *Bedroom in Arles*: Van Gogh. *American Gothic*: Grant Wood.

🎭	Small spaces, being safe, the notion of family just as much as the building. Duets. Physical theatre. Some great set work. A Doll's house on stage.
⚠	Know Your Students.
🔗	006, 022, 051, 052, 065, 077–080, 083, 084, 087, 089, 106, 107, 112, 114, 126, 152, 156, 183, 192, 196.

086   Online dating

	'I can barely even run a computer. God knows what I'd get on online dating' (Stockard Channing – American actress).
👥	14+ Mixed groups.
🚩	**Workshops/games:** *Levels of tension. Emotion memory.* Plucking up the courage to 'ask someone out', 'for a date'. **Questionnaire:** What questions would you include in an online dating app? The risk factor of being turned down, disappointed or embarrassed. Natural feelings that we can avoid? But should we?
💡	The first official online dating site 'Match' started in 1995. There are now over 2,500 online dating companies worldwide. **Look at the language:** that we use online. Personality quizzes and filtered searches take the pain out of the process but how honest are people? **More controversial:** Has internet dating made people more disposable?

Stimulus		
	📱	Dating App on your phone. A Valentine's Day card. A red rose. The heart/love images.
	📖	*The Soulmate Equation:* Christina Lauren. *How to Hack a Heartbreak:* Kristin Rockaway. *The Woman Who Took a Chance:* Fiona Gibson.
	✍️	*Love's Language:* Ella Wheeler Wilcox.
	🎭	*Signals:* Marv Siegel. *Girls Like That:* Evan Placey. *Mobile Phone Show:* Jim Cartwright.
	🎬	*The One:* 2021 (15) TV series Netflix. *You've Got Mail:* 1998 (PG). *Must Love Dogs:* 2005 (12A).
	🎵	*A Dream of You and Me:* Future Islands. *Crazy Little Thing Called Love:* Queen. *The First Time Ever I Saw Your Face:* Roberta Flack.
	🎨	*The Lovers:* Rene Magritte. *Yvonne and James:* Jordan Casteel.

🎭	Juxtaposition of the natural and multimedia. Physical/dance piece. Technology led. Katie Mitchell, Eddie Ladd. Some of the routines from *Love Song* by Abi Morgan (Frantic Assembly). **Look at:** The idea of faceless freedom.
⚠️	Students should not join any of the sites or fill out personal details online. Be wary.
🔗	018, 051, 054, 070, 078, 087, 088, 092, 107, 113, 123, 135, 151, 152, 160, 163, 184, 185, 186, 196.

087   The Heart (A Case study unit, see Chapter 5)

	'The heart is forever making the head its fool' (François de La Rochefoucauld – French Cardinal).
	Older students. Small groups of 2–4.
	The OED has an entry of 15,000 words for the word heart. Most of these are as metaphors. See details in Case study, Unit 87, Chapter 5.
	The ancient Romans made a big connection between the heart and love (goddess Venus). **Research**: How images/icons of the heart are used in media and advertising. American Heart Association. British Heart Foundation.
Stimulus	**Look at**: The imagery. Try this. Search for images of the heart. Now search for images of the heart as a metaphor . . . Discuss differences/similarities.
	The Heart: Maylis de Kerangal. *The Book of the Heart*: Eric Jager. *Heart: A History*: Sandeep Jauher.
	When I Was One-and-Twenty: A. E. Housman.
	Iambic pentameter. Feel the heartbeat. di-DUM di-DUM di-DUM di-DUM di-DUM.
	Seven Pounds: 2008 (12A). *I Daniel Blake*: 2016 (15). *Big Fish*: 2003 (PG). *The Power of the Heart*: A Documentary drama.
	The list here would be endless. Search with your students in mind and what is topical. Think about using classical music.
	From early anatomical studies (da Vinci) to modern prints. **Look at**: The work of Chanelle Walshe.
	See details in Case study, Unit 87, Chapter 5.
	Get them to commit their artistic intentions to paper at an early stage.
	027, 034, 051, 052, 077, 086, 151, 181.

088   The Stranger

	'Do not neglect to show hospitality to strangers, for by doing that some have entertained angels without knowing it' (Hebrews: 13:2).
	All ages (so many possibilities!).
	Workshops/games: *Fear, Levels of tension.* A stranger! We are warned against them, taught to fear them . . . Yet asked to treat them kindly, with compassion. We can talk to total strangers more freely than those we know. You can be that stranger in a strange land. Just a stranger on the bus?
	Look at the language: Stranger danger! A tall, handsome stranger. Mysterious. Were we all strangers wearing masks during the pandemic? When you are the stranger, not speaking the language, unaware of the customs and traditions. *'A stranger is someone with whom you feel strange'* (Robert Mandel-American film producer).

Stimulus		A dark mask. A silhouette.
		(L'Étranger) The Outsider: Albert Camus. *The Stranger*: Harlan Coben. *The Perfect Stranger*: Megan Miranda.
		To a Stranger: Walt Whitman.
		The Playboy of the Western World: J. M. Synge. *The Train Driver*: Athol Fugard. *An Inspector Calls*: J. B. Priestly.
		Strangers on a Train: 1951 (A). *Mother!* 2017 (18). *Bad Times at the El Royale*: 2018 (15).
		The Kindness Of Strangers: Nick Cave And The Bad Seeds. *The Stranger Song*: Leonard Cohen. *Goodbye Stranger*: Supertramp.
		Most famous portraits are of people who are strangers to us and possibly the painter too!

	T.I.E about stranger danger for younger students. Older students can look at strangers and fears (Xenophobia). Minimalist. Duologues with strangers on trains/planes. Character work. Stanislavski.
⚠	Stranger danger should be reinforced. In particular with younger students.
🔗	016, 028, 031, 040, 041, 064, 076, 106–109, 112, 114, 128, 129, 134, 155, 160, 161, 184, 187, 189, 190, 192.

089   Your hometown

		'In my hometown memories are fresh' (Adele – English singer and songwriter).
👥		All ages Groups of 2–4.
🏳		**Workshops/games**: *Emotion memory. Soundscapes.* **Look at**: A photograph of your town. Ask for a story. Each student comes up with their own (narrated). Play Chinese whispers with one of the stories. Take an event (local) and form a freeze frame of it. Re-tell a local story.
🔅		What's happening in your neighbourhood/Street/Town/School? The idea is to take something very local and make a piece of theatre about it. It could be historical or very current. Ask around, especially, the older folk. **What the papers say**: Check those local papers! It's worth searching!
Stimulus	🐚	Local for photos and old local newspapers.
	📖	*The Hate U Give:* Angie Thomas. *Salvage the Bones:* Jesmyn Ward. *Boy:* Roald Dahl.
	📝	*I Often Passed The Village:* Emily Dickinson.
	🎭	*A Memory of Lizzie:* David Foxton. *Gone Too Far:* Bola Agbaje
	🎞	*Stand by Me* 1986 (15). *True Stories* 1986 (PG).
	🎵	*My Hometown:* Bruce Springsteen.
	🎨	**Look at**: Children's drawing of events like Aberfan, UFO's 9/11.
🎭		I once saw an excellent piece of work in a centre in Buckinghamshire, England. Apparently the students had told their teacher, 'Nothing has ever happened here'. Their research came up with the Great Train Robbery 1963. The piece was docudrama which reflected their own research and discoveries about their local story!
⚠		Never make it personal!
🔗		008, 065, 068, 079, 106, 107, 139, 160, 161, 172, 196.

090   A pair of shoes

	'If the shoe fits, wear it' (Idiom).
⚥	All ages ranges.
▣	**Workshops/games:** *Stereotypes.* **Questionnaire:** How many pairs of shoes, your favourite, why etc. '*One shoe can change your life*' (Cinderella). '*Walk a mile in someone else's shoes*' (Mary Lathrap). Shoes connect people, they tell others about us and remind us of our own lives. What do your shoes say about you?
☀	It is believed we have been covering/protecting our feet for around 40,000 years. **Research:** Shoe tossing (shoes on a wire), gangs/organised crime and other meanings. **Search for:** Shoes hidden in homes to ward off evil. The V&A (Victoria and Albert museum) has produced a fantastic timeline 'A History of Shoes'. Shoes on or off . . . Different cultures and beliefs.

Stimulus	🐌	Think of all the types of footwear!
	📖	*Those Shoes:* Maribeth Boelts (illustrated by Noah Jones). *Ballet Shoes:* Noel Streatfeild. *Tess of the d'Urbervilles:* Thomas Hardy.
	📝	*Will You Tie My Shoes When I Grow Old?:* Rachel Kovacs.
	🎭	*What Are They Like?:* Lucinda Coxon *Fear and Misery of the Third Reich (The Black Shoes):* Bertolt Brecht. *The Caretaker:* Harold Pinter (opening scene, DAVIES' shoe monologue).
	🎞	*The Wizard of Oz:* 1939(A). *Back to The Future:* 1985 (PG) (The Nike shoes scene). *Dirty Dancing:* 1987 (15) (The bridge scene).
	🎵	*These Boots Are Made for Walkin':* Nancy Sinatra. *Diamonds on the Soles of Her Shoes:* Paul Simon. *Blue Suede Shoes:* Elvis Presley. *Boots of Spanish Leather:* Bob Dylan.
	🎨	Van Gogh painted a number of Still Lifes of shoes and boots. Andy Warhol made the shoe the focus of a number of his works. **Look at:** Many of the classic paintings and sculptures and pay attention to what's on their feet. Even some of the nudes have footwear!

🎭	Consider a range of ideas from fashion and sexuality, to working shoes and shoes you need to wear. Emotional drama where people's shoes are what's left, a legacy as with Jojo Rabbit's mother's shoes or the shoe memorial of the Holocaust.
⚠	Students get swept along by the shoe as an object of desire. There is more!
🔗	112, 051, 055, 060, 099, 114, 135, 176, 188, 194, 196.

091 Coal

		'Here, are the stiffening hills, here, the rich cargo, Congealed in the dark arteries, Old veins' (Mervyn Peak – English author).
⚐		15+ Mixed groups.
⚑		**Workshops/games;** *Confinement. Status.* Play the list from *The Price of Coal* by David Alexander (YouTube). Or, *Ar Dori Ad Dydd Hen Alaw Gymreig* by Rhos Male Voice Choir. Mining is world's deadliest industry, it kills 15,000 miners a year.
☼		National Coal mining museum. UK. The National Mining Hall of Fame. USA. **Look at:** The heyday of coal mining, the industrial revolution to 1960s. **Research:** Coal mining disasters. Worldwide or just your own country. Look at how mines have closed and coal fired industry has ended. Contrast with Bitcoin mining. Class and privilege.
Stimulus	🎲	Coal. Coal sacks. A miner's helmet and torch/lamp. NCB recruitment posters.
	📖	*King Coal:* Upton Sinclair. *GB84:* David Pearce. *Coal: A Human History:* Barbara Freese.
	✑	*Miners:* Wilfred Owen.
	🎭	*Billy Elliot: The Musical:* Lee Hall and Elton John. *Land of Our Fathers:* Chris Urch. A Monologue by Ifor ap Glyn, *Mamgu's Letter* (Aberfan).
	🎞	*Billy Elliot:* 2000 (15). *Blue Scar:* 1949 (U). *The Last Miners:* 2016 (BBC series).
	♫	*We Work the Black Seam:* Sting. *Solidarity:* from *Billy Elliot: The Musical.* *North Country Blues:* Bob Dylan.
	🎨	*Three Miners:* Josef Herman (1953). *Coalface Conversation:* Valerie Ganz. Pit Head ART UK
🎦		Darkness and light; torches on faces. Ensemble piece with strong rhythms. Male voice choir. Political.
⚠		Some stories of horrific injuries and accidents.
🔗		093, 101, 115, 116, 117, 159.

092   The Media onslaught

<table>
<tr>
<td></td>
<td colspan="2">'It's in our biology to trust what we see with our eyes. This makes living in a carefully edited, overproduced and photoshopped world very dangerous'
(Brené Brown – American writer and professor).</td>
</tr>
<tr>
<td>👥</td>
<td colspan="2">15+ Suits large ensemble.</td>
</tr>
<tr>
<td>🚩</td>
<td colspan="2">Workshops/games; Chinese whispers.
'Get connected! Be connected! Stay connected!' Sound familiar? . . . and if we don't?
Questionnaires: About time spent on your phone/tablet etc . . .
Our smartphone/tablet/laptop/smart speaker is constantly telling us what to do, buy, use, and even feel. Before any of this was real Jim Morrison once said 'Whoever controls the media, controls the mind'. Think carefully about this and today's media bombardment.</td>
</tr>
<tr>
<td>🔆</td>
<td colspan="2">Research: The News, Commercials, Social Media, The Internet, even your GPS . . .
Are we happily dancing to someone else's tune? Where are we being led?
Are we amusing ourselves to death?</td>
</tr>
<tr>
<td rowspan="7">Stimulus</td>
<td>💀</td>
<td>All of the offending tech!</td>
</tr>
<tr>
<td>📖</td>
<td>I'm Trying to Reach You: Barbara Browning.
The Ghost in the Shell: Masamune Shirow.
iBrain: Surviving the Technological Alteration of the Modern Mind: Gary Small.</td>
</tr>
<tr>
<td>📝</td>
<td>When Les Linked In: Brian Bilston.</td>
</tr>
<tr>
<td>🎭</td>
<td>The Suicide: Nikolia Erdman (adapted by Suhayla El-Bushra).
Chatroom: Enda Walsh.
This Is Your Brain on Social Media: Ian McWethy and Carrie McCrossen.</td>
</tr>
<tr>
<td>🎬</td>
<td>The Social Network: 2010 (PG-13).
The Truman Show: 1998 (PG-13).
Men, Women and Children: 2014 (15).</td>
</tr>
<tr>
<td>🎵</td>
<td>Candy Everybody Wants: 10,000 Maniacs.
Follow Me: Sean Paul.
Crawl: Childish Gambino.</td>
</tr>
<tr>
<td>🎨</td>
<td>Look at: The Starry night exhibition: Culturespace.
Alternatives: Espen Kluge.</td>
</tr>
<tr>
<td>🎭</td>
<td colspan="2">Ensemble work. Berkoff. Grotesque, Meyerhold. Highly stylised. All following one piper!
Projections/multimedia. Katie Mitchell.</td>
</tr>
<tr>
<td>⚠️</td>
<td colspan="2">Respect digital privacy/security.</td>
</tr>
<tr>
<td>🔗</td>
<td colspan="2">024, 033, 040, 070, 075, 086, 094, 099, 102, 109, 125, 151, 152, 156, 162, 164, 165, 185, 187, 188, 189, 193.</td>
</tr>
</table>

093 The Industrial Revolution

	'The Industrial Revolution was another of those extraordinary jumps forward in the story of civilisation' (Stephen Gardiner – British architect).
	14+ Mixed groups 5–10.
	Workshops/games: *Status. Soundscapes.* The Industrial Revolution began around 1760. It led to many of the biggest changes of the Victorian era. List the benefits. In hindsight, has it been a disaster? Poverty and squalor abounded, but the Industrial Revolution had positive impacts too. It all started in Britain, with coal, freedom of scientific ideas and inventors!
	historycrunch.com BBC Bitesize History have an excellent unit. The National Museum of Industrial History Virtual museum of industrial history. **Search for** 10 Facts about the Industrial Revolution. **Research** 'Ragged Schools'. **More controversial:** What about all that pollution?

Stimulus		
		A lump of coal. Images of Isambard Kingdom Brunel and his designs.
		Hard Times: Charles Dickens. *Silas Marner:* George Elliot. *Huckleberry Finn:* Mark Twain.
		The Cry of the Children: Elizabeth Browning.
		An Inspector Calls: J. B. Priestley. Musical theatre and Vaudeville.
		Modern Times: 1936 (U). Educational Film: *Industrial Revolution – Great Britain around 1800* (YouTube). *North and South:* 2004 TV Mini Series (12).
		The Industrial Revolution Song: History Music Video. Horrible Histories (YouTube).
		In the Workshops/games, Eugène Buland. L. S. Lowry's works. **Research:** Romanticism and Impressionism.

	Satire. Dark satanic mills. Ensemble work with grotesque mask and exaggerated movement. Pain and poverty against the backdrop of wealth and exploitation (Berkoff).
	Not just a British thing!
	001, 076, 091, 101, 110, 114, 115, 116, 119, 121, 122, 125, 169, 174, 176, 182, 189.

094   Reality TV

	'Truth is stranger than fiction, which is why reality TV is so popular' (Heather Dubrow – American actress).
👥	14+ Mixed groups. From duologues up to large ensemble.
🚩	**Workshops/games**; *Status. Repetition.* Voyeurism! From *Big Brother* to *Love Island*, reality TV is a genre in its own right. But why is it so popular? **Questionnaire:** How many do you watch? How Often? Why? Film a lesson, do we behave differently? So is it reality? Acting up or being honest? Are we laughing at people or being taken for fools?
💡	Creating and belonging to a community. A shared experience. There is a great deal of reality TV available on YouTube. Look at the format of *Big Brother*. Compare to later reality TV shows. Ratings and statistics. **What the papers say:** How can shows like *Love Island* make headlines in some papers?
Stimulus	📺 TV advertising for whichever shows you decide to focus upon.
	📖 *Nerve:* 2016 (Jeanne Ryan) (15). *The Real Real:* Emma McLaughlin and Nicola Krauss. *Something Real:* Heather Demetrios.
	✍️ *Reality TV:* Phil Soar.
	🎭 *The Jailer's Daughter:* Esther Joy Mackay. *The Guffin:* Howard Brenton.
	🎬 *The Truman Show:* 1998 (PG-13). *Nerve:* 2016 (15). *Wanda Vision:* TV Mini-series Disney/Marvel.
	🎵 *It's Easy:* Mia Sable. *Unreal Reality:* The Kinks. Title theme tunes of the various reality shows.
	🎨 **Research:** *Work of Art: The Next Great Artist* (YouTube).
🎭	Verbatim with an eye for the comedic! Parody. Character work. Naturalism, heightened realism. Good set opportunities. Boal. Imaginary Body.
⚠️	Beware of art imitating nothing special! Some reality content is unsuitable for younger students.
🔗	014, 033, 062, 076, 077, 078, 080, 086, 088, 089, 092, 097, 102, 109, 110, 113, 125, 135, 151, 152, 160, 172, 185, 187, 189, 190, 191.

095   Holidays and travel

	'Tourists don't know where they've been, travellers don't know where they're going' (Paul Theroux – American writer).
👥	Groups of 4–5. Any age.
🚩	**Workshops/games:** *Levels of tension. Stereotypes, Soundscapes.* Suitcases and excitement. **Questionnaire:** Favourite destinations. What you love/hate about holidays. Role play tourists in new places. Write a monologue/stream of consciousness about the airport, the holiday, long car journey. *'Are we there yet?'* Write the story behind a simple *Wish You Were Here* postcard . . .
💡	The average person in the United Kingdom has visited ten countries. On average, Germans have been to eight, and the average French person has travelled to five. Only 29% of Americans have even been abroad. Does this say something about the people or the countries they live in?
Stimulus	🧳 Suitcases, passports, postcards and sun lotion. Travel brochures.
	📖 *Five Total Strangers:* Natalie D. Richards. *The Beach:* Alex Garland.
	📝 *I Wandered Lonely as a Cloud (Daffodils):* William Wordsworth.
	🎭 *The 39 Steps:* Patrick Bucham (adapted by P. Barlow). *The Curious Incident of the Dog in the Night-Time:* Mark Haddon. Adapted by Simon Stephen. *The Journey to London* (physicalised).
	🎬 *Summer Holiday:* 1963 (U). *Diary of a Wimpy Kid: The Long Haul:* 2017 (U).
	🎵 *Driving Anthems:* (Album) Various artists. *Summer Holiday:* Cliff Richard and the Shadows.
	🎨 *Rhyl Sands:* David Cox. *Nighthawks:* Edward Hopper. *A Bigger Grand Canyon:* David Hockney.
🎭	Two themes. Travel, long flights, car/train journeys, lend themselves to observational monologues and character work. Frantic Assembly (Chair duets). A pair on a Train Journey London to Edinburgh. (Strangers/lovers/mother and son.) Holidays, relaxing, having fun, getting a tan. Larger groups, ensemble, dance. Narrated storytelling
⚠	Some of your students go on far flung exotic holidays and others stay at home. Can be an issue. *Travelling* is a more levelling topic.
🔗	060, 076, 084, 085, 088, 089, 101, 114, 115, 118, 121, 122, 154, 166, 167, 188.

096   Alcohol

		'To alcohol! The cause of . . . and solution to . . . all of life's problems' (Matt Groening – American cartoonist).
♟	15+ Mixed groups	
🚩	**Workshops/games:** *Guide me. Trust games.* With 'Beer goggles' from a PSHE lesson. Try walking a straight line, tying a shoelace. The pleasures of moderate social drinking weighed against the associated risks: health, crime, road accidents and alcohol dependence. Globally its consumption is responsible for 2.8 million deaths a year. **Look at the language:** Social dinking, drinking problem, alcoholism, alcohol dependency, alcohol abuse. List the different expressions for being drunk, from the polite to the profane. Form a group tableau that depicts each.	
💡	**Research** the beginning of the 18th century when the UK passed a law to encourage the manufacture of Gin. US Government's prohibition in the 1920s. Is alcohol advertised responsibly? What about underage drinking.	
Stimulus	🎨	Beer cans, wine bottle, whisky bottle, alcopops, Vodka (all empty!). Advertising for alcohol. Images of social drinking at parties, toasts at weddings etc. and results of drunken behaviour including shocking images of drink drive (from police drink drive campaigns).
	📖	*Marlena:* Julie Buntin. *Shadow Tag:* Louise Erdrich. *The Girl on the Train:* Paula Hawkins.
	📝	*To Celia:* Ben Jonson.
	🎭	*A Taste of Honey:* Shelagh Delaney. *Tonypandemonium:* Rachel Trezise. *Too Much Punch for Judy:* Mark Wheeller.
	🎬	*The World's End:* 2013 (15). *The Angels' Share:* 2012 (15). *Leaving Las Vegas:* 1995 (18).
	🎵	*Alabama Song:* The Doors. *Red, Red Wine:* UB40. *Whiskey in the Jar:* Thin Lizzy.
	🎨	*Beer Street* and *Gin Lane:* Hogarth. *Bacchus:* Millot. *Los Borrachos (The Drunks):* Valasquez.
🎦	T.I.E. alcohol abuse/drink drive. *Too Much Punch for Judy* is a great inspiration and tackles some of the more difficult aspects of performing as a drunk and keeping it real. Ensemble piece based on the devastating effect of alcohol on the Aboriginal peoples of Australia.	
⚠	Know your students. In some cultures alcohol is forbidden.	
🔗	009, 025, 045, 055, 071, 077, 097, 104, 126, 130, 135, 143, 156, 160, 181, 182, 184, 188.	

097   Addiction

	'Fall seven times, stand up eight' (Japanese proverb).
👥	15+ Mixed able groups of no more than three or four.
🚩	**Workshops/games:** *Trust games.* Addiction may not be drugs. **Questionnaire:** List things we loosely call our addictions . . . Look at addiction and the struggle to rehabilitate.
☼	**Research:** The Victorians and drug addiction. Charles Booth's London. Laudanum (Opium) addiction in particular. United Nations World Drug Report 2021. teens.drugsabuse.gov/teachersaddictioncenter.com/addiction/addiction-statistics/ World Health Organisation. who.int/health-topics/drugsourworldindata.org/drug-use drugfreeworld.org **What the papers say:** Look how drugs and related crimes are reported.

Stimulus		
	☠	Syringes (removed sharp end!). Pills and tablets (M&M's/Smarties). Black and white images of Addict's faces (explore links with homelessness).
	📖	*Beautiful Boy:* David Sheff. *Moth Smoke:* Mohsin Hamid. *Smacked:* Eilene Zimmerman. *Go Ask Alice:* Beatrice Sparks.
	✍	*Give Me What I Need:* John Cooper Clarke. The Narrative verse *Goblin Market:* Christina Rossetti.
	🎭	*People, Places and Things:* Duncan Macmillan. *Jerusalem:* Jez Butterworth. *That Face:* Polly Stenham.
	🎞	*Trainspotting:* 1996 (18). *28 Days:* 2000 (15). *Ben Is Back:* 2018 (15). *Beautiful Boy:* 2018 (15). *Top Boy:* 2011 (15) TV.
	🎵	*The A Team:* Ed Sheeran. *Rehab:* Amy Winehouse. *Cocaine:* Jackson Browne. *Sister Morphine:* The Rolling Stones. Tango re-mix music (Tango Chill sessions) *Fusion A Distancia.*
	🎨	The paintings of Jean-Michel Basquiat. Psychedelia art. Peter Max, Bonnie Maclean, Stanley Miller.

🎦	Students took Rosetti's *Goblin Market* (Narrative verse) and used the idea of the girls being addicted to the Goblin's fruits. They fully exploited the themes of drugs, sex and innocence, portraying the Goblins as dealers. It was performed by three girls on a bare stage covered by white sheets under which Goblin bodies moved. The entire set was strewn with hundreds of Poppies from Poppy Day appeal. See also Unit 178 (literature).
⚠	Many of the links and themes when researching addiction and rehab are disturbing and shocking.
🔗	045, 057, 071, 075, 098, 099, 104, 109, 112, 130, 156, 185.

098   Gambling

		'The sure way of getting nothing for something' (Wilson Mizner – American writer).
👥	16+ Mixed groups.	
🚩	**Workshops/games**; *Soundscapes. Control games.* The sounds of a bookies and a horse race. A harmless 'flutter'. How many people do you know who use scratch cards, enter the lottery? Compare the romantic image of Poker in Casino Royale with the card game in Lock, Stock and Two Smoking Barrels. Can you be addicted to gambling? Risk and the hope of gain.	
🔆	Most countries have an organisation to help people with gambling addiction problems. NHS. SMART Recovery. Gamblers Anonymous. Gamecare. UCLA Gambling Studies Program have a useful PDF Self-help workbook. **helpguide.org** have an excellent article *Gambling Addiction and Problem Gambling*.	
Stimulus	💀	A lotto ticket, a scratch card, a pack of cards, a set of dice, poker chips, betting slips, a four-leaf clover.
	📖	*Casino Royale:* Ian Fleming. *The Gambler:* Dostoevsky. *Titanic Thompson: The Man Who Bet on Everything:* Kevin Cook.
	📝	*Card of Fate: Poems of Gambling Addiction:* Duke of Quails.
	🎭	*Dealer's Choice:* Patrick Marber. *The Odd Couple:* Neil Simon. *Gambling:* George Cohan.
	🎞	*The Gambler:* 2014 (15). *Lock, Stock and Two Smoking Barrels:* 1998 (18). *Casino Royale:* 2006 (12A).
	🎵	*Luck Be A Lady:* Frank Sinatra. *The Gambler:* Kenny Rogers. *House of the Rising Sun:* The Animals.
	🎨	*At The Roulette Table:* Edvard Munch. *Slot Machine Queen:* Shelly Wilkerson. *Card Players:* Paul Cézanne.
🎪	Forum theatre in which the audience are encouraged to bet/have an opinion on the outcome. In the round with a collection of gamblers, from the funny/pathetic to the professional and the addicted. All led by an MC to keep the pace.	
⚠	Students could be introduced to potentially harmful material/concepts. Know your students.	
🔗	045, 063, 071, 077, 96, 97, 104, 107, 113, 135, 151.	

099 Shopaholic

	'Buying is a profound pleasure' (Simone de Beauvoir – French writer, philosopher and feminist).	
	13 onwards. Mixed groups.	
	Workshops/games: *Soundscape. Repetition exercise.* Twenty or more carrier bags (not supermarket) stuffed with boxes and clothes. Scatter around the space in brands . . . Play *'I want it all'* by Queen. Discuss the joys of shopping v. the evils of consumerism. Class is usually fairly divided leading to some good discussions. **Questionnaire**: Do you enjoy shopping? Does it make you feel good? Etc. Shopping addiction, also known as compulsive buying disorder.	
	Search for: History of Consumerism (History Crunch has an excellent resource). Recently there have been a number of news stories/articles on how online shopping is accelerating shopping addiction. Did the Pandemic contribute to this? We laugh and call it 'Retail Therapy', but can we afford it? Links with debt and mental health issues. Is online shopping more addictive?	
Stimulus		Named shopping bags, designer logos and advertising. Advertising for high-end, luxury goods. Images of homelessness, famine, refugees. Use contrast to question.
		The Secret World of a Shopaholic: Sophie Kinsella. *Kingdom Come*: J. G. Ballard. *The Story of Stuff*: Annie Leonard. *Buyology*: Truth and Lies about Why We Buy. M. Lindstorm.
		Shopping Addict: Roger Turner.
		*Shopping and F***ing*: Mark Ravenhill. *Abigail's Party*: Mike Leigh.
		Priceless: 2006 (PG-13). *Uptown Girls*: 2003 (12A). *Crazy Rich Asians*: 2018 (12A).
		Mercedes Benz: Janis Joplin. *Price Tag*: Jessie J. *Feel Good Inc*: Gorillaz.
		Research: Gabriel Kuri: *The Art of Consumerism*. **Look at**: Banksy's *'Sale Ends Today'*.
	Dance/physical theatre, music, glitz and designer labels. More controversial: Cheap labour and poverty behind some famous designer labels. Theatre of the Oppressed. Boal.	
	Shopping addiction is recognised as a serious disorder.	
	025, 027, 030, 045, 062, 063, 071, 090, 092, 097, 101, 104, 105, 135, 151, 152, 164, 188, 194.	

100   Sorry

		'If sorry is such a difficult thing to say, why is it said so often?' (Jason Hanlan – Welsh writer).
👥		Any age. Small (able) groups.
🚩		**Workshops/games:** *Sorry. That hurt!* **Look at the language:** Feeling sorrow is not the same thing as feeling sorry. Discuss nuance, meaning, delivery.
💡		**Search for** '10 Public Apologies by World Leaders'. **Look at:** National Sorry day in Australia. Old English word sārig meaning 'pained or distressed'. The idea that little children have to 'learn' to say sorry.
Stimulus	💀	A bunch of flowers to say 'I'm sorry'. A card 'Sorry for your loss'. **Search for** 'Sorry' (images). Lots of cuddly teddies and hearts . . . Now search for 'Sorrow' (images).
	📖	*My Grandmother Asked Me To Tell You She's Sorry:* Fredrick Backman. *Sorry Not Sorry:* Alyssa Milano. *Sorry:* Trudy Ludwig (for younger students).
	📝	*To a Mouse:* Robert Burns.
	🎭	*The Remorse of Judas:* Play 32. Editor Clifford Davidson. *An Inspector Calls:* J. B. Priestley. *Beside Herself:* Sarah Daniels.
	🎞	**Look at:** movie-sounds.org/sorry for an excellent resource of over 200 quotes from movies (with audio sound clips) about saying sorry.
	🎵	*Swallow my Pride:* The Ramones. *Sorry Seems to be the Hardest Word:* Elton John. *Purple Rain:* Prince.
	🎨	**Look at:** Roy Lichtenstein's *I . . . I'm Sorry.* *The Penitent Magdalene:* Guido Reni.
🎭		Look at the way a word can change meaning through context and delivery. Often text led. Comedy opportunities based on being British and 'dreadfully sorry'.
⚠		Do not undermine or trivialise school policies on apologising.
🔗		003, 004, 024, 025, 043–046, 051, 052, 061, 063, 077, 080, 097, 107, 123, 126, 131, 135, 141, 144, 175, 182, 183, 186, 192.

101 Poverty and inequality

		'You will always have the poor among you' (Jesus. Matthew 19:23–24).
⚥		All ages. Suits large groups/mixed ability. Some performance genres demand a more mature performer and can dictate group size.
⚑		**Workshops/games:** *Status* Almost half of the world is living on less than \$5 (£3.70) approx. per day! **More contentious:** *'Inequality is not unavoidable – it's a political choice'* Oxfam.
💡		**Look at:** The Old Testament, Proverbs 31:8–9 (NIV). **Research:** The *Playing for Change* foundation. Oxfam. When you look at poverty anywhere in the world, you can't fail to see the inequalities which exist. **What the papers say:** 'Poverty in the UK is a marginal issue in mainstream media' JRF.
Stimulus	🎨	Look at the photography of Gordon Parks (Flávio da Silva). See photo by Eleanor Farmer of Oxfam (*Beggar outside Louis Vuitton*).
	📖	*The Grapes of Wrath:* John Steinbeck. *Down and Out in Paris and London:* George Orwell. *Oliver Twist* and *Great Expectations:* Charles Dickens.
	✒️	*Poor Children:* Francis Duggan.
	🎭	*Road:* Jim Cartwright. *Jerusalem:* Jez Butterworth. *Our Day Out* and *Blood Brothers:* Willy Russell.
	🎞️	*Elysium:* 2013 (15). *The Boy Who Harnessed the Wind:* 2019 (PG). *Shameless:* UK and US TV
	🎵	*Ghost of Tom Joad:* Bruce Springsteen. *Mr Banker:* Lynyrd Skynyrd. Watch the video *'Anthem RED – Voice against poverty and inequality.'* Warning, this video has disturbing images.
	🎨	**Look at** paintings from Picasso's Blue period. Artists against poverty (The Borgen Project). Think about how many great artists died in poverty.
🎭		Grotowski. Actor focussed. Show inequality by performance not costume (older students). Younger students, levels and costume/props. Masks and puppets. Verbatim. Research based.
⚠️		Know your students. Some charity/fundraising videos contain upsetting images.
🔗		008, 105, 106, 111, 112, 115, 125, 194.

102 Fake news

<table>
<tr>
<td></td>
<td colspan="2">'A lie can travel half way around the world while the truth is putting on its shoes' (Mark Twain – American author).</td>
</tr>
<tr>
<td>👥</td>
<td colspan="2">12+ Groups of 3–5.</td>
</tr>
<tr>
<td>🏳</td>
<td colspan="2">Workshops/games: Lying (The burden of a lie). Chinese whispers. Start with an opinion. 'I think that . . .' What happens to your opinion? Ask each person to write it as a headline . . . Start with the notion that, if enough people say it, it becomes true. If you see it printed, it becomes even more true! So if it appears on TV!!!! It has to be true: right? The more sensational it is, the more we want to believe it!
Try selling a story/lie to each other. What can you do to make it believable/credible?</td>
</tr>
<tr>
<td>💡</td>
<td colspan="2">What the papers say: Are newspapers honest?
Do our Politicians tell us the truth? How can you tell a fake news story from a real news story? Look at the language: The language of fake news tends to be simple and colloquial, making it easy to understand. It is emotive/sensational and tends to discredit other news sources.
There are some fun fake news/meme generators available online. Break your own news.
Research: How Churchill used fake news during WWII.</td>
</tr>
<tr>
<td rowspan="7">Stimulus</td>
<td>📰</td>
<td>Newspaper headlines.</td>
</tr>
<tr>
<td>📖</td>
<td>Voodoo Histories: David Aaronovitch.
Restless: William Boyd.
Nineteen Eighty-Four: George Orwell.</td>
</tr>
<tr>
<td>📝</td>
<td>Look at: http://fakenews-poetry.org/</td>
</tr>
<tr>
<td>🎭</td>
<td>Sink the Belgrano: Steven Berkoff.
Fake News: Osman Baig.
Fake News!: Werner Trieschmann.</td>
</tr>
<tr>
<td>🎬</td>
<td>Wag the Dog: 1997 (15).
Fake News: 2017 (Not rated).
Fake News: A Trump Story: 2019 (TV Movie).</td>
</tr>
<tr>
<td>🎵</td>
<td>Bullet in the Head: Rage Against the Machine.
Chained to the Rhythm: Katy Perry featuring Skip Marley.
Please Forgive Us: 10,000 Maniacs.</td>
</tr>
<tr>
<td>🎨</td>
<td>Search for: Fake news photography; images.</td>
</tr>
<tr>
<td>🎭</td>
<td colspan="2">Expressionism/stylised depiction of emotional experience rather than physical reality. Berkoff/Lecoq.
Simple and uncluttered set. Projections/multimedia. Katie Mitchell.
Chinese whispers choral piece, dance.</td>
</tr>
<tr>
<td>⚠</td>
<td colspan="2">Respect privacy.</td>
</tr>
<tr>
<td>🔗</td>
<td colspan="2">005, 040, 076, 092, 105, 109, 110, 111, 116, 121, 125, 156, 189.</td>
</tr>
</table>

103   The Sea

	'Even the upper end of the river believes in the ocean' (William Stafford – American poet).
♣	All ages. Large groups
🏁	**Workshops/games**: *Soundscapes*. *Control games*, moving as an ensemble. The sound of the sea is enough to generate a discussion. A darkened room with a recording! What does this mean to you? For some it means summer holidays and sandcastles, a source of food, of inspiration, a means to travel and trade. We worry about it rising, fight over it, plunder it and generally dump our waste into it.
☼	**Research**: History of the Ocean – MarineBio Conservation Society. cousteau.org Check out local Aquariums and their educational resources. NASA Oceanography. Schmidt Ocean Institute (education resources). **Look at the language**: English idioms that use sea-related words. **More controversial**: If Aliens came to Earth why would they contact us? Dolphins and Whales inhabit much more of the planet than we do. They don't pollute or fight wars and their system of communication may be a lot more understandable than our own.

Stimulus		
	☠	Sand, a bucket and spade, seashells, a ship in a bottle.
	📖	*Songs for the Blue Ocean*: Carl Safina. *Life of Pi*: Yann Martel. *The Sea Around Us*: Rachel Carson.
	✍	*By the Sea*: Emily Dickinson.
	🎭	*The Sea*: Edward Bond. *The Lady from the Sea*: Ibsen. Shakespeare uses the sea as a dramatic device in many of his plays. *The Tempest, Hamlet, The Merchant of Venice, Twelfth Night*. How often does he use the sea as a metaphor?
	🎞	*Waterworld*: 1955 (12). *Finding Nemo*: 2003 (U). *Blue Planet*: BBC Documentary series.
	🎵	*The Ocean*: Led Zeppelin. *This is the Sea*: The Waterboys. **Research**: Sea Shanties. Vaughan Williams' *A Sea Symphony*.
	🎨	*The Great Wave off Kanagawa*: Hokusai. *Stormy Sea in Étretat*: Claude Monet. **Research**: *Artists 4 Oceans*.

🎦	Younger students: Pollution of the sea and endangered species, or pirates and ship wrecks! Older students: Stevie Smith's poem, *Not Waving But Drowning*. Blue and green silk sheets, movement based. The drowning being a metaphor for the rising tides of global warming.
⚠	A vast subject with many stories/issues. Be specific, in particular with young students.
🔗	037, 076, 079, 082, 093, 095, 106, 114, 121, 125, 153, 155, 166, 167, 168, 178.

104   Debt

<table>
<tr>
<td></td>
<td colspan="2">'I want it all and I want it now'
(Queen: British rock band).</td>
</tr>
<tr>
<td>👥</td>
<td colspan="2">Older students (15+). Small mixed groups.</td>
</tr>
<tr>
<td>🚩</td>
<td colspan="2">Workshops/games: levels of tension. Look at the stress/tension felt when you owe something. Debt can damage families and friendships. How do we get in to debt? Credit card overuse, ill health, redundancy, low income, divorce, gambling.
More controversial: Student loans and debt! Welcome to the world of Debt.</td>
</tr>
<tr>
<td>💡</td>
<td colspan="2">Research: The origins of 'Pop goes the Weasel'.
Barclays Bank have produced a Life Skills resource 'Understanding and managing debt'. Connected with poverty, homelessness, gambling alcoholism and drugs. Depression and other mental health issues. Wealthy people also have debts!
Look at the language: A moral debt. In the red. Up to my eyeballs in debt. Drowning in debt. You can owe someone honesty, honour, love or vengeance!
Research: Charles Dickens and debtor's prison.
Some nations have massive (sovereign) debts.</td>
</tr>
<tr>
<td rowspan="6">Stimulus</td>
<td>💀</td>
<td>Search for: Symbols of debt. The images show debt as either imprisoning, a burden, dangerous or toxic.
A Pawnbrokers sign (3 Balls). Research the meaning!
They're popping up on all of our high streets.</td>
</tr>
<tr>
<td>📖</td>
<td>Debt: A Novel: Rachel Carey.
Payback: Margaret Atwood.
The Limit: Kristen Landon.</td>
</tr>
<tr>
<td>📝</td>
<td>The Debt: Paul Laurence Dunbar. (In this case 'debt' and 'interest' are metaphors and worth exploring as another form of debt.)</td>
</tr>
<tr>
<td>🎭</td>
<td>A Doll's House: Ibsen.
Blood Brothers: Willy Russell.
Antigone: Sophocles (The debt we owe the dead).
The Merchant of Venice: Shakespeare.</td>
</tr>
<tr>
<td>🎬</td>
<td>Love and Debt: 2009.
Belfast: 2021 (12A).
The Debt Collector: 2018 (15).</td>
</tr>
<tr>
<td>🎵</td>
<td>Money's Too Tight to Mention: Simply Red.
Pawnbroker: B. B. King.
Livin' on a Prayer: Bon Jovi.</td>
</tr>
<tr>
<td>🎨</td>
<td colspan="2">Research: The artwork of Niki Enright 'Crushing Debt'.
Look at: Hogarth's illustration Arrested for Debt from 'A Rakes Progress'.</td>
</tr>
<tr>
<td>🎦</td>
<td colspan="2">No set (Grotowski) with little or no props. Poor theatre.
Physical work and facial expressions to show the agony/weight of debt in a very literal manner. Levels/status.</td>
</tr>
<tr>
<td>⚠️</td>
<td colspan="2">Be very sensitive to student family history.</td>
</tr>
<tr>
<td>🔗</td>
<td colspan="2">006, 025, 029, 030, 045, 063, 068, 071, 077, 085, 095, 097, 098, 099, 101, 105, 107, 109, 112, 136, 149, 183, 188.</td>
</tr>
</table>

105 Money

	'Money doesn't talk, it swears' (Bob Dylan – American singer/songwriter).
	All ages, mixed groups.
	Workshops/games: *Status games. Body Sculpture.* **Questionnaire**: What would you do with a million pounds (or more). Does money make you happy, what can and can't you buy?
	Look at the language: Dirty money, Hush money, Blood money, Easy money, Money talks, Money is power, Money heist, Money makes the world go round, The colour of your money, and Thirty pieces of silver. The Bible mentions money more than 800 times! **What the papers say**: *Your Money* bbc.com/news. **Research**: The history of money and then consider the future. From barter to banknote to bitcoin. The Royal Mint royalmint.com NatWest Bank: *Money sense teaching resources 8–12's.* *The Evolution of Money*: YouTube.

Stimulus		
		A purse, a wallet, bankcards, money (notes and coins of any currency.
		Refund: Karen Bender. *The Richest Man in Babylon*: George S. Clason. *The Soul of Money*: Lynne Twist and Teresa Barker.
		Ten Pence Story: Simon Armitage.
		Volpone: Ben Jonson. *Money*: Edward Bulwer. *Tons of Money*: Alan Ayckbourn.
		The Big Short: 2015 (15). *Trading Places*: 1983 (15). *Dirty Money*: 2018 (Netflix).
		The Money Song from the musical *Cabaret*. *Money, Money, Money*: ABBA. *Money*: Pink Floyd.
		Look at the works of artists like Andy Warhol and Ben Allen or the graffiti artist Alec Monopoly. Photographic works by David Lachapelle and Tyler Shields.

	Physical work with characters moving around a Monopoly board. Greed, theft and bankruptcy, thirty pieces of silver. Great set opportunities: full size props and projections. Music/dance.
	Encourage any artifacts brought in, to be copies.
	093, 98, 099, 101, 104, 112, 115, 132, 136.

106   Emigration and immigration

<table>
<tr><td></td><td>'We the people of this continent are not afraid of foreigners because many of us were once foreigners'
(Pope Francis – Argentine).</td></tr>
<tr><td></td><td>All ages and abilities.</td></tr>
<tr><td></td><td>Workshops/games: Alienation. Columbian hypnosis. Control games. Filling the space.
Questionnaire: Where did we come from/where did we go? Sensitively survey the group.
Ensemble work, moving as one. Focus on one group and follow their journey.
Look at: What immigrants bring to a new land and how they change.
Consider how some stay in tightly closed communities while others embrace the new culture.</td></tr>
<tr><td></td><td>World population reviews by country. The IOM International Organisation for Migration.
Look at the language: In particular the language of the British tabloids, but also politicians; Tide; Illegal; Number; Stay; Eu; Thousands; Coming; Stop; Seekers; Eastern; Terrorists; Wave; Invasion; Suspected; Arrived; Houses; Influx; Housing; Sham.
What the papers say: Examine the North American media and how it deals with migrants from Mexico, Central and South America.
Consider the masses who emigrated to the USA, Australia, New Zealand, but also the lesser known like the Welsh to Patagonia (Argentina).
Look at: The countries with the highest number of emigrants and compare with the most immigrants. What conclusions could you draw from this?
More controversial: 'I will build a great wall and nobody builds walls better than me' (Former US President Donald Trump).
Research: Conditions at US/UK border detention centres.</td></tr>
<tr><td rowspan="6">Stimulus</td><td>Suitcases, passports, maps, a compass.
A map of the world or globe. Plot some of the journeys.
Image of Ellis Island/Statue of Liberty and contrast with immigration/detention centres.</td></tr>
<tr><td>The Good Immigrant: Nikesh Shukla.
Behold the Dreamers: Imbolo Mbue.
Brick Lane: Monica Ali.
Immigrant Nations: Paul Scheffer.</td></tr>
<tr><td>Immigrant Blues: Li-Young Lee.</td></tr>
<tr><td>A View from the Bridge: Arthur Miller.
Pigeon English: Stephen Kelman.
True Brits: Vinay Patel.</td></tr>
<tr><td>In America: 2002 (15).
Spanglish: 2004 (12A).
Far and Away: 1992 (PG-13).</td></tr>
<tr><td>City of Immigrants: Steve Earle.
This is Your Land: Woody Guthrie.
Englishman in New York: Sting.</td></tr>
<tr><td></td><td>Minneapolis Institute of Art's work on 'Global Movements'.
'Migration and Art' at The Tate. The 'Migration Series' of 60 paintings by Jacob Lawrence 1941.
The Statue of Liberty, often referred to as The Immigrant's Statue.</td></tr>
<tr><td></td><td>Starting with a soundscape/canon of voices speaking the languages of your chosen peoples (use the tongues of you community).
National dress/costume/music/flags . . .
A multicultural city using: immersive multimedia, binaural sound and storytelling, sound manipulation. Gareth Fry.</td></tr>
<tr><td></td><td>Think about the language used. Is it correct? Is it kind?</td></tr>
<tr><td></td><td>08, 085, 089, 101, 107, 108, 110, 111, 112, 114, 140, 155, 172, 174.</td></tr>
</table>

107   Tension

	'Every director will tell you that you have to create conditions that create tension, because tension is what makes drama feel real' (Paul Greengrass – English writer and film director).
♣♀	15+ Small mixed groups of 4 or 5.
⚑	**Workshops/games**: *Tension exercises. Body sculpture.* Look at: The rising action in studied play texts. Good theatre is created when we explore tension . . . The tension of keeping a secret/hiding a truth. Of waiting and not knowing. The tension created by a timely pause.
☼	**Look at the language**: Release tension. Feel the tension. Explore the tension. A moment of tension. Sexual tension. Racial tension. Stress head. Family tensions. *Dramatic tension* refers to the moment(s) in a play when the audience feels a heightened sense of anticipation/fear about what is going to happen next. For example, significant dramatic tension can be felt when ARTHUR KIPPS reaches out to the door handle in *The Woman in Black*.

Stimulus	🎻	Pluck the string of a guitar/violin. Tension!!!
	📖	Tension/suspense is used in crime and horror novels by writers like: Stephen King, Gillian Flynn (*Gone Girl*), Agatha Christie or Sir Arthur Conan Doyle.
	📝	*The Raven:* Edgar Allan Poe.
	🎭	*The Woman in Black:* Susan Hill (adapted by Stephen Mallatratt). *The Maids:* Jean Genet. *The Dumb Waiter:* Harold Pinter.
	🎬	*The Birds:* 1963 (X). *The Woman in Black:* 2012 (15). *Alien:* 1979 (X).
	🎵	*Under Pressure:* Queen and David Bowie. *Breathin:* Ariana Grande. *The Way I am:* Eminem.
	🎨	**Research**: Visual tension in art.

🎭	Pieces that explore rising tension (perhaps through the seven levels). Complicité/Lecoq. Mime/ mask. Choral movement. Physicalisation and proxemics. The tension of silence. The release of tension through comedy.
⚠	Show only selected scenes from the suggested movies.
🔗	This is the theatre! There is tension in everything!

108   Human Trafficking

	'You may choose to look the other way but you can never say again that you did not know' (William Wilberforce – British politician and abolitionist).
👥	15+ Mixed groups.
⚑	**Workshops/games;** *Status. Confinement. Control games.* Slavery has been with us forever, and has persisted throughout our history. Focus on modern-day slavery involving the illegal transportation of people by force or deception for the purpose of exploitation, either, sexual, labour including as soldiers or for the financial benefit of others.
🔅	**Research:** The Exodus Road (Non-Governmental Organisation). ICAT (Inter-Agency Coordination Group against Trafficking in Persons. UN. CAST (Coalition to Abolish Slavery and Trafficking). The A21 Campaign. www.antislavery.org BBC Panorama '*The hunt for Britain's slave gangs*'. Debt bondage, forced labour (involuntary servitude) and sex trafficking. **More controversial:** Are the clothes, trainers, electrical good, you bought on the high street, the product of forced labour?

Stimulus	🐌	There are the historical images of slavery but **search for** images of modern slavery. It has not 'gone away'.
	📖	*Sold:* Patricia McCormick. *I Am Nujood, Age 10 and Divorced:* Nujood Ali. *Disposable People:* Kevin Bales.
	📝	*Between Two Worlds:* Nazreen Mohamed (see reading on YouTube).
	🎭	*She Has A Name:* Andrew Kooman. *Ruined:* Lynn Nottage. *Useless:* Saviana Stanescu.
	🎞	*7 Prisoners:* 2021 (15). *Trafficked:* 2017 (18). *Not My Life:* 2011 (Documentary).
	🎵	*Don't Walk Away (Human Trafficking Song):* Meg Ammons (YouTube). *All God's Children:* Tauren Wells (see official video). *Mass Manipulation:* Steel Pulse. Artists Unite Against Human Trafficking UNDOC #artistsUNiteXhumantrafficking
	🎨	**Research:** Artworks for Freedom and Artworks For Change. Look at: The Anti Human Trafficking posters.

🎭	Through research, students like to tell individual stories of survivors of trafficking as well as present the bigger picture. Shock and/or inform. Narration and projected images. Verbatim.
⚠	Searches including the words *people trafficking* will result in references to the sex trade. Some materials will be shocking.
🔗	008, 010, 015, 044, 064, 076, 097, 101, 103, 104, 105, 106, 107, 109, 130, 136, 140, 146, 149, 155, 174, 182, 194.

109 Secrets and lies

	'Three may keep a secret, if two of them are dead' (Benjamin Franklin – American statesman).
⚇	15+ mixed. Small groups.
⚑	**Workshops/games**: *Lying (The burden of a lie). Fear. Super objectives.* Improv games with role play cards but one contains a secret. The others try to look for signs. Nobody knows who holds the secret. Works well with a hidden objective. **Questionnaire**: Define honesty. Who do you trust? A policeman, a politician, your parents/teachers?
☀	**Look at**: Some of society's common lies. The drive to be rich, to be successful. The secrets to success! Or the little lies we tell ourselves, our friends, parents, teachers. Is anyone honest? **Research**: History's greatest lies. Does keeping a secret make you a liar? Secrets in families. The Official Secrets Act. Can you keep a secret? **What the papers say**: Explore how papers love 'an exposé!'.

	🎨	A mirror.
	📖	*History's Greatest Lies:* William Weir. *The Great Gatsby:* F. Scott Fitzgerald. *Everything I Never Told You:* Celeste Ng.
	📝	*The Secret:* John Clare.
	🎭	*Who's Afraid of Virginia Woolf?* Edward Albee. *Bruised:* Matthew Trevannion. Most of Shakespeare's plays hinge upon a lie.
Stimulus	📽	*The Blacklist:* 2013 (TV Series) (15). *True Lies:* 1994 (15). *The Invention of Lying:* 2009 (12A).
	🎵	*Little Lies:* Fleetwood Mac. *Suspicious Minds:* Elvis Presley. *Secret:* Seal.
	🎨	**Search for**: '4 famous works of art that lied to you about historical events.' Consider all art is a lie!

🎭	Character work. Carrying a secret. Secrets and lies in relationships and families. Some great dance/physical theatre opportunities. Mime. Duets. How lies physically distort us. Berkoff (Kvetch).
⚠	Students should respect each other's secrets and truths.
🔗	003, 004, 005, 029, 044, 061–064, 071, 073, 074, 075, 077, 088, 092, 097, 098, 102, 104, 107, 108, 121, 128, 129, 130, 131, 183, 184, 189.

110   Society

	'Society is like a stew. If you don't stir it up every once in a while then a layer of scum floats to the top' (Edward Abbey – American author and essayist).
👥	13+ Mixed groups (ensemble).
🚩	**Workshops/games:** *Alienation. Control games. Soundscapes. Status games.* **Questionnaire:** Start by asking for definitions from the group. Get one agreed statement and write it down. Look at it as a series of tableaux.
🔆	**Research:** Different societies (cultures). What is common to all/most? **Look at the language:** A menace to society. To pay a debt to society. Polite society. Climb the social ladder. Society's ills. Café society. High society. Corporate society. Secret society. Multicultural society. My tribe. Gangs. A feeling of belonging. **More controversial:** *'There is no such thing as society'*, Margaret Thatcher 1987. What did she mean?

Stimulus	💡	Post-it notes with quotes about the meaning of society.
	📖	*Saturday Night and Sunday Morning:* Alan Sillitoe. *The Remains of the Day:* Kazuo Ishiguro. *Sapiens: A Brief History of Humankind:* Yuval Noah Harari.
	📝	*Do You Live in a Community:* Francis Duggan.
	🎭	*The Importance of Being Earnest:* Oscar Wide. *The Servant of Two Masters:* Goldini and Hall. *Mother Courage and her Children:* Brecht.
	🎬	*Nightcrawler:* 2014 (15). *Zootopia (Zootropolis):* 2016 (PG). *The Wolf of Wall Street:* 2013 (18).
	🎵	*The Sounds of Silence:* Simon and Garfunkel. *A Day in the Life:* The Beatles. *Society:* Eddie Vedder.
	🎨	Art is a reflection on society. Look at the paintings of Pieter Breughel. Consider abstract art and an abstract society.

🎭	Ensemble/chorus. Narrated. Moving as one, physical work. Le coq. Also can look at our multicultural society, lots of colour/costume, music/dance.
⚠️	Be sensitive to cultural differences.
🔗	001, 002, 017–021, 068–071, 077, 078, 079, 081, 085, 088, 089, 093, 094, 101, 106, 107, 112, 126, 130, 132, 133, 136, 138, 149, 156, 160, 161, 174, 175, 185, 187, 188, 196, 198, 199, 200.

111   World hunger

	'Hunger never saw bad bread' (Benjamin Franklin – American statesman).
👥	All ages. Small groups. (Teacher differentiates.)
🚩	**Workshops/games;** *Emotion memory. Status.* 1 in 9 children goes to bed hungry every night. About 690 million people globally are undernourished. With older children (consent required), Ask them to skip breakfast. How do they feel by morning break? Imagine feeling much worse pangs than this every day. Get them to describe hunger, can they physicalise the feeling? List all the things you eat in one day . . .
🔆	**Research:** Article 25 of The Universal Declaration of Human Rights. worldhunger.org. Hunger is a vast topic. If we look at world hunger we almost drown under the statistics. Devised work needs a more precise focus. Suggestions could include: The Great Hunger (Ireland 1845–1849) or Somalia, Ethiopia, Cambodia or the streets of London and New York amidst the wealth. **What the papers say:** How do we respond to media coverage of world hunger? **More controversial:** 'The cure for hunger is not available to the poor.'

Stimulus	📷	Shutterstock.com images of children holding a sign 'I'm hungry'.
	📖	For younger students, *Yard Sale:* Eve Bunting and Lauren Castillo. For older students, Dickens describes hunger with a very sharp focus in *A Tale of Two Cities.* *The Grapes of Wrath:* Steinbeck.
	✍️	*Hunger:* Arthur Rimbaud.
	🎭	*Black Harvest:* Nigel Gray. *Famine:* Tom Murphy. *Mother Courage:* Brecht.
	🎬	*The Boy Who Harnessed the Wind:* 2019 (PG). *Live and Become:* 2005 (Unrated). *Black 47:* 2018 (15).
	🎵	*Another Day in Paradise:* Phil Collins. *Them Belly Full:* Bob Marley. *The Famine Song:* Jonny McEvoy.
	🎨	**Research:** The art of the Irish Famine (the Great Hunger). Van Gogh's *The Potato Eaters.* Sculpture: *The Hunger March* by Jens Galshiøt.

🎭	Ensemble pieces to show the vast scale of the problem. Small intimate studio pieces to focus on the individual suffering. Combine the two with a stark focus on the individual. Light can play an important role in making figures and faces gaunt and drawn, as can the subtle use of makeup.
⚠️	Some images and art depicting starving people can be graphic and upsetting.
🔗	008, 075, 101, 104, 105, 106, 112, 114, 115, 121, 150, 174.

112   Homelessness

	'It can be refugees, it can be a pregnant mother, it can be a 15-year-old . . . homelessness can happen to everybody' (Giles Deacon – British designer).
👥	15+ Mixed groups of 2 or 3
🚩	**Workshops/games:** *Status. Fear. Silent Screams. Control games.* I put an old sleeping bag and a cardboard box outside my studio, followed by a **questionnaire;** What was your emotional response? **Research:** How homeless people are portrayed by the media, particularly in wealthy countries. What are the reasons why a person may leave home/become homeless. Stereotypes. **More controversial:** Lazy, or even an object of jokes. Social media, homeless selfie.
💡	**Research:** The history of the railways and tramps/hobos riding the rails in search of employment. SHELTER (The Charity) https://shelter.org.uk NATIONAL HOMELESS.ORG Teaching resources . . . Why do you think a homeless person might spend their money on alcohol or drugs? **What the papers say:** *The Big Issue.* A hand up not a hand out? **Research:** The work of the foundation bigissue.com/foundation/

Stimulus	💀	Large cardboard boxes and household rubbish. Carrier bags. Empty cider cans/bottles. A torn family photo.
	📖	*No and Me:* Delphine de Vigan. *Stone Cold:* Robert Swindells. *Where I Live:* Brenda Rufener.
	📝	*Homeless:* Peter Marshall.
	🎭	*The Bench:* Robert Galinsky. *Home:* Nadia Fall. *Frozen Dreams:* Robert Ainsworth. Watch *Homeless Shakespeare.* A short film by Steve DeVorkin 2016.
	🎬	*The Pursuit of Happyness.* 2006 (PG). *The Same Kind of Different as Me:* 2017 (12). *Dark Days:* 2000 (Documentary).
	🎵	*The A Team:* Ed Sheeran. *Angels with Dirty Faces:* Los Lobos. *Homeless:* Paul Simon.
	🎨	Look at *Santa on His Bench:* Banksy. Brian Peterson's paintings of the homeless.

🎭	Boal. Theatre of the Oppressed, Invisible theatre. Ensemble piece. Simple set with cardboard boxes and black stage blocks/scaffolds/levels. Stark lighting. Physical theatre pieces work well. Dance/DV8. Frantic Assembly.
⚠️	Direct communication with homeless people in you locality should be thoroughly researched and always supervised. Seek the advice/assistance of local charities.
🔗	008, 071–075, 077, 101, 111, 130, 161.

113   Chairs!

	'There is always something melancholic about the empty chairs' (Mehmet Murat Ildan – Turkish playwright).	
⚭♀	11+ Small groups (pairs).	
🏳	**Workshops/games**; *Super objective. Status.* Not just a furniture/prop. The relationship between the actor and the chair. Spotlight a lone chair. What does it say? How can you alter it? In relation to you, to another chair, the rest of the set. Improvise with it. A simple chair can become so many things and so many things can become a chair! If I sit on it one way, I can make it a throne. Another way, a car seat, the electric chair, the dentist's chair, an interview chair . . . A Rocking chair. Musical chairs . . . How an empty chair at a table can speak volumes.	
💡	Chairs are everywhere! Imagine life without them! Cultural significance. **Research**: Famous chairs in movie and pop culture. Shakespeare's Courting chair . . . Famous Director's chairs . . . Thrones . . . Stephen Hawking's wheelchair . . . Ian Fleming's writing chair. A seat for 'whites only' on a bus, not so long ago . . .	

Stimulus		
	🐌	A chair and your imagination . . . Nothing else!
	📖	*The Silver Chair*: C. S. Lewis. *Now I Sit Me Down*: Witold Rybczynski. *Down the Back of the Chair*: Margaret Mahy.
	📝	*The Table and the Chair*: Edward Lear.
	🎭	**Look at**: How chairs are used in *Billy Elliot, Cabaret, Chicago*. The rocking chair in *The Woman in Black*. Chair duets (Frantic Assembly).
	🎞	Look at the featured chairs in movies like: *The Matrix*, The Bond films, Austin Powers' chair for Dr Evil, The Egg chairs in *Men In Black*.
	🎵	*The Mercy Seat*: Nick Cave. *Empty Chairs*: Don McLean. *The Empty Chair*: Sting.
	🎨	Look at the chair in art: Van Gogh's Chair, Paul Gauguin's Armchair (both by Van Gogh), The Chair by Salvador Dali. Also consider iconic chair designs.

🎭	Physical theatre, dance, Frantic Assembly. Explore the flexibility of the chair. Minimalist. Relationships, character work. Polished improv. Da Vinci's Last Supper. Just the chairs.	
⚠	Physical work/dance with chairs takes careful practice and supervision.	
🔗	002, 009, 018, 024, 060, 062, 074, 077, 086, 094, 098, 123, 142, 151, 154, 185.	

114   Journeys

	'The journey of a thousand miles begins with one step' (Lao Tzu – Chinese philosopher).
♟	Any age. Suits large groups.
⚑	**Workshops/games**; *Super objective. Soundscapes.* Often used as a metaphor for life . . . also: a pilgrimage, tour, travel, trek, trip, voyage. Improvise 'my journey to work/school'. Now improvise 'my journey to stardom/despair'. How did they differ? **Questionnaire**: What was your most difficult journey?
☀	**Look at the language:** A journey of discovery, journey's end, journey to work, to your heart, of a lifetime. An essential journey or epic, daring, pointless, *'Life is a journey, not a destination.'* **Research**: Famous journeys, historical journeys. **What the papers say**: How the media covers the long dangerous journeys made by refugees.

Stimulus		
	🐚	A passport, a suitcase, a compass.
	📖	*Long Walk to Freedom*: Nelson Mandela. *The Grapes of Wrath*: John Steinbeck. *The Odyssey*: Homer.
	✍	*The Night Mail North*: Henry Cholmondeley Pennell.
	🎭	*Kindertransport*: Diane Samuels. *Pink Mist*: Owen Sheers. *The Curious Incident of the Dog in the Night-Time*: Mark Haddon/Simon Stephens.
	🎬	*The Motorcycle Diaries*: 2004 (15). *Thelma and Louise*: 1991 (15). *The Trip*: 2010 (15).
	🎵	*Carolina in My Mind*: James Taylor. *Highway to Hell*: AC/DC. *Travelin' Man*: Lynyrd Skynyrd.
	🎨	*Between the Two my Heart is Balanced*: Lubaina Himid (Painting). *La Route des Alpes*: Tristram Hillier (Painting). *Last Journey*: Vasily Perov.

🎭	Ensemble, physical. Berkoff/Lecoq. Works very well as a dance piece. Whites sheets (Sails), movement. Projections.
⚠	From the start they should decide on a real journey or metaphor. Write it down and stick to it.
🔗	002, 008, 012, 027, 055, 056, 057, 072, 090, 095, 103, 106, 108, 118, 119, 122, 139, 140, 153, 155, 167, 171, 172, 173.

115   Class

<table>
<tr>
<td></td>
<td></td>
<td colspan="2">'Or could it be what we, the English, have come to know as class'
(The Narrator – Willy Russell's Blood Brothers).</td>
</tr>
<tr>
<td></td>
<td colspan="3">15+ Small groups. Mixed to higher ability.</td>
</tr>
<tr>
<td></td>
<td colspan="3">Workshops/games; Status. Soundscapes.
Blood Brothers is a good starting point as students may be familiar with the text/play which clearly contrasts the class differences in the 1970's in Liverpool, UK.
Consider 1st-class travel and VIP status being about the ability to pay more.
Discuss whether class is less about money and more about opportunities, living conditions, health, education and occupation.</td>
</tr>
<tr>
<td></td>
<td colspan="3">Watch the BBC's Great British Class Survey Experiment.
SAGE publishing. The British Sociological Association.
The 'Up' series. British longitudinal study. SBS.
More controversial: Aberfan Unit 117, 'A symbol of corporate negligence towards the working classes.' Or Unit 118 on the Titanic.</td>
</tr>
<tr>
<td rowspan="6">Stimulus</td>
<td></td>
<td colspan="2">A first class train/air ticket.
Emblems like Rolls Royce and VIP compare with The Big Issue and Oxfam.</td>
</tr>
<tr>
<td></td>
<td colspan="2">Great Expectations: Charles Dickens.
Pride and Prejudice: Jane Austen.
Chavs: The Demonization of the Working Class: Owen Jones.</td>
</tr>
<tr>
<td></td>
<td colspan="2">Song of the Shirt: Thomas Hood</td>
</tr>
<tr>
<td></td>
<td colspan="2">An Inspector Calls: J. B. Priestley.
Blood Brothers: Willy Russell.
Volpone: Ben Jonson.
Road: Jim Cartwright.</td>
</tr>
<tr>
<td></td>
<td colspan="2">The Class System sketch from 1966 The Frost Report. (BBC Television).
The Grapes of Wrath: 1940 (A).
Shameless: Both the UK and US TV series.</td>
</tr>
<tr>
<td></td>
<td colspan="2">Talkin' bout a Revolution: Tracy Chapman.
Jonny 99: Bruce Springsteen.
Like a Rolling Stone: Bob Dylan.</td>
</tr>
</table>

<table>
<tr>
<td></td>
<td>Man at the Crossroads: A Fresco: Diego Rivera.
Look at the John Bull prints on social class.
Woman Ironing: Pablo Picasso.</td>
</tr>
<tr>
<td></td>
<td>Physical theatre. Stark Brechtian set.
Ensemble, using levels and masks to exaggerate differences.
Berkoff, Lecoq.</td>
</tr>
<tr>
<td></td>
<td>Know your students.</td>
</tr>
<tr>
<td></td>
<td>025, 038, 062, 063, 085, 089, 093, 095, 101, 110, 111, 112, 117, 118, 125, 126, 130, 132, 140, 147, 175, 182.</td>
</tr>
</table>

116   Energy

		'Energy is liberated matter, matter is energy waiting to happen' (Bill Bryson – American writer).
♣♀		14+ Works well with large and small groups.
⚑		**Workshops/games**: *Energy games. Levels of tension.* Suppressed energy and tension. Look at the energy of movement and the power of words. Levels of tension. Tension is energy, anger is the release of tension. Suppressed energy, tension and rage. I used the song/dance *Electricity* from the musical *Billy Elliot* to get them to develop the idea. To consider the energy in a painting or a poem, for example, requires students to think and discuss in a more abstract manner.
☀		**Look at**: The energy of healing (Reiki). *'The energy of the mind is the essence of life'* (Aristotle). worldenergy.org **Research**: Types: Kinetic, potential, mechanical, chemical and a thousand metaphorical meanings! Energy is constant, dangerous and vital. Theatre is the exploration of energy and tension. **What the papers say**: The rising cost of energy! **Look at the language**: Phrases and expressions that use energy either literally or as a metaphor.
Stimulus	💡	A lightbulb, the sun, a plant, an energy drink, a pair of trainers.
	📖	*Energy Magic*: Eric and Katrina Rasbold. *The Boy Who Harnessed the Wind*:William Kamkwamba and Bryan Mealer. *Burning Bright*: Kelsey Patel (Reiki).
	✍	*On Love*: Bliss Carman.
	🎭	*Britannia Waves the Rules*: Gareth Farr. Shakespeare understood the power and energy of words. 'We waste our lights in vain, like lamps by day', MERCUTIO, *Romeo and Juliet* 1:4
	🎬	*Doctor Strange*: 2016 (12A). *Avatar*: 2009 (12A). *Eternals*: 2021 (12A). *Lifeforce*: 1985 (18).
	🎵	*Electricity*: from *Billy Elliot*. *High Voltage*: AC/DC. *You Light Up My Life*: Debby Boone. *Electric Avenue*: Eddy Grant. *Physical Energy*: Vangelis.
	🎨	**Research**: Energy Art (Energy paintings). The Land Art Generator initiative (LAGI). Think about the energy in a piece of art. Spiritual or more obvious. **Look at**: The work of mixed media artist Susan Wahlrab. Energy in nature.
🎭		Dance and physical theatre to describe that inner power. Use the idea of the energy of a spirit being as real and indestructible (constant) as heat or kinetic energy. The unseen energy of genius.
⚠		Take care with energy sources.
🔗		007, 025, 027, 032, 035, 036, 041, 042, 051, 061, 074, 087, 091, 103, 107, 121, 125, 151–154, 158, 171, 173, 177, 197.

117   Aberfan (A Case study unit, see Chapter 5)

		'The past is a foreign country: they do things differently there' (L. P. Hartley British novelist).
👥	11+ Mixed groups.	
🚩	116 Children and 28 adults. 'Buried alive by the National Coal Board.' See details in Case study, Unit 117, Chapter 5.	
💡	Look at the findings of The Aberfan Disaster Tribunal Report. The National Library of Wales Education Services. https://hwb.gov.wales TES Aberfan – The story of a disaster. https://www.tes.com (Teacher resources pack). *The Price of Coal* by David Alexander (YouTube) **What the papers say:** Look at the original article in the *Weekly Merthyr Express*. *Aberfan – Valley of Sorrow:* 1966 (British Pathé).	
Stimulus	🐌	NCB (National Coal Board) recruitment poster. The images of the children's coffins. A candle. A doll/teddy bear, a toy car. Primary school desk and chairs. A school clock stopped at 9:13 am.
	📕	*Black River:* Louise Walsh. *Aberfan: A Story of Love and Community in One of Britain's Worst Disasters:* Gaynor Madgwick.
	📝	*Oh Aberfan:* John Murray (set to music). *Aber-Fan gan:* T. Llew Jones.
	🎭	*The Revlon Girl:* Neil Anthony Docking. A monologue by Ifor ap Glyn *Mamgu's Letter.* *Land of Our Fathers:* Chris Urch.
	🎞	*The Crown:* Season 3, Episode 3 (Netflix). *Sorrow:* 2017 (Short) (5 mins). *The Green Hollow:* 2016. *Aberfan: The Fight for Justice:* BBC Cymru Wales.
	🎵	The album *Cantana Memoria:* Karl Jenkins. *Jesu, Lover of My Soul:* Charles Wesley. *We Work the Black Seam:* Sting. *I Grieve:* Peter Gabriel. *Gone too Soon:* Michael Jackson.
	🎨	Cofiwch Aberfan Mural 2020. *Aberfan* by Dorothie Field. *Partially Buried* by James Rielly. Sculpture *21. 10. 1966 144 9:13AM* by Nathan Wyburn at the Rhondda Heritage Park, South Wales.
🎦	See details in Case study, Unit 117, Chapter 5.	
⚠	There is much printed and many short films and documentaries, in particular on YouTube. Caution students that some may be distressing, whilst others are not entirely accurate. Remind them that some dramatisations are just that.	
🔗	057, 091, 115, 118, 123, 133, 157, 177, 182, 183.	

118   Titanic

		'SOS Titanic calling. We have struck ice and require immediate assistance' (Telegram of the RMS Titanic) 15 April 1912.
🐾		Mixed ability groups. 11–16.
🚩		**Workshops/games:** *Status. Soundscapes.* The meaning of the word 'Titan'. The idea that something was unsinkable, hence not enough life boats. 1,517 died. What do students know apart from the story of Jack and Rose! Clips of said Movie.
💡		**Look at:** The work of Robert Ballard. National Geographic's explorer-in-residence (*Restore the Titanic*). **What the papers say:** The Titanic Disaster Newspaper Archive. *The Washington Times, The New York Times, The Times.* How well did the Working classes fare? There are many sub plots scandals and stories. Research news/dispatches.
Stimulus	💀	Images of original posters advertising the maiden voyage (look at the class price structure).
	📖	*A Night to Remember:* Walter Lord. *I Survived the Sinking of the Titanic 1912:* A graphic novel: Lauren Tarshis. *Midnight Watch:* David Dyer. *Shadow of The Titanic (survivors' stories):* Andrew Wilson.
	📝	*The Convergence of the Twain:* Thomas Hardy.
	🎭	Reference by BIRLING in Priestley's *An Inspector Calls* (A good example of class divisions at the time). *Titanic:* A Musical by Peter Stone.
	📽	*Titanic:* 1997 (12). *Titanic:* 1943. TV, *Titanic:* 1984. *SOS Titanic:* 1979. *Secrets of the Titanic:* 2020 (Full documentary YouTube).
	🎵	*For those in Peril on the Sea*: William Whiting. *Nearer, My God, to Thee:* Sarah Flower Adams. *The Titanic:* Lead Belly.
	🎨	*Titanic Sinking:* Willy Stöwer (1912 engraving). **Look at:** The paintings of Ken Marschall. *Sinking of The Titanic:* Max Beckmann (1912).
🎭		We chose to look at the class system and how it cost lives. Using projections and SFX/music. Marc Rees/Katie Mitchell. Worked well in a small black box studio space (Immersive).
⚠		Avoid re-telling Jack and Rose's story. Please!
🔗		052, 103, 114, 115, 117, 133, 183.

119 History

	'A generation which ignores history has no past – and no future' (Robert A. Heinlein – American author).	
👥	Any age. Suits larger mixed groups.	
🚩	**Workshops/games**: *Story circle. Soundscapes.* **Questionnaire:** Have you a story passed down in your family? What is the biggest event so far in your life/personally or in the world? For many it will be the pandemic. Take an event from history, research it and select a moment. Create a tableau of known or imaginary characters and ask each one to prepare a thought. From these, try to create a story. A reporter on the scene. Look at storytelling.	
💡	Use online history timelines. Timelines of humanity. 'History is about people not dates.' There are some specific historical units already in this book. Titanic, Hiroshima, The Holocaust, Aberfan which will offer further ideas on presenting historical events. Consider your local history.	
Stimulus	💀	Choose artifacts/images from your chosen event, person.
	📖	*Wolf Hall:* Hilary Mantel. *Brooklyn:* Colm Tóibín. *Horrible Histories:* series Terry Deary.
	✍️	*Ozymandias:* Percy Shelley.
	🎭	Act 1 of *Top Girls:* Caryl Churchill. *Four Nights in Knaresborough:* Paul Webb. *Our Country's Good:* Timberlake Wertenbaker. Shakespeare's Histories.
	🎬	*Braveheart:* 1995 (15). *Zulu:* 1964 (PG). *Oppenheimer:* 2023 (15).
	🎵	*American Pie:* Don McLean. *We Didn't Start the Fire:* Billy Joel. *The Rising:* Bruce Springsteen. Any of the *Horrible Histories* Songs BBC/YouTube.
	🎨	**Research:** 'History Painting'. Paintings from the Creation and the Last Supper to World Wars and the Pandemic.
🎭	First person narration. Storytelling. Ensemble work. Character work. 'Magic If.' Stanislavski. Projections/multimedia, music (Katie Mitchell). Immersive sound (Gareth Fry).	
⚠️	A vast subject. Be clear about artistic intent from early on.	
🔗	001–008, 011, 012, 013, 015, 028, 030, 032, 036, 037, 056, 076, 084, 090, 093, 101, 109, 117, 118, 122, 125, 129, 140, 143, 148, 150–155, 169, 170, 171, 174, 176, 178–183, 189, 190, 192, 196.	

120   The Seasons

		'The Seasons come up undisturbed by crime and war' (George A. Smith – American politician).
♟		Younger students in particular. Large groups. Older students could look at mood.
🚩		**Workshops/games;** *Filling the space. Levels of tension.* Spring, Summer, Autumn and Winter: depending on where you live, mean different things. Create a still image for each of the seasons. What are the characters thinking/doing? Not just how we dress but consider how the different seasons make you feel? Why?
☀		**Research:** News articles covering climate change and how the seasons are changing. Unit 121. Livescience.com Earth's seasons. National Geographic resource library have a great resource 'Season'. NASA's https://spaceplace.nasa.gov/seasons/ **More Controversial:** Health issues like (SAD) Seasonal Affective Disorder. A type of depression related to changes in season,
Stimulus	💀	**Search for:** Images of Christmas cards in Australia and California and compare them with ones from the UK and New York State. **Look at:** The colours of the seasons where you live.
	📖	*Cider With Rosie:* Laurie Lee. *Outline:* Rachel Cask.
	📝	Shakespeare's *Sonnet 104*.
	🎭	*Colder Than Here:* Laura Wade. *Things I Know to be True:* Andrew Bovell. *The Four Seasons:* Arnold Wesker.
	🎬	*The Four Seasons:* 1981 (15). **Look at:** How movies use the seasons to show the passing of time. See *Notting Hill* 1999 (15) when William (Hugh Grant) walks through the market as the seasons rapidly change, to the song *Ain't no Sunshine* (Bill Withers). Watch clip on YouTube.
	🎵	*Four Seasons in One Day:* Crowded House. *A Hazy Shade of Winter:* Simon and Garfunkel. *The Four Seasons:* Vivaldi.
	🎨	**Look at:** Giuseppe Arcimboldo's Cornucopic portraits. *The Four Seasons:* Chagall. Watch the NGV production (video) of David Hockney's *Four Seasons*.
🎭		Students chose the seasons as a metaphor for a man/woman's life. They projected images and played music to accompany each season whilst performing key moments/confrontations/ realisations through life. Rather like Shakespeare's Seven Ages from *As You Like It*.
⚠		There are a number of companies using the name Four Seasons.
🔗		027, 030, 031, 056, 071, 095, 103, 112, 114, 121, 123, 151, 153, 156–159, 163, 166, 176, 179, 192.

121   Climate change

		'Extreme weather is Earth's "chorus of anguish"' (Pope Francis – Argentine).
👥	11+ Larger mixed groups.	
🚩	**Workshops/games**: *Status. Control games.* Projected images, news/weather reports. Students are usually very well informed about climate change and its causes. Research scenarios: A farming family facing drought, a ski resort without snow, a river flooding a town, mud slides, a coastal town facing rising tides. As a group write a statement based on how you feel about your research results. Improvise a short scene/still image that best represents the group's feelings. Give it a title.	
💡	**Research**: The difference between weather and climate. Fossil fuels and greenhouse gasses. Climate refugees. The following agencies: Earth Guardians, Boulder, CO. Greenpeace. WWF – Australia. Ocean Conservancy – USA. Earthjustice – USA. C40 Cities, International. Climate Alliance, International. Extinction Rebellion (XR). **Questionnaire**: Take a carbon footprint calculator test. Available online. Gov.UK Carbon calculator or EPA for example. **What the papers say:** Those scary headlines. **Look at**: BBC Future Planet. Greta Thunberg's full speech to the UN in 2019. And responses. **More controversial**: Fracking. Superstars in their private jets. The price of mining for Bitcoin.	

Stimulus		
	💀	An extreme weather report. Newspaper headlines of storms, floods.
	📖	*Something New Under the Sun:* Alexandra Kleeman. *The Sea and Summer:* George Turner. *The History of Bees:* Maja Lunde.
	✍️	*Let Them Not Say:* Jane Hirshfield.
	🎭	*The Heretic:* Richard Bean. *The Contingency Plan:* Steve Waters. *Crown Prince:* John Godber.
	🎬	*Interstellar:* 2014 (12A). *Avatar:* 2009 (12A). *An Inconvenient Truth:* 2006 (Documentary) (U).
	🎵	*Feels Like Summer:* Childish Gambino. *All the Good Girls go to Hell:* Billie Eilish. *Despite Repeated Warnings:* Paul McCartney.
	🎨	**Research**: *Climate change art.* 'I DON'T BELIEVE IN GLOBAL WARMING' Graffiti piece by Banksy.

🎭	Dreamlike, surreal. Imaginary Body. Magical realism. Forkbeard Fantasy. Multimedia/projections. Complicité, DV8. Smoke machine with spotlights.
⚠️	Use government *approved* online carbon calculator.
🔗	023, 027, 054, 061, 064, 082, 093, 101, 102, 103, 109, 110, 111, 124, 125, 154, 155, 163, 166, 189, 194.

122   The Train

		'The train is a small world moving through a larger world' (Elisha Cooper – American writer).
👥		Any age! Everyone loves trains!
🚩		**Workshops/games:** *Soundscapes.* Start with a simple train ticket. What does it mean to you? The train as a metaphor for life. The train as a means of transport, a romantic interlude, a means of escape, a journey to hell, from hell, to work, to school, to shop, to a holiday, an interview, a new beginning! The Great Train Robbery! Improvise around the rhythms of a train.
🔅		**Research:** Locomotion No 1 (Stockton and Darlington). Trains get a lot of bad press, but look at how popular they are in cultures all over the world. Look at the part they played in the Industrial Revolution. www.trainhistory.net Museum of the American Railroad www.historictrains.org. London Transport Museum www.ltmuseum.co.uk **More controversial:** Trains are romantic, nostalgic, a symbol of progress. However, from India to Africa, and the Americas, the train has also represented Oppression for many groups.
Stimulus	🐌	Images of the splendid steam trains of old, of the cattle trucks that transported the victims of the Holocaust. A train set.
	📖	*Orphan Train:* Christina Baker Kline. *Outbound Train:* Renea Winchester. *The Old Patagonian Express:* Paul Theroux.
	📝	*The Whitsun Weddings:* Philip Larkin.
	🎭	*Kindertransport:* Diane Samuels. *The Train Driver:* Athol Fugard. *Strangers on a Train:* Craig Warner *The 39 Steps:* Patrick Barlow adaptation.
	🎬	*Murder on The Orient Express:* 2017 (12A). *The Darjeeling Limited:* 2007 (15). *Unstoppable:* 2010 (12A). Look at the wonderful train scenes in the *Harry Potter* movies.
	🎵	*Love Train:* The O'Jays. *Downtown Train:* Rod Stewart. *Downbound Train:* Bruce Springsteen.
	🎨	*The Travelling Companions:* Augustus Egg (1862). *The Railway Station:* William Powell Frith (1863). *The Railway:* Edouard Manet (1873). **Look at:** railart.co.uk
🎞		Simple props aided by sound and light. Rhythm/sounds and movements of trains to create physical pieces.
⚠		Rail lines and crossings are dangerous places.
🔗		008, 012, 017, 080, 085, 088–091, 093, 087, 095, 107, 114, 115, 139, 180, 196.

123   A Moment

	'Be happy in the moment, that's enough. Each moment is all we need, not more' (Mother Teresa – Albanian-Indian Catholic nun).	
👥	Small groups. A difficult concept but students of any age get it at their own level.	
⚑	**Workshops/games**; *Emotion memory.* Use a photograph to capture a moment. Freeze frame/still image. Define moments in your day/life. **Questionnaire**: The moment I: passed my driving test/my exams, met my best friend, fell in love. Realise moments can never be recaptured, even in a photograph, there is a feeling too. The drama should be about that.	
💡	Defined as a very short period of time: a particular time: a precise point in time: the present time We collect moments, that's our life. Moments are memories and so much more. **Look at the language**: A moment in time/history, take a moment, defining moment, careless moment, awkward moment, never a dull moment, spur of the moment, moment of truth, living in the moment. Each could be the inspiration for a piece of drama!	
Stimulus	💀	A photograph of a special moment. Ask students to bring one in. What makes it a special moment.
	📖	*I Know Who You Remind Me Of*: Naomi K. Lewis. *The Book Thief*: Markus Zusak. *Cider with Rosie*: Laurie Lee.
	📝	*Moment in Time*: Cynthia Kepp
	🎭	*100*: Diene Petterle, Neil Monaghan and Christopher Heimann. *Moment of Grace*: Bren Gosling.
	🎞	*Groundhog Day*: 1993 (PG). *A Moment to Remember*: 2004 (PG-13). Also consider significant/special moments in your favourite movies.
	🎵	*Stuck in a Moment*: U2. *You're Beautiful*: James Blunt. *Photograph*: Ed Sheeran.
	🎨	Great art captures a moment.
🎭	Juxtaposition. Same moment different people's perspectives. Look at the story within a moment. Freeze frame. Character work. Flashback/forward to define a moment.	
⚠	Ensure any photographs students bring in are with the necessary permissions (photocopy and return original).	
🔗	002, 004, 007, 022, 025, 030, 040, 045, 047, 050, 055, 059, 063, 065, 066, 067, 078, 084, 100, 113, 117, 120, 126, 127, 128, 142, 151, 170, 176.	

124   The Amazon rainforest

	'We are, quite literally, gambling with the future of our planet – for the sake of hamburgers' (Peter Singer – Australian philosopher).
⚷	All ages. Larger groups work well.
🏁	**Workshops/games:** *Status. Control games. Soundscapes.* Project images of a treetop canopy, sound effects of the rainforest. Camouflage materials. Simple Gobos. Look at the size on a map and compare it to countries; i.e. the UK would fit in it 17 times.
☀	**Research:** earth.org greenpeace.org The Politicians and the indigenous people. Broken promises. globalforestwatch.org nature.com earth.google.com See the Rainforest Alliance for teacher resources. **Look at:** The Amazon River. **More controversial:** Greenpeace claim one third of deforestation in the Amazon rainforest is linked to land grabbing, mainly by meat producers. List the 10 Major companies responsible for deforestation.

Stimulus		
	👁	Liken the rainforest to an image of a pair of lungs.
	📖	*State Of Wonder:* Ann Patchett. *World Burn Down:* Steve Cole. *The Great Kapok Tree:* Lynne Cherry.
	🎭	Younger students *The Rumpus In The Rainforest* from Bad Wolf Press (musical). **Research:** The Manaus Opera House: Amazon Theatre in the heart of the rainforest.
	🎞	*The Emerald Forest:* 1995 (15). *Embrace of the Serpent:* 2015 (12A). *The Sacred Science:* 2011 (Documentary).
	🎵	Soundtrack from the movie *The Mission.* *In The Rainforest:* Ricardo Williams. *Don't Give Up:* Peter Gabriel and Kate Bush.
	🎨	**Look at:** The photography/artwork of Phillippe Echaroux (*The Blood Forest*). World Rainforest Day WRD 2021 Art Gallery. **Research:** Environmental Art Movement. The works of Agnes Denes.

🎭	Younger students. Dance/music based piece celebrating the diversity and beauty of the rainforest. Older students. Darker pieces using well know beefburger logos from around the world questioning the meat industry's role in deforestation. Brechtian theatre.
⚠	This could be a simple celebration of the beauty and diversity of the rainforest. Some of the issues should only be tackled by older students.
🔗	05, 101, 102, 105, 121, 125, 155, 174.

125   Future world

	'The future starts today, not tomorrow' (Pope John Paul II - Polish).
⚇	All ages. Suits larger groups.
⚑	**Workshops/games:** *Story telling. First person narration.* **Questionnaire:** What are your hopes for the future of mankind? The unit is about hopes and plans for the future. Make it a positive piece. What do you think the world will be like in one hundred years' time? What will have changed? Inventions, ways of thinking, laws, borders, alliances . . . religion. Will we have become an interplanetary species? Ask your older relatives what the big changes have been in their lives. Consider how fast our progress has been. How will we live? Where will we live?
☼	**Research:** Quantum computers. Post-biological humanity. www.futuretimeline.net/ Why does most literature and film about the future portray it as dystopian? **Look at:** BBC Future Planet.
Stimulus	<table><tr><td>☺</td><td>Project images of utopian/dystopian futures.</td></tr><tr><td>📖</td><td>*1984:* George Orwell. *Brave New World:* Aldous Huxley. *The Giver:* Lois Lowry.</td></tr><tr><td>📝</td><td>*A Vision:* Simon Armitage.</td></tr><tr><td>🎭</td><td>*The Beauty Manifesto:* Nell Leyshon. *The New Galileos:* Amy Berryman. *In the Know:* Mark Kenneally.</td></tr><tr><td>🎬</td><td>*The Fifth Element:* 1997 (PG-13). *Oblivion:* 2013 (PG-13). *Interstellar:* 2014 (12A).</td></tr><tr><td>🎵</td><td>*The Future:* Leonard Cohen (adult content). *In The Year 2525:* Zager and Evans. *Here Comes the Sun:* The Beatles.</td></tr><tr><td>🎨</td><td>*Infinity Rooms:* Yayoi Kusama. **Look at:** The art photography of Andreas Gursky.</td></tr></table>
🎭	Flashback and forward. Dance/ensemble. Docudrama. Good set/costume design opportunities.
⚠	Requires a clear shared vision.
🔗	014–022, 027, 057, 076, 092, 101, 102, 103, 111, 112, 119, 121, 142, 152, 162–166, 170, 171, 183, 190.

126   Domestic Violence (A Case study unit, see Chapter 5)

	'Domestic violence is an epidemic, and yet we don't address it. Until it happens to celebrities' (Nelsan Ellis – American actor and playwright).
👥	14+ Mixed ability groups. Encourage but do not insist on mixed groups. Works well with students who are comfortable with one another.
🚩	**Workshops/games:** *That hurt. Sorry. Control games.* See details in Case study, Unit 126, Chapter 5.
💡	bbc.com/news/topics/c008ql15dvgt/domestic-abuse **What the papers say:** Involving celebrities and high-profile cases. **Search for:** Art-sheep.com domestic violence. (This resource is a link to twelve very powerful videos/works Watch them first and select according to your students.) ndvc.org.uk domestic violence against men. socialsolutions.com/blog/domestic-violence-statistics Consider also how the police (The Law) deals with Domestic abuse. Historically and today. **More controversial:** '*Culture is no excuse for abuse*' (Davinder Kaur).
Stimulus	Wedding photograph (in a broken frame?). Plasters, bandages, make up (to cover up), broken crockery.
	Extract from *'The Woman Who Walked into Doors'*: Roddy Doyle. *A Woman Torn:* Stewart Stafford. *Into the Darkest Corner:* Elizabeth Haynes.
	The lyrics to Tracey Chapman's song '*Behind the Wall*' (see song/music section).
	Circles: Rachel De-lahay. *Bruised:* Matthew Trevannion. *Punch and Judy* (Violence towards women in Commedia dell'arte) *Blue Remembered Hills:* Dennis Potter contains some examples of a child's eye view of abuse within families.
	Once Were Warriors: 1994 (18). *Dangerous Intentions:* 1995 (Unclassified). Watch piece from *France's Got Talent:* 2018. Dakota and Nadia dance against domestic violence on YouTube.
	Behind the Wall and *Sorry:* Tracy Chapman. *My name is Luka* Susanne: Vega. (Watch the official video.) *The Ballad of Hollis Brown:* Bob Dylan. *Rain on me:* Ashanti. *Sposa Son Disprezzata:* Cecilia Bartoli.
	Mexican artist Alberto Penagos, series of works entitled 'Violence against women' Italian artist and activist aleXsandro Palombo's paintings using Marge Simpson, Wonder Woman and Wilma Flintstone as victims of abuse from their partners.
🎭	See details in Case study, Unit 126, Chapter 5.
⚠	Sensitive treatment of domestic violence issues is essential. Know your students.
🔗	001, 009, 018, 021, 061–064, 071, 073, 075, 077, 078, 084, 085, 096, 104, 105, 107, 109, 112, 130, 139, 143, 174, 175, 181, 199, 200.

127 Knife Crime

		#*DitchTheBlade* (Staffordshire Police campaign).
⚘		Able, mature students. Although the piece can be aimed at younger students (T.I.E.), I would not use students younger than 15 on this project.
⚑		**Workshops/games:** *Repetition exercises. Mirror imaging.* Chalked outline of a body on the floor. Discover a crime scene. What has happened? Knife (safe). Gang graffiti, tags. Stage blood. 'It's for my own protection.' **More controversial:** Snapchat and social media's role in knife crime. Knife crime and social deprivation.
☼		Most police forces/departments have a knife crime website with useful information and advice. **Research:** Ben Kinsella Trust. Operation Sceptre (UK). **What the papers say:** News headlines are sadly all too easy to find. But are they selectively using a convenient label? **Look at:** The statistics and stories behind each tragedy.
Stimulus	💀	Photos. Knives (safe). Public amnesty knife bin.
	📖	*When I was Joe:* Keren David. *Dead Boy Talking:* Linda Strachan. *Cut Short:* Ciaran Thapar.
	📝	*'Unarmed, A Spoken Word Poem About Knife Crime':* Video YouTube
	🎭	*The Long Road:* Shelagh Stephenson. *Gone Too Far:* Bola Agbaje. *Pigeon English:* Stephen Kelman (adapted by Gbolahan Obisesan).
	🎬	*Shank:* 2010 (15). *Hood:* 2011 (Short film) (12A) *I'm Out:* 2020 (A series of three shorts on the impact of knife crime.) Ross Kemp *'Living with Knife Crime':* (full episode) 2019 (YouTube).
	🎵	*Ceasefire:* Cecil (see Project Ceasefire video on YouTube). *Knife Crime:* Y. Shadey. *Words Over Weapons:* Nathan Grisdale.
	🎨	See Art against Knives. *The Knife Angel* which was made of 100,000 confiscated knives.
🎭		Using the assassination of Julius Caesar in Shakespeare's play, we put the words to a rap beat and a very physical piece set in an inner city estate. Costumed all in black hoodies with fight sequences based on the work of Frantic Assembly.
⚠		The risks with this one are obvious but be aware of hidden dangers, gang and peer pressure issues.
🔗		014, 016, 017, 020, 021, 024, 052, 061, 079, 080, 084, 096, 101, 106, 107, 128, 133, 135, 137, 144.

128   Hate crime

	'Why is it that, as a culture, we are more comfortable seeing two men holding guns than holding hands?' (Ernest Gaines – American author).
♟	15+ I recommend this unit for small groups.
⚐	**Workshops/games**: *Control games. Levels of tension.* Begin with some power/status games. Look at being powerless and afraid. Then at having a lot of power, yet ignorant/afraid of something unknown. Discuss hate crime as the use of violence against something we fear and therefore hate.
☀	Crime Stoppers UK Standing up to hate crime. www.stophateuk.org www.CommunitiesAgainstHate.org **Research**: Hate crimes against: traveller communities, religious and ethnic minorities, disability, or due to transgender identity and sexual orientation. Hate Speech. **What the papers say**: Is 'hate crime' yet another convenient press label? **More controversial**: Does social media fan the flames of hate?

Stimulus		
	🐌	Disabled parking sign. Racist graffiti. Consider the places where hate crimes often occur.
	📖	*We Have Always Been Here*: Samra Habib. *The Anatomy of Organised Hate*: Lonnie Lusardo. *Home is Not A Country*: Safia Elhillo.
	📝	George The Poet On Hate Crime (YouTube). Works as a strong monologue.
	🎭	*Tomorrow I'll be Happy*: Jonathan Harvey. *The Laramie Project*: M. Kaufman and S Belber. *Five – A play about Hate Crime*. Footlight Theatre Company.
	🎞	*Boys Don't Cry*: 1999 (18). *The Mathew Shepard Story*: 2002 (TV-14). *Targeted: The Truth about Disability Hate Crime*: BBC iPlayer or YouTube.
	🎵	*Birmingham Sunday*: Richard Fariña. *Paint it Black*: The Rolling Stones. *Heal The World*: Michael Jackson.
	🎨	**Search for**: Artwork against Hate Crime (images). **Look at**: The work of multidisciplinary artist Amanda Phingbodhipakkiya (TED).

🎭	Verbatim. Docudrama. Forum. Go for shock! Highly choreographed ensemble pieces. Break the tension by laughing and encourage the audience to join in. Or start with laughter . . . Tickle and Slap/Brecht.
⚠	This unit is not for younger students! A lot of the material online and film contains distressing images and language.
🔗	001–004, 016–021, 023, 052, 053, 057, 060–066, 079, 080, 088, 096, 100, 106, 107, 109, 112, 123, 127, 130, 135, 138, 144, 148, 160, 161, 174, 175, 182, 186, 189.

129   Serial Killers

	'It strikes me profoundly that the world is more often than not a bad and cruel place' (Bret Easton Ellis – American author and screenwriter).
⚖	Older students only (16+). Small groups
⚑	**Workshops/games**; *Control games. Body sculpture.* Serial killers have become a cultural obsession. We are actually glamorising them? The movie industry is all over it, and the media reports every detail, name, place and drop of blood, but why? Should we give them the attention they crave or stop giving them so much headline space and making so many movies and TV shows about them?
☼	Men largely attack strangers, whereas studies show that 80% of women know their victims. **Search for**: An article in the *Observer* newspaper 2018 'Inside the Creepy Underground world of Serial Killer Art'. **What the papers say**: The Gale Review; Are we Obsessed with Serial Killers? Media treatment of cases of mass murder. **More controversial**: What did Charles Manson hear in the Beatles song *Helter Skelter*?

Stimulus	☠	They look like any ordinary man/woman in the street. Or do they. Photographs of some of the most notorious serial killers are a chilling starting point.
	📖	*American Psycho*: Bret Easton Ellis. *The Talented Mr Ripley*: Patricia Highsmith. *A History of British Serial Killing* David Wilson.
	📝	*3 Kinds of Serial Killers*: Anna Niemus.
	🎭	*Rope*: Patrick Hamilton. *The Pillowman*: Martin McDonagh. *A Memory of Lizzie*: David Foxton.
	🎞	*The Silence of the Lambs*: 1991 (16). *Solace*: 2015 (15). *See no Evil: The Moors Murders*: 2006 (TV mini-series).
	🎵	*Midnight Rambler*: The Rolling Stones. *Jack The Ripper*: Nick Cave. *Ted, Just Admit It . . .*: Jane's Addiction. *Psycho Killer*: Talking Heads.
	🎨	**Look at**: The Paintings of John Wayne Gacy (in particular 'Pogo'). Also look at the amount of Charles Manson art merchandise, in particular T-shirts which have almost made his face as iconic as that of Che Guevara.

🎭	I saw a group of A-level Students' devised piece which focussed solely on Myra Hindley. They had photocopied many images of her face in an Andy Warhol style repeated all over their studio. They didn't have one actor playing the part but rather all four performers wore a mask of her likeness. The Focus was on the reporting of her as a woman. Projected headlines and commentaries, likening her press coverage to that of Marilyn Monroe with a clever changing of masks at the end of the piece.
⚠	Look at the psychology rather than the details of the crime. Focus on why we seem fascinated and the media attention.
🔗	020, 025, 029, 042, 057, 063, 064, 074, 088, 107, 109, 119, 130, 134, 142, 144, 151, 160, 184.

130   Violence against women and girls

	'Violence against women isn't cultural, it's criminal' (Samantha Power – Irish-American academic, author and diplomat).
👥	13+ Small groups. The gender mix of the group should be very much a student led decision.
🚩	**Workshops/games;** *Control games. Repetition exercises. Mirror imaging. Body sculpture. Levels of tension.* Begin with sensitively led discussion. Show pieces from the television campaign '*Enough*'. Together we can end violence towards women and girls. One in three women will experience some sort of violence in their lifetime. What kind of world/culture allows this to happen?
☼	Oxfam. Say enough to violence. www.sayenoughtoviolence.org The Pixel Project. UNESCO **Search for:** We will stop femicide. **What the papers say:** Examine coverage of 'The Shadow Pandemic', violence against women during the pandemic. Media reporting of violence against women and girls in different countries. **More controversial:** Why are so many TV crime series focussed heavily on extreme violence towards women?
Stimulus	💀 On the sayenoughtoviolence.org website there is a diagram exploring the different causes.
	📖 *An Excess Male:* Maggie Shen King. *Fried Green Tomatoes at the Whistle Stop Café:* Fannie Flagg. *The Colour Purple:* Alice Walker. 📝 *Red Sky:* Poetry on the global epidemic of violence against women. By Sable Books. 🎭 *Staging Violence against Women and Girls Plays and Interviews:* Isley Lynn, Raúl Quirós Molina, Bahar Brunton, Karis E. Halsall, Dacia Maraini and Renato Chiocca, Authors). *Circles:* Rachel De-lahay. *Bruised:* Matthew Trevannion. *Girls:* Theresa Ikoko.
	🎬 *The Handmaid's Tale:* 1990 (18). *Lost Girls:* 2020 (15). *Three Billboards Outside Ebbing Missouri:* 2017 (15). 🎵 *Right through You:* Alanis Morrissette. *I'm OK:* Christina Aguilera. *Behind the Wall:* Tracy Chapman. 🎨 The Wall of Dolls in Milan 2014, and in the same city in 2012 'Zapatos Rojos'. Mexican artist Alberto Penagos, series of works entitled 'Violence against women'. Italian artist and activist aleXsandro Palombo's paintings using Marge Simpson, Wonder Woman and Wilma Flintstone as victims of abuse from their partners.
🎪	Forum theatre. Focus on the causes, in particular: attitudes and beliefs, controlling male behaviours, discrimination and outdated laws. Theatre of the Oppressed. Boal. Careful use of comedy, Brecht's Tickle and Slap (Spass).
⚠	Research of this subject matter will trigger references to gendered and sexual violence. Check school policies.
🔗	001, 008, 009, 111, 118, 121, 032, 161–164, 071, 077, 080, 096, 106–110, 112, 123, 128, 132, 143, 156, 181, 182, 186, 191, 196, 199, 200.

131 Miscarriages of justice

	'Injustice anywhere is a threat to justice everywhere' (Martin Luther King Jnr – American clergyman, activist and leader in the American Civil Rights Movement).
⚖	14+ Mixed groups.
🚩	**Workshops/games**; *Accusation. Control games. Confinement. Levels of tension.* Begin with accusing a student of doing something they could not possibly have done. (This can be acted, with their help or for real.) You know your students! Eventually admit you are mistaken. Discuss false accusation. What it feels like. Now ask '. . . and what if you had been executed for that'. Causes of wrongful conviction could be: misidentification, official misconduct, false testimony, false accusation, perjury and false confession.
☀	**Research**: These Infamous cases: Alfred Dreyfus 1894. Sam Sheppard 1954. Derek Bentley 1953. Dewey Bozella 2011. Darryl Burton 2008. Darryl Hunt 1984. The Roscetti Four 1986. The Guildford Four and the Maguire seven 1975 and 1976. The Birmingham Six 1975. Randall Dale Adams 1976. The Central Park Five 1989. Has modern forensic science (DNA testing) led to a fall in cases? justicedenied.org Miscarriages of Justice Organisation MOJO.

Stimulus	💀	Newspaper headlines for any number of infamous cases, consider how definite they are!
	📖	*Atonement:* Ian McEwan. *The Central Park Five:* Sarah Burns. *The Count of Monte Cristo:* Alexandre Dumas.
	📝	*Colossal Miscarriage of Justice:* Chinedu Dike.
	🎭	*Your Ever Loving:* Martin McNamara. *The Brownsville Raid:* Charles Fuller.
	🎬	*At The Death House Door:* 2011 (An investigative documentary). *Let Him Have It:* 1991 (15). *When They See Us:* 2019 (15) Netflix (4 part series).
	🎵	*Let Him Dangle:* Elvis Costello. *Angel Down:* Lady Gaga. *Murder in the Red Barn:* Tom Watts.
	🎨	*A Dog's Breakfast* by Blak Douglas. **Look at**: The paintings of Zhang Yuhuan *(Summer Snow).*

🎭	Storytelling. Kneehigh. Verbatim. Students engage very quickly with individual stories. Strong monologues narration ensemble movement, Lecoq Complicité.
⚠	Details of crimes contain disturbing images and descriptions.
🔗	004, 044, 052, 061, 063, 076, 100, 109, 119, 123, 133, 136, 137, 138, 142, 144, 175, 181.

132   Power

	'The object of power is power' (George Orwell - English author and journalist).
👥	All ages.
🚩	Start the session by loudly saying 'RIGHT' then wait. Discuss the power of silence, pause, and the tension of expectation. **Workshops/games:** *Status games. Levels of tension.* **Research:** What does power mean to you? List types of power. The power to change/control/influence others. How do you physically represent power? Look at the power behind silence or stillness on stage.
🔆	**Look at the language:** The power of love. I have the power. 'Power corrupts.' Abuse of power. Power to the people! Flower power. Knowledge is power. PowerPoint. Power nap. Black power. Girl power. *'Power does not corrupt. Fear corrupts. Perhaps the fear of a loss of power'* (John Steinbeck) *"With great power comes great responsibility".*

Stimulus		
	💀	Compare the different results from a search for images of *power* and images of *powerful people*.
	📖	*Conclave:* Robert Harris. *The Table of Less Valued Knights:* Marie Phillips. *The 48 Laws of Power:* Robert Greene.
	✍️	Power is a key theme in much of greatest literature: kingly power in Shakespeare's history plays, the power of magic in classic fantasy, and the power of the gods in ancient epic poetry.
	🎭	*Risk:* John Retallack. *Agnes of God:* John Pielmeier. *The Dumb Waiter:* Harold Pinter.
	🎬	*Superman* or any superhero film. *Goodfellas:* 1990 (18). *Citizen Kane:* 1941 (A).
	🎵	*Soul Power:* James Brown. *We Are the Champions:* Queen. *Power to the People:* John Lennon.
	🎨	Artists who challenge power, for example, Banksy.

🎪	Younger students will be more literal. Small groups. Status. Levels. Character work. Older students like the metaphor. Larger ensemble physical work or small group, character based. Stanislavski. Dance and choral movement. Stylised/physical theatre. Gecko. Lecoq. Berkoff.
⚠️	The confusion between literal and a more metaphorical power is not a bad thing and students like to work with this double meaning. However, get that artistic intention down on paper!
🔗	001–008, 021, 023, 024, 025, 026, 032, 033, 042, 045, 051, 057, 064, 074, 081, 087, 089, 091, 093, 097, 101, 103, 105, 107, 112, 116, 119, 126, 130, 137, 145, 153, 158, 159, 167, 186, 197.

133   Justice

	'Justice is what love looks like in public' (Cornel West – American philosopher).
♟	12+ Mixed groups of 4–6.
⚑	**Workshops/games**: *Confinement. Levels of tension. Status.* Can you think of other words for justice? What does it mean. What is injustice? Improvise a brief scene/tableau based on the words, 'They got what they deserved'.
☼	*'An eye for an eye makes the world blind'* (Attributed to Mahatma Gandhi). **Research**: The following; social justice, restorative/corrective justice, retributive justice, environmental justice, distributive justice and procedural justice. Ethics. **Look at the language**: To do it justice. A travesty of justice. To bring to justice. Justice is blind. Poetic justice. Rough justice. Sweet justice. Justice league.

Stimulus		
	⚖	A set of scales/blind justice. A hammer.
	📖	*Anna Karenina:* Leo Tolstoy. *To Kill a Mockingbird:* Harper Lee. *A Time to Kill:* John Grisham.
	✍	*Justice Avenges:* Alice Cary.
	🎭	*The Caucasian Chalk Circle:* Brecht. *Death and the Maiden:* Ariel Dorfman. *A View from the Bridge:* Arthur Miller.
	🎬	*In the Name of the Father:* 1993 (15). *The Accused:* 1988 (18). *12 Angry Men:* 1957 (U).
	🎵	*Higher Ground:* Stevie Wonder. *Hurricane:* Bob Dylan. *Redemption Song:* Bob Marley and The Wailers.
	🎨	**Look at**: The various paintings/sculptures and images entitled 'Lady Justice'

🎦	Ideas of poetic justice work well with physical theatre/mime. Theatre of Cruelty. Artaud. Mask work. Levels/status.
⚠	Know your students and their family situations.
🔗	003, 004, 011, 012, 013, 015, 016, 017, 041, 043, 044, 101, 102, 126–150, 175, 182, 183, 187, 197.

134   Monsters

<table>
<tr>
<td></td>
<td colspan="2">'It's the monsters that don't wear costumes that scare me the most at Halloween'
(Anthony T. Hincks – British writer).</td>
</tr>
<tr>
<td>👥</td>
<td colspan="2">15+ From monologues to large ensemble.</td>
</tr>
<tr>
<td>🚩</td>
<td colspan="2">Workshops/games; Fear. Gestus.
Consider the following quote by Edgar Allan Poe: 'The scariest monsters are the ones that lurk within our souls.' Look in the mirror.
Make a list of 10 things that we're afraid of.
Humans create fictional and real monsters; this can be about either . . .</td>
</tr>
<tr>
<td>💡</td>
<td colspan="2">Look at the language: Evil monster, little monster, monster sale, monster truck, green eyed monster, monsters of the deep, of the mind, from history and rock 'n roll.
What the papers say: How the tabloids use the word monster!</td>
</tr>
<tr>
<td rowspan="6">Stimulus</td>
<td>🎃</td>
<td>A carved Halloween pumpkin, a clown's face, a skull.</td>
</tr>
<tr>
<td>📖</td>
<td>The Ocean at the End of the Lane: Neil Gaiman.
The Silence of the Lambs: Thomas Harris.
The Odyssey: Homer.</td>
</tr>
<tr>
<td>📝</td>
<td>The Raven: Edgar Allen Poe.</td>
</tr>
<tr>
<td>🎭</td>
<td>Monsters*: Niklas Rådström.
Adult Child, Dead Child: Andy Hamilton and Claire Dowie.
Macbeth/Titus Andronicus: William Shakespeare.
Collected Grimm's Tales: Carol Anne Duffy and Tim Supple.</td>
</tr>
<tr>
<td>🎬</td>
<td>The Silence of the Lambs: 1991 (18).
Pan's Labyrinth: 2006 (15).
A Clockwork Orange: 1971 (X).</td>
</tr>
<tr>
<td>🎵</td>
<td>He's Back (The Man Behind the Mask): Alice Cooper.
The Thing that Should Not Be: Metallica.
I See a Darkness: Jonny Cash.</td>
</tr>
<tr>
<td></td>
<td>🎨</td>
<td>The Nightmare: Henry Fuseli.
Medusa: Caravaggio.</td>
</tr>
<tr>
<td>🎭</td>
<td colspan="2">Stylised/physical theatre, epic! The complexity of human nature, emotional.
Gecko. Absurd.</td>
</tr>
<tr>
<td>⚠️</td>
<td colspan="2">Know your students!
*Monsters the play is not suitable for younger students.</td>
</tr>
<tr>
<td>🔗</td>
<td colspan="2">025, 031, 032, 034, 036, 037, 040, 042, 044, 047, 048, 049, 061, 062, 064, 071, 073, 074, 076, 082, 097, 104, 129, 157, 159, 160, 173, 190, 192, 197.</td>
</tr>
</table>

135   Peer pressure

	'Ultimately peer pressure can lead people to bully, but peer pressure can also say bullying is not acceptable' (Barack Obama – American President).
♣♦	11–14. 4–5 per group.
⚑	**Workshops/games**; *Control games. Get out of my way!* Tell the story of *The Emperor's New Clothes.* **Questionnaire**: Name the peer pressures that affect your life. Which are positive and negative? Why do you conform/give in to any of them? What about the pressure just to feel accepted and normal?
☀	Watch on YouTube *The Peer Pressure Experiment – Part 1* WISN.com. Watch and discuss. Childnet.com have some excellent teaching (PSHE) resources on peer pressure. Adults are pressured to conform too. What we drive, wear, drink, eat and watch.

Stimulus	💀	In groups, make posters. When put into words, some peer pressures look daft, because they are.
	📖	*Face:* Benjamin Zephaniah. (The scene before the accident when Martin's friends convince him to get in the car.) *One of the Boys:* Scott Johnson. *The Body of Christopher Creed:* Carol Plum-Ucci.
	✍	*Peer Pressure, Peer Pressure:* Kikodinho Edward Alexandros.
	🎭	*DNA:* Dennis Kelly. *I Am the Brother of Dragons:* Gillette Elvgren. *Girls Like That:* Evan Placey.
	🎞	*Finding Nemo:* 2003 (U). *Mean Girls:* 2004 (12A). *Thirteen:* 2003 (18).
	🎵	*Under Pressure:* Queen. *Peer Pressure:* James Bay. *One Step Closer:* Linkin Park.
	🎨	Search for peer pressure art (images). Consider your own posters.

🎭	Peer pressure can be negative or positive. Narrated/Storytelling. Verbatim (T.I.E.). Physical theatre to give 'pressure' a presence on stage.
⚠	Be aware of the group's dynamics. Some songs on the subject use explicit language.
🔗	021, 024, 025, 045, 062, 070, 071, 075, 096–099, 107, 109, 127, 128, 185, 186, 189.

136   Corruption

<table>
<tr>
<td colspan="3">'The duty of youth is to challenge corruption'
(Kurt Cobain – American singer and songwriter).</td>
</tr>
<tr>
<td>👥</td>
<td colspan="2">14+ Small groups.</td>
</tr>
<tr>
<td>🚩</td>
<td colspan="2">Workshops/games, Status. Control games. Super objective.
Look at the language: The politician was corrupt. A corrupt Police force. The file was corrupted. He had corrupted their values. Her words had been corrupted. Darkness and corruption. Morally corrupt. Bribery. Cover-up!
When you think of a corrupt person, what do you see? Draw the image . . . Discuss what you each came up with. Think about stereotypes. Consider this image as a Brechtian character.</td>
</tr>
<tr>
<td>💡</td>
<td colspan="2">Corruption can happen anywhere!
Dictionary definition: Dishonest or fraudulent conduct by those in power, typically involving bribery.
Corruption is: The abuse of entrusted power for private gain.
Research: Transparency International.
CPI; The Corruption Perception Index.
What the papers say: Whistle blowers.</td>
</tr>
<tr>
<td rowspan="7">Stimulus</td>
<td>💀</td>
<td>Look for image of corruption. What do you notice? Hidden money and handshakes!</td>
</tr>
<tr>
<td>📖</td>
<td>The Girl with the Dragon Tattoo: Stieg Larsson.
Filth: Irvine Welsh.
Bare-faced Messiah: The True Story of L. Ron Hubbard: Russell Miller.</td>
</tr>
<tr>
<td>📝</td>
<td>Be Angry at the Sun: Robinson Jeffers.</td>
</tr>
<tr>
<td>🎭</td>
<td>Macbeth: Shakespeare.
The Resistible Rise of Arturo Ui: Brecht.
The Government Inspector: Nikolia Gogol.</td>
</tr>
<tr>
<td>🎬</td>
<td>Line of Duty: 2012 (BBC TV series). (15).
Changeling: 2008 (15).
Mr Smith Goes to Washington: 1939 (U).</td>
</tr>
<tr>
<td>🎵</td>
<td>Absolutely Sweet Marie: Bob Dylan.
A Song about Corruption: Josie R.
Fight the Power: Public Enemy.</td>
</tr>
<tr>
<td>🎨</td>
<td>Cartoon of Boss: Thomas Nast.</td>
</tr>
<tr>
<td>🎭</td>
<td colspan="2">Narration. Gestus. Non-naturalism, stereotypes. Brecht.
Elements of commedia and physical comedy. Performers study the physicality of their character – how they walk and move about the stage. Vocal tone and pace. Meyerhold.</td>
</tr>
<tr>
<td>⚠️</td>
<td colspan="2">A large and confusing subject. Younger students may need more teacher input.</td>
</tr>
<tr>
<td>🔗</td>
<td colspan="2">044, 045, 062, 063, 101, 104, 105, 107–112, 132, 147, 175, 183, 184.</td>
</tr>
</table>

137 Prison

<table>
<tr>
<td></td>
<td colspan="2">'We who live in prison, and in whose lives there is no event but sorrow, have to measure time by throbs of pain, and the record of bitter moments'
(Oscar Wilde – Irish writer and poet).</td>
</tr>
<tr>
<td></td>
<td colspan="2">14+ Small groups.</td>
</tr>
<tr>
<td></td>
<td colspan="2">Workshops/games: Confinement. Control games. Soundscapes. Guide me. Fear.
Questionnaire: Why should people be sent to prison?
Look at the language: Banged up, doing time, going down, the slammer, nicked!</td>
</tr>
<tr>
<td></td>
<td colspan="2">The prison population of England and Wales quadrupled in size between 1900 and 2018, with around half of this increase taking place since 1990.
The US has the highest prison rate in the world.
WPB, The World Prison Brief is an online database providing free access to information on prison systems around the world.
Research: What Dostoyevsky said about prisons and society.</td>
</tr>
<tr>
<td rowspan="6">Stimulus</td>
<td></td>
<td>Prison clothes. Handcuffs, prison bars. A bunch of large keys on a chain. Cobwebs. Numbers scratched on a wall. A judge's wig. A Prison Guard. Barbed wire (images).</td>
</tr>
<tr>
<td></td>
<td>Solitary: Albert Woodfox.
Go-Boy! Roger Caron.
A Life Inside: A Prisoner's Notebook: Erwin James.</td>
</tr>
<tr>
<td></td>
<td>The Ballad of Reading Gaol: Oscar Wilde.</td>
</tr>
<tr>
<td></td>
<td>Holloway Jones: Evan Placey.
Not about Nightingales: Tennessee Williams.
Short Eyes: Miguel Piñero.</td>
</tr>
<tr>
<td></td>
<td>Shawshank Redemption: 1994 (15).
Time: 2021 (British TV Series).
Orange is the New Black: 2013–2019 (US TV Series).</td>
</tr>
<tr>
<td></td>
<td>Folsom Prison Blues: Jonny Cash.
One Love: Nas.
Chain Gang: Sam Cooke.

Locked in a Dark Calm: Tameca Cole.
Research: Prison Art.</td>
</tr>
<tr>
<td></td>
<td colspan="2">Minimalist. Stark lighting. Gobo/projection of prison bars.
Ensemble works well.
Good monologue opportunities. Physical/dance work.</td>
</tr>
<tr>
<td></td>
<td colspan="2">Be aware of family circumstances.</td>
</tr>
<tr>
<td></td>
<td colspan="2">017, 020, 021, 025, 044, 048, 061–064, 071, 073, 074, 077, 081, 085, 088, 097, 104, 107, 123, 126–144, 149, 151, 156–160, 170, 174, 181, 182, 183, 187, 199, 200.</td>
</tr>
</table>

138   The Police Force

		'It's like a government agency that really works' (Peter Kreeft – American philosopher).
👥		14+ Mixed groups of 4 or more.
🚩		**Workshops/games:** *Control. Status games.* **Questionnaire:** List the qualities that make a good Police officer. Do the Police make you feel safe or threatened? **Look at the language:** The nicknames we give the police. Some affectionate, some, not so much! Why do we call them so many different things? We don't have a host of other names for fireman or teachers?
🔅		In France 1666 Paris, Louis XIV created the first efficient police service. 1789 US Marshals Service. Robert Peel London 1822. **What the papers say:** Police in the news. How does TV portray the modern police force? **Search for:** Safe4me Introduction to the police. https://nycpm.org Metropolitan Police Heritage Centre. SAPS Museum S. Africa. AFP Museum Australia.
Stimulus	💀	Police sirens. Blue flashing lights. Handcuffs, truncheon/gun. Uniform. If you **search for** Police officer you tend to get smiling images and illustrations. If you search for Police force, the resulting images are very different.
	📖	*The Choirboys:* Joseph Wambaugh. *Busting Bad Guys* (true stories): Mark Langan. *The Great British Bobby: A History:* Clive Emsley.
	📝	*A Constable Calls:* Seamus Heaney.
	🎭	*Monsters:* Niklas Rådström. *Accidental Death of an Anarchist:* Dario Fo. *The Curious Incident of the Dog in the Night-Time:* Mark Haddon (adapted by Simon Stephens).
	🎬	*The Sweeney:* 2012 (15). *Black and Blue:* 2019 (15). *Line of Duty:* (Netflix).
	🎵	*The Laughing Policeman:* Charles Penrose. *American Skin (41 Shots):* Bruce Springsteen. *I Fought the Law:* The Clash.
	🎨	**Look at:** Many of the Murals and prints of Banksy. **Research:** Leonard Freed's photography of the NYPD. Portrait of a Policeman by Charles F. Tunnicliffe (UK). **Search for:** *Saturday Evening Post* Police posters (USA).
🎭		A lot of work I've seen has been based on the physical control the police have over us. Some great ensemble opportunities.
⚠		Groups are often divided over whether to portray the police as heroes or tyrants. Be wary that your introduction might sway this. Remember you will teach the children of police officers.
🔗		017, 021, 023, 029, 044, 045, 063, 066, 089, 096, 097, 100, 101, 107, 108, 126–134, 136, 137, 146, 154, 161, 174, 184, 187, 191, 197.

139   Runaway

	'I could still turn back before I pass the last houses and really have to commit to this' (Claire Wong – Singapore-Malaysian actor).
👥	All ages. Small mixed groups. Differentiate by age.
🚩	**Workshops/games**: *Status. Control games. Body sculpture.* **Questionnaire**: Why would you run away from home? Where would you go? How would you live? What would you take? Write a letter telling someone why you left. Read your letter aloud. Turn it into a monologue to a group of others who have run away. Improvise a family receiving the letter. Tell your story after one month. Diary entries of a runaway.
☀	**Research** the statistics for child run-aways in your country/state/county. The figures are alarming. The risks, for young women, young men. Runaway youth shelters and charities. What is the attraction of the big city?

Stimulus		
	💀	A rucksack. A diary. A letter.
	📖	*The Adventures of Huckleberry Finn:* Mark Twain. *Jump the Cracks:* Stacy DeKeyser. *Runaway:* Wendelin Van Draanen.
	📝	*What Has Happened to Lulu?:* Charles Causley.
	🎭	*Leaving Home:* David French. *Circles:* Rachel De-lahay. *Runaways (musical):* Elizabeth Swados.
	🎞	*Inside Out:* 2015 (U). *Stand by Me:*1986 (15). *The Runaways:* 2019 (12A).
	🎵	*She's got her Ticket:* Tracy Chapman. *She's Leaving Home:* The Beatles. *Born to Run:* Bruce Springsteen.
	🎨	*Leaving Home:* William Turner. *Santa on His Bench:* Banksy

🎭	Verbatim theatre. Physical theatre. Mime, body props. Levels. Minimal set. Monologues. Stanislavski for character work.
⚠	Know your students!
🔗	020, 021, 025, 034, 061, 063, 065, 069, 071, 073, 075, 088, 089, 090, 097, 101, 104, 105, 107, 108, 109, 112, 114, 123, 126, 130, 135, 149, 161, 163, 182, 183, 186.

140   Transportation of convicts to the Colonies

<table>
<tr>
<td colspan="2"> 'Perish or Prosper'
(Jeremy Bentham – English philosopher, jurist and social reformer). </td>
</tr>
<tr>
<td>👥</td>
<td>11+ Mixed groups of 4 and above.</td>
</tr>
<tr>
<td>🚩</td>
<td>Workshops/games; Control games. Status. Confinement. Circle of attention.
Imagine being sent to the other side of the world because you stole two candles. If you didn't go you would be sentenced instead to death!
Confined to a prison ship on a journey below decks which would last between 3 to 5 months.
For older students look at LIZ MORDEN'S Monologue from Our Country's Good, Act 2, Scene 1.</td>
</tr>
<tr>
<td>💡</td>
<td>Before Australia convicts/undesirables were sent to North America and the Caribbean. Transportation to the penal colonies occurred between 1788 and 1868 when 165,000 convicts were transported to Australia alone. For our work, we focussed solely on Australia's penal colonies.
Research: The journal of the real Arthur Phillip, Governor of New South Wales 1791.
Also The First Fleet.
The State Library of New South Wales has an excellent resource.
More controversial: Do we still send undesirables to other lands?</td>
</tr>
<tr>
<td rowspan="7">Stimulus</td>
<td>🖥   Search for: Transport to the colonies paperwork (images). Print off and age . . .</td>
</tr>
<tr>
<td>📖   Great Expectations: Dickens.
The Playmaker: Thomas Keneally.
The Fatal Shore: Robert Hughes.
Convicts in the Colonies: Lucy Williams.</td>
</tr>
<tr>
<td>📝   Convict Poem: George Barrington. (Wisehammer*).</td>
</tr>
<tr>
<td>🎭   Our Country's Good: Timberlake Wertenbaker.
Female Transport: Steve Gooch.</td>
</tr>
<tr>
<td>📽   Banished: 2015 (TV Mini Series) (15).</td>
</tr>
<tr>
<td>🎵   Botany Bay: John Williamson.
Van Dieman's Land: U2.
Six Months in a Leaky Boat: Split Enz.
Research: The Convict Voice – songs of transportation by Don Brian.</td>
</tr>
<tr>
<td>🎨   The Convict Ship: Alexander Ignatius Roche.
'The Discovery.' Convict Ship (Lying at Deptford). Etching by E. W. Cooke.</td>
</tr>
<tr>
<td>🎭</td>
<td>Lecoq/Berkoff. Minimalist. Bars/grating gobo/lights from above to interior/hold of a ship.
SFX.
Monologues.</td>
</tr>
<tr>
<td>⚠</td>
<td>Some adult themes/language in source materials.</td>
</tr>
<tr>
<td>🔗</td>
<td>015, 036, 063, 064, 079, 101, 103, 114, 115, 133, 141, 149, 155, 174, 178–183.</td>
</tr>
</table>

141 Mercy

	'Mercy in the promise is as the apple in the seed' (William Gurnall – English author and Anglican clergyman).
♟♟	14+ Small groups (duologues).
⚑	**Workshops/games**: *Control games. Body sculpture. Mirror imaging.* What does mercy look like?. What does it mean to be merciful? Explore in tableau, the act of showing mercy; for example, in a sporting context, a battle, a law court, a parent, a doctor, a god! Can you think of others? **Questionnaire**: Have you ever been shown mercy, or shown mercy to someone? How did it feel?
☀	**Look at the language**: No mercy. At their mercy. Have mercy. God's mercy. Her death was merciful. Mercy me! Merciless judgment. Angel of mercy. Beg for mercy. **Research**: Mercy in different cultures and religions. Mercy, forgiveness and redemption. 'The quality of Mercy', Portia's speech from Shakespeare's *The Merchant of Venice*.

Stimulus	☠	Images of angels, scales of justice.
	📕	*Just Mercy:* Bryan Stevenson. *Mercy:* Jodi Picoult. *A Very Old Man with Enormous Wings. A Tale for Children:* García Márquez.
	📝	Look at Portia's speech from Shakespeare's *The Merchant of Venice*, Act 4, Scene 1.
	🎭	*Children of Killers:* Katori Hall. *The Merchant of Venice:* William Shakespeare. *The Mysteries:* Tony Harrison.
	🎬	*Just Mercy:* 2019 (12A). *Joyeux Noël:* 2005 (12A). *Tsotsi:* 2005 (15).
	🎵	*The Sisters of Mercy:* Leonard Cohen. *Mercy:* Duffy. *The Mercy Seat:* Nick Cave.
	🎨	*The Seven Acts of Mercy:* Caravaggio.

🎭	Magic realism. Minimalist set. Stark lighting. Good opportunities for set/props/costume. SFX. Some good duologue work. Physicalised. Dance. DV8. Boal. Imaginary Body.
⚠	A difficult concept which may need more teacher input.
🔗	021, 026, 041, 051, 066, 087, 113, 123, 132, 133, 142, 144, 174, 175, 181.

142   The death penalty

		'There is no justice in killing in the name of Justice' (Desmond Tutu – South African Anglican bishop).
👥		16+ Mature able groups.
🚩		**Workshops/games:** *Control games. Fear. Body sculpture.* 16 countries still impose the death penalty. China executes more people than the rest of the world combined. **Questionnaire:** Do you think there are some crimes that deserve the death penalty? **Research:** The methods of execution different countries use. Are there some crimes which deserve the death penalty?
💡		British Institution of Human Rights banned the Death penalty in the UK in 1965. The DPIC (Death Penalty Information Centre). USA deathpenaltyinfo.org Cornell Centre on death penalty worldwide. deathpenaltyworldwide.org. The United Nations Human Rights Committee and Amnesty International have both produced excellent resources. Christ was sentenced to death. Leviticus 24:19–21. *An eye for an eye.* "*An eye for an eye will make the whole world blind*" (Ghandi).
Stimulus	🕯️	A hangman's noose. A last meal. An execution warrant. Letters to and from family.
	📖	*Ketchup Clouds:* Annabel Pitcher. *Death Row Letters:* Charles M. Lesley. *The Death Penalty:* Stuart Banner.
	✍️	*The Death Penalty is Murder:* Francis Duggan.
	🎭	*Female Transport:* Steve Gooch. *Our Country's Good:* Timberlake Wertenbaker (the science of hanging scene). *The Hangman:* Martin Mc Donagh.
	🎬	*The Green Mile:* 1999 (18). *The Life of David Gale:* 2003 (15). *Clemency:* 2019 (15). *Pierrepoint: The Last Hangman:* 2005 (R). *At the Death House Door:* 2011 (An investigative documentary).
	🎵	*The Mercy Seat:* Nick Cave. *Dead Man Walkin':* Bruce Springsteen. *Let Him Dangle:* Elvis Costello.
	🎨	Look at the work of Julie Green '*Last Meals*' *Electric Chair:* Andy Warhol. Look at the work of Goya on executions.
🎭		Realism (Stanislavski). Emotion/tension. Or an ensemble dance/physical theatre piece. Highly choreographed and stylised. Use of light and shadow. **More controversial:** Use of mask and comedy (Commedia dell'arte). Puppets or children's soft toys as the executed. Grand Guignol.
⚠️		Research online should be supervised.
🔗		023, 035, 044, 057, 058, 063, 125, 131, 133, 137, 143, 144, 148, 174, 175, 183.

143 Commedia dell'arte

	'Wherever there are witty servants and domineering masters, young wives and old husbands, pompous pedants, thwarted lovers or bragging soldiers, the Commedia is there in spirit and also very often form' (Simon Callow – English actor, writer and director).
	Any age. Groups of 2–5. Ensemble with older students.
	Workshops/games; *Energy Games. Stereotypes.* Introduce students with fast-paced physical workshops/games. Improvise the stock characters, using exaggerated movement, voice and mannerisms of the stereotypes. Using the breath. Grammelot (gibberish language that satires dialects). Masks and props. **Research**: The stock characters and relationships between them. Explore classic lazzi, burle or meccanismi.
	Usually improvised comedy, stock characters, stylised and recognisable characters and costumes, mask and exaggerated gesture, panto/slapstick, 'lazzi', originated in 15th-century Italy. A not too subtle blend of stereotype, sketch and shtick passed down through circus, pantomime, vaudeville and burlesque. Shakespeare's Fools were often zanni character types and his romantic leads were inspired by Commedia's innamorati (the Lovers). **More controversial**: Look at how women are portrayed in Commedia dell'arte. Consider punch and Judy and violence against women and girls.

Stimulus		
		A slapstick. Punch and Judy set/images. Half masks.
		The Commedia Dell'arte: Giacomo Oreglia. *Punch and Judy: A History:* George Speaight. *Commedia Dell'Arte: An Actor's Handbook:* John Rudlin.
		Commedia Dell'arte: Charl Landsberg.
		The Servant of Two Masters: Carlo Goldini, adapted by Lee Hall. *Accidental Death of an Anarchist:* Dario Fo. *The Rover:* Aphra Behn.
		Commedia dell'arte: The story of the style. 2007 TV Documentary. And of course *The Simpsons*. The stock characters; ARLECCHINO: Homer and Bart. COLOMBINA: Marge and Lisa. PANTALONE: Mr. Burns. PIERROT: Smithers. BRIGHELLA: Moe!
		Listen to late Renaissance music. Brighella the lute/guitar. The music helped to set mood. Popular instruments were; the lute, viola, sackbut, shawm, mandolin, recorder and zither.
		A Commedia dell'Arte Scene Depicting Pantalone and Brighella: A painting by Sebastian Vrancx.

	Ensemble. Mask. ERS and Melodrama. Works well outdoors, where people are gathered. Site specific (outside a church, a market place etc.). Take a modern topic and give it the commedia treatment! Pantomime.
	Gain permission for public performances.
	016, 018, 031, 034, 044, 051, 063, 066, 068, 083, 109, 126, 130, 136, 138, 144, 160, 178, 179, 180, 184, 190, 195, 196, 197.

144   Revenge

		'Before you embark on a journey of revenge, dig two graves' (Confucius – Chinese philosopher).
⚥	15+ Mixed groups.	
⚑	**Workshops/games**: *Levels of tension. Body sculpture.* **Questionnaire**: Someone makes you look silly in front of friends, do you want pay back? If they harmed a member of your family, would you seek revenge? Consider the quote by Confucius, what does it mean? Does the law offer enough or do you need to take your own action? What are the emotions that fuel revenge?	
☀	**Research**; Cycles of violence. Revenge in other cultures. Voodoo dolls. Turning the other cheek. *'It is mine to avenge; I will repay'*, says the Lord. Paul in *Romans 12*. Revenge is cited as a factor in one in five murders. **Search for**: The complicated psychology of revenge. **What the papers say**: Trump's presidential victory was due to 'revenge of working-class whites'. (*Washington Post*) **Look at the language**: Vengeance is mine. I will have bloody revenge. Vengeance is sweet. Payback!	
Stimulus	🍷	The hammer is the symbol of revenge but it is also the symbol of justice and destruction.
	📖	*The Twits*: Roald Dahl. *Gone Girl*: Gillian Fry. *Wuthering Heights*: Emily Brontë
	📝	*A Poison Tree*: William Blake.
	🎭	*Blood Wedding*: Lorca. *Boudica*: Tristan Bernays. *Death and The Maiden*: Ariel Dorfman. *Titus Andronicus*: Shakespeare.
	🎬	*The Godfather*: 1972 (X) 'Revenge is a dish which tastes best when served cold.' *Kill Bill Volumes 1 and 2*: 2003–2004 (X). *Gladiator*: 2000 (15).
	🎵	*You Oughta Know*: Alanis Morissette (explicit lyrics). *Rolling in the Deep*: Adele. *Better than Revenge*: Taylor Swift.
	🎨	**Look at**: The work of Artemisia Gentileschi (*Judith Slaying Holofernes* in particular). And then there's spite, Michelangelo painted an official who criticised his work, as a naked oaf with donkey's ears, in hell!
🎭	The theme of revenge and tragedy in the theatre. Thirst for vengeance bringing no relief, in fact more pain. Berkoff/Lecoq ensemble with masks and stylised movement.	
⚠	Don't allow students to make it personal.	
🔗	003, 007, 025, 034, 044, 061, 062, 063, 074, 080, 100, 107, 109, 127, 133, 142, 157, 175, 192.	

145 The Monarchy

	'It's vital that the monarchy keeps in touch with the people' (Princess Diana – Princess of Wales).
	14 + Mixed groups.
	Workshops/games: *Status. Control games.* A throne, set up on a raised level. Discuss Queen Elizabeth II and the 70th (Platinum) Jubilee. The outpouring of love and sorrow at her passing. Decide upon an artistic intention. What do you want to show/question? Once cruel tyrants now people's hero? Fair/democratic, worth the money? Their role historically, their place in a modern world?
	Consider the success of the TV series, *The Crown*. **Research**: The 44 sovereign countries around the world have a monarch as their head of state. **What the papers say**: Look at media coverage of Royal events around the world.

Stimulus		
		A crown and Sceptre. A throne. Robes. Horse drawn carriages.
		The Secret Bride (In The Court of Henry VIII): Diane Haeger. *Murder Most Royal:* Jean Plaidy. *Kings, Queens, Bones and Bastards:* David Hilliam.
		When I Was Fair and Young: QUEEN ELIZABETH I.
		Boudica: Tristan Bernays. *The Empress:* Tanika Gupta. *The Madness of George III:* Alan Bennett. Shakespeare's Kings.
		The Crown: Netflix TV Series. *Marie Antoinette:* 2006 (PG-13). *The Young Victoria:* 2009 (PG).
		It's Good to be King: Tom Petty. *God Save the Queen:* Sex Pistols. *The Queen and The Soldier:* Susan Vega.
		Henry VIII: Hans Holbein the Younger. *The Queen:* Justin Mortimer. *The Queen:* Gerald Scarfe CBE.

	Pomp and ceremony. Character work (Stanislavski). Chorus work. Lecoq. Levels.
	Have fun if you want to but remain respectful. Consider your school and audience.
	015, 021, 034, 066, 074, 084, 101, 113, 123, 132, 175, 178, 180, 189, 196, 198, 199, 200.

146   Riot and Protest

	'Those who make peaceful revolution impossible will make violent revolution inevitable' (J. F. Kennedy – American President).
♟	13+ Suits large ensemble.
⚑	**Workshops/games;** *Status games. Control games. Soundscapes. Colombian hypnosis. Get out of my way!* **Questionnaire:** Think of something profound and unjust. (Like the unlawful killing of George Floyd). You complain and nobody listens, what would you do to get attention?
🔅	Riot is a violent offence against public order involving three or more people, usually springing from some kind of grievance. **Research:** Los Angeles Riots of 1992. The Capitol riots/protest in Washington, January 2021. The history of riots in the UK range from 1391 (Baker's riots) to 2011 UK riots. In many cases injustice is the catalyst. The theatre and protest are often closely interlinked in the contemporary culture. **What the papers say:** Look at the way the press headline riots. 'Mob rule.'

Stimulus		
	🎭	Police batons and shields. Banners. SFX Sirens, shouts/chants, smashing glass. Sirens.
	📖	*Kent State:* Deborah Wiles. *Blindness:* José Saramago. *High-Rise:* J. G. Ballard.
	📝	*Protest:* Ella Wheeler Wilcox.
	🎬	*Les Misérables:* Victor Hugo. *Advice for the Young at Heart:* Roy Williams. *Billy Elliot:* Lee Hall and Elton John.
	🎞	*Billy Elliot:* 2000 (15). *Harlan County: USA:* 1976 (A). *V for Vendetta:* 2005 (15).
	🎵	*Get Up, Stand Up:* Bob Marley and the Wailers. *We Shall Overcome:* Joan Baez. *The Times They Are a-Changin':* Bob Dylan.
	🎨	**Look at:** The BLM street art. Banksy. **Research:** The Performance Art of Pyotr Pavlensky.

🎭	Forum theatre. Encourage students to mirror the madness of riots through physical work. DV8/Frantic Assembly. Katie Mitchell. Expressionism. Mask work.
⚠	Insist students get their main artistic intentions down on paper and stick to them.
🔗	001–005, 017, 023, 053, 066, 079, 101, 102, 115, 130, 147, 149, 150, 174, 175, 178, 181, 187, 189, 197.

147 Politics

	'Politicians are the same all over. They promise to build a bridge even where there is no river' (Nikita Khrushchev – Former leader of the Soviet Union).
	14+ Small mixed groups.
	Workshops/games: *Status games.* **Questionnaire**: Who is your local MP/representative/member of congress? How many didn't know? When you hear the word Politician, what do you immediately think of? Each write one word on a piece of paper. How does the list read? Is it negative or positive? Think about a piece of drama which either challenges or demonstrates these feelings.
	From the Greek: Πολιτικά, politiká, 'affairs of the cities'. **Research**: 10 Common Forms of Government. Look at real-world examples of each. Think about recent events in world politics. Have the politicians behaved well? Do they set a good example? What would happen without politics? What are the alternatives? **Look at the language**: Students who have studied persuasive speaking in English will have looked at Politician's use of *alliteration, repetition, rhetoric, statistics* and the use of 1st person pronouns (these work well in parody). **What the papers say**: Examine the political leanings of leading newspapers.

		Images of your Government in session.
		Animal Farm: George Orwell. *Fahrenheit 451:* Ray Bradbury.
		The New Colossus: Emma Lazarus. *London, 1802:* William Wordsworth.
Stimulus		*The Resistible Rise of Arturo Ui:* Bertolt Brecht. *Julius Caesar:* William Shakespeare. Look at playwrights like: Sean O'Casey, Caryl Churchill, Arthur Miller or Dario Fo.
		All the President's Men: 1976 (PG). *In the Loop:* 2009 (15). *Scandal:* 1989 (18).
		Fortunate Son: Creedence Clearwater Revival. *Ronnie, Talk To Russia:* Prince. *Get Up, Stand Up:* Bob Marley and The Wailers.
		Man at the Crossroads: Mural by Diego Rivera. *We Don't Need Another Hero:* Barbara Kruger. *Flower Thrower:* Graffiti art by Banksy.

	Boal, Theatre of the Oppressed. Forum. Brecht, Godber (using comedy), Berkoff. Max Stafford-Clark. Political/ensemble. Use of levels. Ensemble, physical theatre. Commentary/narration/docudrama. Comedy/Subtext. Short sketches.
	At first many students shy away from 'politics' citing it as 'boring'. It takes a lively approach to challenge this. Comedy/parody is often a good tool.
	001, 005, 022, 023, 066, 076, 101, 102, 109–113, 121, 132, 146, 163, 174, 187, 196.

148   Assassination

	'Assassination is the extreme form of censorship' (George Bernard Shaw – Irish playwright).
♟	13+ Groups of 3–5
🚩	**Workshops/games**: *Control games. Repetition exercises.* Projected image of witnesses pointing in the direction of the shots that killed Martin Luther King. It's such a powerful image; not showing the victim, rather the location of the assassin. I put together a PowerPoint of some famous assassinated people to Marvin Gaye's song, *Abraham, Martin and John*.
🔅	**Research**: It's not just politicians: civil rights leaders, singers, monarchs, royalty, fashion designers, warriors, Emperors, conservationists, poets, playwrights, theatre directors, activists, and assassins! Assassination is murder! https://www.thefamouspeople.com/assassinated.php (a staggering list of over 450 people). **More controversial**: Osama bin Laden was also assassinated? Is assassination ever justified? And the usual conspiracy theories!.

Stimulus	💀	A montage of the faces of assassination victims (Google images).
	📕	*The Day of the Jackal*: Frederick Forsyth. *The Eiger Sanction*: Trevanian. *The Pelican Brief*: John Grisham.
	📝	*The Genius of the Crowd*: Charles Bukowski.
	🎭	*Julius Caesar*: William Shakespeare. *The Father and the Assassin*: Anupama Chandrasekhar. *Assassins*: (Musical) Sondheim and Weidman.
	📀	*JFK*: 1991 (15). *The Killing of John Lennon*: 2006 (Unrated). *The Day of the Jackal*: 1973 (PG).
	🎵	*Abraham, Martin and John*: Marvin Gaye. *Murder Most Foul*: Bob Dylan (watch official video). *I Just Shot John Lennon*: The Cranberries.
	🎨	*The Death of Julius Caesar*: Vincenzo Camuccini.

🎭	Ensemble, Lecoq/Berkoff. Also lends itself to Verbatim and Physical theatre. Boal/Brecht. Multi role. Simple set.
⚠	Some images/news footage/details are disturbing.
🔗	006, 023, 044, 057, 061, 071, 079, 100, 102, 119, 123, 128, 133, 144–147, 175, 189, 198.

149   Freedom!

		'Freedom is the oxygen of the soul' (Moshe Dayan – Israeli military leader and politician).
⚥		15+ Mixed groups.
⚑		**Workshops/games** *Confinement. Levels of tension.* Freedom means different things to different people. What do you think freedom is? Define it as a group tableau (or individually).
☼		**Look at the language:** Freedom of speech. As free as a bird. Free of doubt. Freedom from debt. Freedom to kill. Free and easy. The freedom of the City. Sexual freedom. The price of freedom. Religious freedom. Sweet liberty. Freedom from pain. Freedom of choice. Freedom from want. To live without oppression, without fear, without pain. Freedom is dancing! **Research:** Different cultures definitions of freedom.
Stimulus	☠	Broken chains. The statue of Liberty.
	📖	*Freedom for the Thought That We Hate:* Anthony Lewis. *Joseph Knight:* James Robertson. *Go Tell It on the Mountain:* James Baldwin.
	📝	*Freedom's Plow:* Langston Hughes.
	🎭	*Games and After Liverpool:* James Saunders. *My Mother Said I never Should:* Charlotte Keatley. *The Cagebirds:* David Campton.
	🎞	*The Patriot:* 2000 (15). *Braveheart:* 1995 (15). *Selma:* 2014 (12A).
	🎵	*Chimes of Freedom:* Bob Dylan. *I'm Free:* The Who. *Freebird:* Lynyrd Skynyrd
	🎨	**Look at:** Norman Rockwell's *Four Freedoms.*
🎭		Good opportunities for dance and choral movement. Berkoff/Lecoq. Levels on stage. Cages/bars. Chains/ribbons. Theatre of the Oppressed. Boal.
⚠		Be aware of cultural/religious differences.
🔗		001, 002, 008, 017, 027, 035, 065, 066, 077, 097, 101, 123, 141, 150, 156, 174, 181.

150   The Easter rising 1916

	Éirí Amach na Cásca *'It's the same old theme since 1916'* (The Cranberries – Irish band)
👥	15+ Mixed groups.
🚩	**Workshops/games:** *Levels of tension. Control. Status.* Also known as the 'Easter Rebellion'. Why do people rise up? What would make you rebel against your government/rulers? Is violence ever justified?
💡	TES *Introduction to the Troubles in Northern Ireland* (a teaching resource). www.historyonthenet.com > worksheets (The troubles). RTÉ- archives: Civil Rights Movement in Northern Ireland. Scoilnet. DES Irish Education. Notable dates: 1641, 1798, 1864, 1916, 1968/9. **Research:** The Potato Famine (The great hunger) 1845–1852. Bloody Sunday. The IRA. The Church. Emigration to the USA.
Stimulus	There are many photographs and paintings available of the Easter Rebellion on Google images.
	Guests of the Nation: Frank O'Connor (Short story). *Women and the Irish Revolution:* Linda Connolly. *1916: A Novel of the Irish Revolution:* Morgan Llwelyn.
	Easter 1916: W. B. Yeats.
	The Shadow of a Gunman: Sean O'Casey. *Joyriders:* Christina Reid. *The Death of Cuchulain:* W. B. Yeats (Poetic form).
	A Terrible Hullabaloo: 2016 (Short animated film). Irish Film Board. *Ryan's Daughter:* 1970 (AA). *Rebellion:* 2016 series (Netflix).
	The Ballad of James Connolly: Derek Warfield. *Sunday Bloody Sunday:* U2. *Zombie:* The Cranberries. *This is a Rebel Song:* Sinead O'Connor.
	Sculpture, *The statue of Cú Chulainn:* Oliver Shepherd. Look at the work of artist Jack B. Yates. *Birth of the Irish Republic* by Walter Paget. *Art of the Troubles:* National Museums NI. *Arts and Culture: Ireland Easter Rising 1916.* An Archive of photographs, artifacts and documents.
🎭	Verbatim/through the eyes of a child. Ensemble work with soundscapes for the battle scenes and riots. Music and song can be important. Images/projections. Dance work, storytelling with flags.
⚠️	Political and religious feelings still run high.
🔗	06, 10, 16, 061, 079, 101, 106, 110, 119, 132, 146, 149, 189.

151 Repeat, repeat

	'Angels converge where patterns are repeated' (Michael Bassey Johnson – Nigerian writer and dramatist).
	14+ Works well with large group.
	Workshops/games: *Repetition exercises. Mirror images.* Get the group to repeat a simple mimed action like opening curtains or stirring a cup of tea. Look at the action in detail and make the repeat an exact copy. Repeat a short sentence like, *'Good morning my love, and how are you?'* Try to keep the exact same tone, pace etc. List the things you repeat every day. Work out a short piece of choral movement that repeats to a pattern. A dance routine for an everyday routine. Give it a rhythm/beat. Work on it as a group.
	Think about how life repeats itself. How we are comforted by routine, yet bored by it too. **Look at the language**: History repeats itself. Same old story. Rinse and repeat. Repeat after me. Re-run. Say again! Déjà vu. Life repeats itself. Over and over and over and . . . We make the same mistakes, personally and as a race/species. Groundhog day. Young children love repetitive literature. Assonance and alliteration. **Research**: Repetition in nature. How natural repetition includes the presence of variation. From schools of fish to forests, fractals and landscapes. Repetition in time, architecture, nature, design, art, dance, games. Repetition and rhetoric in persuasive speaking. **Look at**: Repetition and comedy. Ritual and repetition. Repetition in mathematics and music. Theatrical Repetition.

Stimulus		
		Images of repetition in nature.
		The Stone Gods Jeanette Winterson. *Repeat:* Neal Pollack. *The Truth Lies Here:* Lindsey Klingele.
		A Pizza the Size of the Sun: Jack Prelutsky.
		Advice for the Young at Heart: Roy Williams. **Look at** repetition in Shakespeare.
		Groundhog Day: 1993 (PG). *The Edge of Tomorrow:* 2014 (12A).
		Joy in Repetition: Prince. *Same Old Story:* BB King. *Repetition:* Au Pairs.
		Heroic Strokes of the Bow: Paul Klee. **Research**: The Importance of Repetition in Art

	Stylised robotic movement to emphasise ritual and repetition. Chorus work, ensemble. Berkoff approach to movement. Dance based. Mime.
	It is important to start with repetition exercises to build focus. Repetition without focus becomes stale.
	024, 027, 030, 033, 056, 067, 074, 080, 084, 087, 097, 103, 107, 109, 119, 152, 153, 162, 163, 164, 166, 168, 170, 179, 181, 185, 186, 192, 196.

152   Our phones (From Bell to Apple!)

	'An invention of the devil which abrogates some of the advantages of making a disagreeable person keep his distance' (Ambrose Bierce – American writer).
👥	Any age. Duologues to large ensemble.
🚩	**Workshops/games**; *Soundscapes. Mirror imaging.* A fun start is to place a bell and an apple at different ends of the stage. It's a good conversation starter. Then fill in the development across the stage in date order, with pictures of phones and designs. Even if we just look at the development of the mobile phone there is a vast amount of change from the early models to our all-knowing smart phones. Life before the phone/the mobile/the smart phone. **Questionnaire**: List all the functions you use on your phone. Do you even make that many phone calls anymore?
💡	**More controversial**: Their darker side; bullying, drugs trafficking and sex. Reports of mobile phones/masts causing cancers. From bans on mobiles in schools to the use of smartphones in lessons. The ITPA has a great history of the telephone page, https://www.nationalitpa.com/history-of-telephone

Stimulus	📷	Different telephones (easily available from jumble/junk shops). Images of telegraph poles across a landscape.
	📖	Look at Short fiction to read on your phone (phone fiction). Or novels like *Quilt* by Nicholas Royle.
	📝	*Long Distance II*: Tony Harrison.
	🎭	Plays in which the phone is a central or important theme. *Bully Boy*: Sandi Toksvig. *Mobile Phone Show*: Jim Cartwright. There are also some great telephone conversation/duologues.
	🎬	*Cellular*: 2004 (15). *Compliance*: 2012 (15). *The Matrix*: 1999 (15). **Look at**: How the phone has a very sinister role in many movies.
	🎵	*Hanging on the Telephone*: Blondie. *Rikki Don't Lose That Number*: Steely Dan. *I Just Called*: Stevie Wonder. Listen to all the different ring tones.
	🎨	Interactive app-driven experiences which enable us to engage with art (The Space). Photography on mobiles/The Selfie . . . *Lobster Telephone*: Salvador Dali. *Recycled Mobile Phone Art*: Rob Pettit. *Concrete Cell Phones*: Will Coles.

🎪	Soundscapes of phone chat and ring tones. Monologues and duologues. Moments when phone calls may have changed/made history . . .
⚠️	Consider your school policies concerning mobile phones, sharing data and phone numbers.
🔗	023, 024, 084, 086, 092, 093, 097, 099, 109, 119, 123, 125, 135, 156, 164, 188,

153   The Moon (A Case study unit, see Chapter 5)

		'He made the moon to mark the seasons' (Psalm 104:19).
☄	A source of wonder for all ages! Groups of 2–22.	
⚑	See details in Case study, Unit 153, Chapter 5.	
☼	NASA Gallery. **Search for**: Moon Facts. *Moon 101* National Geographic – YouTube. How the moon affects our behaviour. The moon's symbolism, signs and meanings in different cultures. Our nearest neighbour! **What the papers say:** Look at the media coverage of the lunar landing in 1969 Apollo 11. **More controversial.** Lunatics and the moon. Full moon and evil/werewolves/pagan worship.	
Stimulus	☾	Moon symbolism is seen in all aspects of life on earth: darkness, mystery, fertility, natural cycles, life/death, emotions, renewal and eternity. A contrast to the sun, sitting between our conscious and unconscious.
	📖	There are far too many to individually name! **Search for** lunar literature. In Science Fiction man has been writing about going to the moon for hundreds of years.
	✍	*Moonrise:* Gerard Manley Hopkins.
	🎭	*The Far Side of the Moon:* Robert Lepage. *Man on the Moon:* John Phillips (Musical). 'O' swear not by the moon, the inconstant moon.' JULIET. *Romeo and Juliet.*
	🎬	*First Men in the Moon:* 1964 (U). *Transformers: Dark of the Moon:* 2011 (12A). *In the Shadow of the Moon:* British-made documentary.
	♫	*Dark Side of the Moon:* Pink Floyd. *Walking on the Moon:* The Police. *The Whole of the Moon:* The Waterboys. *Moonlight Sonata:* Beethoven.
	🎨	*Road with Cypress and Star:* Van Gogh. *Moonlit Shipwreck at Sea:* Thomas Moran. *Moonlight, a Study at Millbank:* Turner.
🎞	See details in Case study, Unit 153, Chapter 5.	
⚠	A vast subject, with younger students there should be a definite focus for groups.	
🔗	031, 032, 034–040, 047, 049, 054, 055, 056, 071, 074, 103, 107, 120, 123, 151, 157, 158, 159, 190, 192, 196.	

154   The Car

	'Cars are the sculptures of our everyday lives' (Chris Bangle – American automobile designer).
👥	Any age. Small groups.
🚩	**Workshops/games:** *Energy games, Soundscapes. Filling the space.* What do you think of when you hear the word 'car'? Apart from driving them we: write about them, sing about them, make movies about them. Explore our love affair with the car. **Look at the language:** Cars are described as: thirsty, conservative, flashy, sexy, ugly, a monster, a rust bucket, a death trap, family, green, sensible, safe, powerful . . . To some it's a statement, to others a necessity. List pros/cons . . .
💡	**Research:** The 1901 Mercedes, designed by Wilhelm Maybach is credited as being the first modern motorcar. In 1908 Henry Ford introduced the Model T and William Durant founded General Motors. Mass production had begun! Think of movies about cars, movies about journeys in cars, cars with personalities, killer cars, people and their cars . . . Pollution and the electric car. Your first car . . .
Stimulus	**Images of famous cars.** Pink Rolls Royce, The Batmobile, James Bond's Aston Martin, Herbie, Scooby Doo's Mystery Machine, The Weasley's flying Ford Anglia, Greased Lightning!!! *Anywhere but Here:* Mona Simpson. *On the Road:* Jack Kerouac. *Clarkson on Cars:* Jeremy Clarkson. *To Motorists:* Rudyard Kipling. *Too Much Punch for Judy:* Mark Wheeller. *Autobahn:* Neil LaBute. *Grease:* The Musical (TRW). *The Fast and The Furious:* Franchise. *The Love Bug:* 1968 (G). *Gone in 60 Seconds:* 1974 (PG). *The Italian Job:* 1969 (U). *Thunder Road:* Bruce Springsteen. *Driving in My Car:* Madness. *Drive My Car:* The Beatles. *Concrete Traffic:* Wolf Vostell (Sculpture). *Trabi:* Birgit Kinder (painted on the Berlin wall). *Rainy Taxi:* Salvador Dali. *In the Car:* Roy Lichtenstein.
🎭	Site specific. A lot of fun can be had with back projections and a performer on a chair with a steering wheel. Movement/physical theatre.
⚠️	Cars are status symbols, know your students!
🔗	033, 040, 051, 060, 079, 093, 095, 096, 113, 114, 116, 119, 125, 132, 138, 149, 160, 181, 187, 191.

155   Explorers

		'Exploration is really the essence of the human spirit' (Frank Borman – American astronaut).
♟		11+ mixed groups. Popular with younger students.
⚑		**Workshops/games**: *In the spotlight. Energy games.* Teacher in role. Take your students on adventures with famous explorers. Christopher Columbus, as he takes his first steps on the American continent: Amy Johnson as she flies solo from London to Australia. Ranulph Fiennes as he crosses the polar ice caps, or climbs Everest. Neil Armstrong as he took those first steps on the Moon. What does it feel like? Write a diary entry for that moment, or a letter home. Roll on wall.
☼		**Research**: Vasco da Gama, Ferdinand Magellan, Marco Polo, Francis Drake, David Livingstone, Captain James Cook, Ernest Shackleton, Leif Ericson, Robert Peary, Amelia Earhart, Idris Hall (AKA Aloha Wanderwell), Xuanzang. Each of these explorers has an inspiring story to tell. Use Google Earth to make your own explorations!
Stimulus	💀	A compass. Walking boots. Climbing equipment. A World Globe.
	📖	*City of the Beasts:* (YA) Isabel Allende. *The Polar Bear Explorers' Club:* Alex Bell. *The Explorer:* Katherine Rundell.
	✍	*The Strength Within:* Rod Walford.
	🎭	*The Explorers Club:* Nell Benjamin. *Gulliver's Travels:* Johathan Swift (adapted by Lowell Swortzell).
	🎞	*Fitzcarraldo:* 1982 (A). *Mountains of the Moon:* 1990 (15). *Queen of the Desert:* 2015 (PG).
	🎵	*Amerigo:* Patti Smith. *Gold Rush:* 10,000 Maniacs. *Columbus:* Mary Black.
	🎨	Darwin's sketches and the works of Conrad Martens. *View of Adventure Bay, Van Diemen's Land, New Holland*, by William Ellis. *Man on the Moon:* Neil Armstrong's iconic photograph.
🎭		Movement based. Good dance opportunities/ensemble. Light and SFX. Soundscapes. Puppets. Or, take it outside! Local woods, beach, fields.
⚠		With teacher in role work, know when to step away.
🔗		015, 016, 017, 056, 066, 072, 076, 079, 088, 103, 106, 114, 119, 124, 125, 153, 161, 167, 172, 174, 183, 197–200.

156   Pandemic

<table>
<tr>
<td></td>
<td colspan="2">'Normal led to this'
(Ed Young – British science journalist).</td>
</tr>
<tr>
<td>👥</td>
<td colspan="2">All ages. Large groups, or pairs/solo for work on isolation monologues.</td>
</tr>
<tr>
<td>🚩</td>
<td colspan="2">Workshops/games: Fear. Guide me. Grief.
The world is temporarily closed! The pandemic has killed millions worldwide A powerful stimulus in itself, another is the isolation, loneliness and mental health issues. (Social distancing and mask wearing, relationship emotions.)
Questionnaire: What are your lasting memories of the pandemic? Negative and positive.
More controversial: The finger of blame. Did governments respond quickly enough? Conspiracy theories.</td>
</tr>
<tr>
<td>🔆</td>
<td colspan="2">What the papers say: There have been many stories in the news that inspire, inform, incite or simply frighten us!
ONS (Office for National Statistics UK). NCHS (National Center for Health Statistics USA). World Health Organisation.
Look at: How online shopping and smart technology increased in popularity during the pandemic.</td>
</tr>
<tr>
<td rowspan="6">Stimulus</td>
<td>💀</td>
<td>A face mask. Images of mass graves in Brazil. The magnified photo of the virus SARS-CoV-2. World map showing distribution of deaths/cases. Government poster/advice. An oxygen bottle. A syringe (made safe). A table set for one (isolation). Emails to loved ones.</td>
</tr>
<tr>
<td>📖

📝

🎭</td>
<td>A Journal of the Plague Year: Defoe 1.
The Andromeda Strain: Michael Crichton.
Love in the Time of Cholera: Garcia Marquez.

Ring a Ring o' Roses (traditional).

Theatre of Lockdown: Barbara Fuchs (Digital and distanced performance art).
Look at: Various publications of Lockdown and Isolation Monologues online.
What Do We Need to Talk About: Richard Nelson.</td>
</tr>
<tr>
<td>🎬</td>
<td>In time there will no doubt be movies. There are many movies already out there which deal with similar scenarios.
Contagion: 2011 (12A).
Songbird: 2020 (15).</td>
</tr>
<tr>
<td>🎵</td>
<td>Let Your Love Be Known: U2 (Video Edit) (YouTube).
Six Feet Apart: Luke Combs.
Living in a Ghost Town: The Rolling Stones.</td>
</tr>
<tr>
<td>🎨</td>
<td>Nature medicine. Art in a pandemic: a digital gallery. nature.com. We looked at famous portraits wearing masks.
Look at: The glass sculptures of Luke Jerram (Covid inspired art). Research the Covid inspired street art (Graffiti) around the world.</td>
</tr>
<tr>
<td>🎭</td>
<td>Ensemble, social distancing and dance. The sorrow of separation, isolation and death. White sheets and Black staging. Theatre masks and Covid masks. Miss You by The Rolling Stones. Monologues and testimonies.</td>
</tr>
<tr>
<td>⚠️</td>
<td colspan="2">Most students will know someone affected by the pandemic.</td>
</tr>
<tr>
<td>🔗</td>
<td colspan="2">004, 019, 033, 052, 057, 060, 064, 066, 068, 071, 085, 092, 101, 102, 104, 110, 15, 119, 126, 130, 133, 147, 152, 157, 160, 176, 184, 187, 189, 197.</td>
</tr>
</table>

157   Shadows

	'Beware that you do not lose the substance by grasping at the shadow' (Aesop – Ancient Greek storyteller).	
	14+ Small groups.	
	Workshops/games *Mirror image. Tension.* Use stage lighting (or improvise) to create shadows. Drama studio/stage space is ideal. Experiment with your shadow. **Look at the language:** Sayings about shadows. How many are positive/negative? To cast a shadow! Like a bad conscience or a faithful dog, they follow us everywhere.	
	BBC Bitesize science. Light and Shadows. **Research**: Chinese/Thai Shadow Puppets. Try making your own. Shakespeare's shadows. Look at the shadows on the walls of Hiroshima (Unit 007).	
Stimulus		Use images of shadows Why are they usually dark in subject? Experiment with making shadows with your hands. Tell a story.
		Shadows are a literary term/device. Foreshadowing for example. *Shadows:* Tim Bowler.
		My Shadow: Robert Louis Stevenson.
		Walking with Shadows: Ben Myers. Look at foreshadowing in *Romeo and Juliet* and *Macbeth*. PUCK 'If we shadows have offended', *A Midsummer Night's Dream*.
		Look at the shadows in *Ghost It* 1990 (15) (spirits from hell). The *Shadow* series of 1940's movies and the many re-makes/spin offs.
		Shadows Fall: The Proclaimers. *Have You Seen Your Mother, Baby? (Standing in the Shadow):* The Rolling Stones. *I See a Darkness:* Jonny Cash.
		Look at shadows in photography. These photographers: Mayer George, Natasha Lee. Cheryl Ramalho and Elena Dijour.
	Opportunities for shadow puppets. Great work with long shadows across stage and cyclorama. Ensemble, dance, Lecoq. Creation of tension suspense (*The Woman in Black*). Ghost/horror stories.	
	Shadows are often associated with the darker side of human nature/psyche.	
	007, 011, 012, 017, 031–035, 039, 040, 042, 044, 047, 049, 055, 059, 064, 071, 084, 088, 097, 107, 109, 117, 123, 134, 153, 156, 158, 159, 166, 176, 192.	

158   Light (the absence of darkness)

		'There is a crack in everything. That's how the light gets in' (Leonard Cohen – Canadian poet and singer-songwriter).
👥	14+ Works well as an ensemble piece with a class split with Unit 159 on Darkness.	
🏳	A dark space. **Workshops/games:** *In the spotlight. Energy games.* **Look at the Language:** 'Light at the end of the tunnel.' 'I am the resurrection and the light.' To shed light upon. Come into the light. Let there be light.	
💡	In many cultures light is an ancient symbol of understanding and thought. Exposure to natural light is good for us. Vitamin D. *Limits of Light – The Secrets of Nature* (YouTube). An excellent resource. **Research:** Diwali, The Festival of Lights.	
Stimulus	🔦	A torch, a candle, a light bulb, theatre lamps, a light switch, a miner's lamp. Image of the sun. Mirrors.
	📖	*The Left Hand of Darkness:* Ursula K. Le Guin. *Playing with Light and Shadows:* Jennifer Boothroyd.
	📝	*Light is the Left Hand of Darkness:* Ursula K. Le Guin.
	🎭	*Dark Comedy:* Peter Shaffer. *The Light:* Loy Webb. **Look at:** How lighting in the theatre is used to indicate time, location and communicate meaning, both abstract and symbolic. Light, seeking light, doth light of light beguile. *Love's Labour's Lost*, Act 1, Scene 1.
	📽	*The Wake of Light:* 2019. *Limits of Light – The Secrets of Nature:* YouTube. The Pixar shorts collection. YouTube. *Luxo Jr.* Light and Dark TV mini-series 2013.
	🎵	*Here Comes the Sun:* The Beatles. *In the Light:* Led Zeppelin. *There is a Light That Never Goes Out:* The Smiths.
	🎨	**Research:** Light Painting. **Look at:** The symbolic use of light in art (historically). The practice of using contrasts between light and dark, known as 'Chiaroscuro' during the Baroque period.
🎪	Both this unit and Unit 159 on Darkness, came together to present an evening of 'Light and Dark' which used lighting and costume; darkness and shadows in a high energy drama/dance ensemble piece. See also Unit 157 Shadows.	
⚠	Take care with naked flames/candles. Ensure students are protected from bright lights and black outs. Adhere to strobe light protocols.	
🔗	007, 026, 028, 033, 035, 041, 044, 050, 116, 120, 153, 157, 159, 166, 176, 179, 198.	

159   Darkness (the absence of light)

	'So the darkness shall be light, and the stillness the dancing' (T. S. Elliot – English author).
♟	14+ Works well as an ensemble piece with a class split with Unit 158 on Light.
⚑	**Workshops/games**: *Fear, Levels of tension.* A darkened space. Use minimal light to highlight how dark the rest of the space is. A small spotlight/torch beam. Why is darkness a metaphor for evil? **Look at the language**: The dark ages. His dark period. A dark horse. Dark days ahead. In the dark. A shot in the dark. A dark cloud. The Dark Net. Dark matter.
💡	**Look at**: How newspapers use the word dark/darkness. **Research**: The experiments of Michel Siffre on humans deprived of light. **Search for**: Scotobiology. How does light and lack of light affect our mental health? **Look at**: Kurayami Matsuri. Tokyo's Darkness festival.

Stimulus		
	☠	Look at light colours and dark colours. Reflective and non-reflective surfaces. Images of night time, the moon. A candle, as a symbol of light which defines darkness.
	📖	*Darkness:* John Saul. *Into the Darkness:* Harry Turtledove. *The Left Hand of Darkness:* Ursula K. Le Guin.
	✍	*Darkness:* Lord Byron.
	🎭	*Dark Comedy:* Peter Shaffer. **Look at**: Dark Comedies like, *The Dumb Waiter* Harold Pinter, or the dark humour in Theresa Ikoko's *Girls*. *Playboy of The Western World:* J. M. Synge. **Look at**: The images/sounds of darkness in *Macbeth*.
	🎬	*The Darkness:* 2016 (15). *Dancer in the Dark:* 2000 (15). *Night on Earth:* Netflix. *Light and Dark:* 2013 (TV mini series).
	🎵	*I See a Darkness:* Jonny Cash. *Beware of Darkness:* George Harrison. *Darkness on the Edge of Town:* Bruce Springsteen. *Darkness:* Eminem.
	🎨	**Look at**: Goya's *Saturn Devouring His Son*, or Van Gogh's *Skull with a Burning Cigarette. Death And Life* by Gustav Klimt is full of colour yet it's so dark!

🎭	See Unit 158 Light, the absence of darkness.
⚠	Beware of some images/content on the web tagged darkness. Take all precautions when using blackout states with students
🔗	032, 034, 042, 044, 071, 091, 103, 109, 117, 120, 153, 157, 166, 176, 179, 184, 192.

160   Stereotypes

	'Don't live up to your stereotypes' (Sherman Alexie – Native American author and film-maker).
⚭♀	Works well at all levels. Groups of 2–5.
🏳	**Workshops/games:** *Stereotypes. Soundscapes. Body sculpture.* **Questionnaire:** Name some modern stereotypes and describe them. They might include: a nerd, a racist, a bully, an overstressed mum/dad, a nosey neighbour . . . Think about gender stereotypes, racial and cultural stereotypes, are they ever positive?
☀	Stock characters are a feature of Commedia Dell'arte (Unit 143) and were instantly recognisable to audiences. **What the papers say:** Look at how the tabloids in particular – sexualise (stereotype) women. **More controversial:** Look at the history of the roles black men and women played in early movies. But also how some persist today . . . In movies Asian people are 'foreign', Russians are criminals and Arab men are villains. Is a stereotype just a cliché?
Stimulus	
	💀 Stereotypical objects/images by association: a walking stick, clown mask, a pair of aviator sunglasses, a pair of jackboots, a hand-held mirror . . .
	📕 *Notes of a Native Son:* James Baldwin. *White Oleander:* Janet Fitch. For younger students, *Red: A Crayon's Story:* Michael Hall.
	📝 *A Little History:* David Lehman.
	🎭 *Mother Figure:* Alan Ayckbourn. *Teechers:* John Godber. *Woyzeck:* Georg Büchner. **Think about:** Shakespeare's SHYLOCK.
	🎬 *Hillbilly Elegy:* 2020 (15). *Bend It Like Beckham:* 2002 (12). *Moonlight:* 2016 (15).
	🎵 *Boys:* Britney Spears. *Stereotype:* The Specials. *The Lumberjack Song:* Monty Python.
	🎨 Look at the photographic art of Lubo Sergeev.
🎭	Stereotyping people is a theatrical device. Comic stereotypes can often be used to highlight a bully, dictator or problems within a system. Brecht. Berkoff ideas of exaggerated movement/characteristics for the stereotype/caricature. Also consider work which challenges stereotypes.
⚠	Stereotyping is widely seen in a negative light, however as actors we display traits as clues to characters and their thoughts/emotions. Whether using stereotypes or challenging them, ensure students have a well-defined set of balanced artistic intentions.
🔗	008, 016–021, 031, 032, 034, 043, 044, 047, 054, 060, 062, 066, 068, 072, 078, 079, 088, 096, 097, 106, 112, 115, 129, 134, 138, 143, 145, 173, 182, 184, 189, 190, 191, 195, 196, 197, 199, 200.

161   The Outsider

		'Outsiders often have an insight that an insider doesn't quite have' (Diane Abbott – British Labour MP).
♟		11+ Suits larger mixed groups.
⚑		**Workshops/games.** *Alienation. Third person narration.* Questionnaire: When have you been or been made to feel like, an outsider? Describe those feelings.
☼		**Discuss:** Types of outsider. The outsider who arrives and finds their place at once, right at the centre of a community. The outsider whose arrival changes everything within the community. And finally the outsider who is never able to become an insider . . . Can we fit these characters to real life situations/events and/or movies/novels/plays? What makes an outsider? Being different? Positive/negative aspects. How an outsider affects a plot.
Stimulus	🎭	A mask. Five yellow Lego figures and one red.
	📖	*Stranger in a Strange Land:* Robert Heinlein. *The Bluest Eye:* Toni Morrison. *The Outsiders:* S. E. Hinton.
	✍	*Outsider:* James Berry.
	🎭	*The Homecoming:* Harold Pinter. *Tomorrow I'll Be Happy:* Jonathan Harvey. *The Playboy of the Western World:* J. M. Synge
	🎞	*Divergent:* 2014 (12A). *Diary of a Wimpy Kid:* 2010 (PG). *The Elephant Man:* 1980 (AA).
	🎵	*Outsider:* Rachel Grae. *Oh You Pretty Things:* David Bowie. *A Strange Boy:* Joni Mitchell.
	🎨	**Look at:** 'Outsider Art' Naïve works by untrained artists. **Research:** The Henry Boxer Gallery.
🎭		Character work. Stanislavski. Use of levels and areas of light and darkness. Brechtian elements. Movement/dance ensemble. DV8/Frantic Assembly. Proxemics/status. Berkoff/Lecoq. Mask work.
⚠		Be aware of issues/relationships within groups.
🔗		008, 009, 013, 016, 020, 021, 023, 028, 064, 069, 071, 088, 095, 106, 107, 108, 112, 134, 155, 160, 171, 172, 173, 180, 184, 186, 187, 190, 191, 192, 196, 197, 199, 200.

162   AI (Artificial intelligence)

		'Artificial intelligence is no match for natural stupidity' (Albert Einstein – German-American physicist).
👥	11+ Small groups 3–5.	
🚩	**Workshops/games**: *The pointing game, Super objective. Third person narration. Silent screams.* Smart? The ability to think and learn. Science fiction or fact? The Tin Man in *The Wizard of Oz?* Can machines think? What makes a machine intelligent? Can it feel emotions? Will they take over?	
💡	**Research**: The history of AI (The rise of the Machine!). From Alan Turing to the present day, the age of 'Big Data!'. AI app called Dream from WOMBO studios. **What the papers say**: Look at the fear/concerns expressed in the press by former advocates and developers. artificialintelligence-news.com AI News. art-ai.io Artificial intelligence festival. **Look at**: The creation and uses of Avatars. Google has Google AI. ai.google/education/ ChatGPT	
Stimulus	💀	Images of robots, *I Robot*. Alexa and Siri. Self-driving cars. Our email spam filters and even Netflix viewing recommendations.
	📖 ✒️	*The Prey Of Gods*: Nicky Drayden. *Machines Like Me*: Ian McEwan. *I Have No Mouth and I Must Scream*: Harlan Ellison (see YouTube video). *Artificial Intelligence*: Susan T. Aparejo.
	🎭	*Improbotics*: a co-creation by robotics researchers from around the world. An improvised theatre experiment. See improbotics.org Robo-drama. *AI*: Chinonyerem Odimba and Nina Segal alongside GPT-3. *Genesis Fellow* and The Young Vic (directed by Jennifer Tang).
	🎬 🎵 🎨	*AI*: 2001 (12). *I Robot*: 2004 (12A) *The Mitchells vs The Machine*: 2021 (PG). The *Terminator*: Films (16). **Look at**: Music/songs created/generated by AI. Example, research AI and Nirvana or the Eurovision song created by AI 'Blue Jeans and Bloody Tears.' **Look at**: The work of Mauro Martino (Visual AI Lab). Lauren McCarthy. Harold Cohen.
🎭	A household machine, like a toaster becoming self-aware. Dance to give the machine freedom and projected images for vision/imagination of 'the machine'. Alone in a darkened kitchen, Siri reaches out to Alexa. 'Hello? Is anyone there?' A mono/duologue. Use AI platforms to generate ideas/suggestions on themes. Combining ideas. Getting AI Apps to write monologues on given topics.	
⚠️	Be aware of age restrictions on some AI applications. As with any search your input prompts should be precise. Any use of AI should be recognised.	
🔗	074, 125, 151, 152, 161, 164, 165, 173, 193.	

163 Change

<table>
<tr>
<td></td>
<td></td>
<td colspan="2">'Change in all things is sweet'
(Aristotle – Classical Greek philosopher).</td>
</tr>
<tr>
<td>⚥</td>
<td colspan="3">11+ Small groups.</td>
</tr>
<tr>
<td>🚩</td>
<td colspan="3">Improv is about accepting change. In Pairs try some simple exercises.
A walks across the space, B forces A to change of direction. What's the result? A ended up somewhere else? How did B effect this change?
Questionnaire: Define different kinds of change. Which are good? Which make us uncomfortable?
Take a well-known script and try changing a line, a stage direction, a super objective, the pace or even a slight difference in inflection, discuss the results.
Older students: Try walking through Hamlet's soliloquy 'To be or not to be'. Change direction, with each punctuation. What does this tell us about his state of mind?</td>
</tr>
<tr>
<td>💡</td>
<td colspan="3">Look at the language: A change for the better. Better change your ways! A welcome change, A leopard never changes his spots. A change of scenery. A change is as good as a rest. A change of role, or circumstance. Climate change!
A costume change, a scene/set/location or lighting change. A change of mood, mind, direction, intention, inflection or pace.
Mahatma Gandhi said, 'Be the change that you wish to see in the world'.
The changes our bodies go through.</td>
</tr>
<tr>
<td rowspan="6">Stimulus</td>
<td>☠</td>
<td colspan="2">A clock. A mirror. A letter. A diary/calendar. A map.</td>
</tr>
<tr>
<td>📖</td>
<td colspan="2">Great Expectations: Charles Dickens.
The Water Knife: Paolo Bacigalupi.
Cider With Rosie: Laurie Lee.</td>
</tr>
<tr>
<td>📝</td>
<td colspan="2">All the World's a Stage: William Shakespeare.</td>
</tr>
<tr>
<td>🎭</td>
<td colspan="2">Britannia Waves the Rules: Gareth Farr (How war changes a man).
Metamorphosis: Berkoff, adaptation of Kafka.
Pygmalion: George Bernard Shaw.</td>
</tr>
<tr>
<td>🎞</td>
<td colspan="2">Inside Out: 2015 (U).
About Time: 2013 (12A).
The Butterfly Effect: 2004 (15).</td>
</tr>
<tr>
<td>🎵</td>
<td colspan="2">Changes: David Bowie.
A Change Is Gonna Come: Sam Cooke.
The Times They Are A-Changin': Bob Dylan</td>
</tr>
<tr>
<td></td>
<td>🎨</td>
<td colspan="2">The Obliteration Room: Yayoi Kusama.</td>
</tr>
<tr>
<td>🏛</td>
<td colspan="3">Dynamic, movement based. Frantic Assembly. Multi role and character work.
Expressionism, Lecoq and Artaud, stylised mime. Masks.</td>
</tr>
<tr>
<td>⚠</td>
<td colspan="3">Some changes in student's lives/bodies may cause embarrassment.</td>
</tr>
<tr>
<td>🔗</td>
<td colspan="3">001, 002, 007, 008, 025, 031, 038, 050, 056, 057, 067, 071, 073, 076, 077, 088, 106, 110, 113, 114, 123, 124, 132, 142, 148, 150, 152, 153, 175, 177–184, 192, 196, 199, 200.</td>
</tr>
</table>

164   Alexa, who is Siri?

		'Once a new technology rolls over you, if you're not part of the steamroller, you're part of the road' (Stewart Brand – American writer).
		Suits all ages. Small groups.
		Workshops/games; *Third person narration. Control games.* The day from Alexa's point of view. **Questionnaire:** Do you use Alexa, Siri or Google assistant? How many smart devices are in your home and how often do you interact with them? The smart speaker is now the most popular smart home device, How well does it know you? The more human they sound, the more we expect of them . . . discuss. Enact/recall the conversations you have with Alexa and co.
		Research: How the pandemic increased the sales of smart technology for the home. **What the papers say:** Smart News with the Smithsonian Magazine. Do Alexa and family learn manners from us, or do we just demand? **More controversial:** Is the gender/accent/ethnicity of your machine important? Have you changed it, and if so why?
Stimulus		Mainly audio. Those familiar commands. 'Hey Siri', 'Ok Google', 'Alexa, . . .'
		Fiction predicted many things we accept today. *1984:* George Orwell. *2001 A Space Odyssey:* Arthur C. Clarke. *Neuromancer:* William Gibson.
		Ode to Technology: Tien Dang.
		Henceforward: Alan Ayckbourn. *1984:* Icke and Macmillan (based on the 1949 novel by Orwell). *Improbotics:* See improbotics.org
		Ghost in the Shell: 1995 (15). *Ex Machina:* 2014 (15). *The Man in the White Suit:* 1951 (U).
		Paranoid Android: Radiohead. *Virtual Insanity:* Jamiroquai. *Rise Up Alexa:* Ariel Sharratt and Mathias Kom.
		For fun. **Search for:** Famous paintings updated with 21st Century gadgets. Also look at how smart technology is being used in museums and galleries.
		Students loved the idea of the stimulus, *Alone in a darkened kitchen, Siri reaches out to Alexa.* *'Hello? Is anyone there?'* Or, look at how we will treat our smart assistants in the future and that one day Alexa may have rights. Very 'techie' or a simple set on a plain/bleak stage.
		Access to Smart technology, like all access to the web should be monitored. Protect privacy
		025, 027, 030, 055, 068, 072, 076, 085, 086, 092, 093, 097, 099, 102, 104, 109, 110, 123, 125, 151, 152, 156, 161, 162, 163, 165, 166, 179, 181, 185, 187, 196, 198.

165 Virtual reality

	'Once you have perfect virtual reality, what else are you supposed to perfect?' (Palmer Luckey – American entrepreneur and inventor).
⚙	11+ All Abilities.
🚩	**Workshops/games;** *Trust games. Super objective.* Fill a space with auditory and visual reality sounds/projections. Blindfold older students and let them identify sounds/feels/smells. Which emotions are easier to recreate virtually? Look at the idea of going on holiday without leaving home.
☼	Science fiction to science fact. **Research:** Possible future uses in pain relief and the treatment of PTSD. **What the papers say:** *New York Times* article on the VR version of *The Tempest.* July 2020. **Look at:** Immersive holographics. Augmented reality.
Stimulus	☠ An old Tamagotchi toy. Projected images of virtual games. Virtual reality goggles/ flight simulator. Blindfold/headphones.
	📖 *The Eye of the Minds:* James Dashner. *Ready Player One:* Ernest Cline. *Neuromancer:* William Gibson. *Storytelling for Virtual Reality:* John Bucher.
	✍ Ask students to write a verse of poetry about their take on Virtual Reality and share.
	🎭 See Beckettian experiments in Virtual Reality. Trinity College Dublin. *Chatroom:* Enda Walsh.
	🎞 The *Lawnmower Man:* films 1 and 2 1992, and 1996 (15 and12). *The Holodeck in Star Trek Next Gen.* *The Matrix* films: 1999 onwards (15). *Reverie:* NBC Science fiction series.
	🎵 Apart from music/songs about VR, many artists/music producers and companies are beginning to involve us in the VR Music experience (see music based VR apps and visualisers). Examples: Intone – Sing. *Virtual Insanity:* Jamiroquai.
	🎨 The notion that art is virtual reality. Look at the augmented reality galleries used during the pandemic. The Van Gogh Immersive experience.
🎭	Works well in the round. Minimal with levels. Frantic style physical work with the changes between fantasy and reality. Imaginary Body. Kneehigh.
⚠	Some virtual reality games contain graphic violence and adult content.
🔗	014, 033, 074, 092, 125, 152, 162, 164, 185, 193.

166   The Weather

<table>
<tr><td></td><td colspan="2"> 'Weather permitting'
(idiom). </td></tr>
<tr><td>☕♀
☯</td><td colspan="2">Any age. Good opportunities for large ensemble pieces.</td></tr>
<tr><td>🚩</td><td colspan="2">Workshops/games: Energy games. Levels of tension. Soundscapes.
Listen to a radio weather forecast. Use SFX of different weather. What do you feel at each sound?
People spend a disproportionate amount of time discussing the weather. We watch the forecast at least twice a day. It influences our plans, our mood, our day. The weather App is on every smartphone as standard and it comes with a 10-day forecast.</td></tr>
<tr><td>🔆</td><td colspan="2">The early Greeks (Aristotle) wrote a summary of meteorology back in 340 BC.
Research: Luke Howard (The Father of Meteorology).
The Tate has a great student resource 'Weather Coursework Guide'.
AMS American Meteorological Society. RMetS Royal Meteorological Society.
What the papers say: Weather headlines; why are they always so dramatic?
Look at: How many beliefs and rituals there are around the world associated with the weather. Think about all the sayings/proverbs about the weather?</td></tr>
<tr><td rowspan="7">Stimulus</td><td>🗺️</td><td>Weather maps and forecasts. Umbrellas, Wellington boots, scarfs, sunglasses and sun tan lotion.</td></tr>
<tr><td>📖</td><td>Weather plays an important role in many novels. To set the mood, to build tension/ suspense, atmosphere and even the pace. Consider: The drought in Steinbeck's Grapes of Wrath. The lightning in Nabokov's Lolita. The mud and rain in Dickens's Bleak House. The storm in Brontë's Wuthering Heights.</td></tr>
<tr><td>📝</td><td>Look at: How Wilfred Owen uses the weather in his war poetry.</td></tr>
<tr><td>🎭</td><td>Neville's Island: Tim Firth.
The Play of the Weather: John Heywood.
Before special effects/lighting, Shakespeare described the weather through words. The howling winds in The Tempest. The thunder and lightning in King Lear. The heat turning to hatred in Romeo and Juliet. The weather on the moor when MACBETH and BANQUO first encounter the WITCHES.</td></tr>
<tr><td>🎬</td><td>The Aeronauts: 2019 (PG).
Groundhog Day: 1993 (PG).
The Perfect Storm: 2000 (12).</td></tr>
<tr><td>🎵</td><td>The Wind Cries Mary: Jimi Hendrix.
Like a Hurricane: Neil Young.
Riders on the Storm: The Doors.
Chopin's Raindrop Prelude. Op. 28, No 15.</td></tr>
<tr><td>🎨</td><td>Reaper with Wheat Field and Sun: Van Gogh. Sunrise: Georgia O'Keefe.
Trees in the Sun, Cyprus: David Bomberg.
Search for: Abstract weather photography (images).</td></tr>
<tr><td>🎭</td><td colspan="2">Weather sound effects work as a great inspiration.
Dance/physical pieces involving large ensemble casts.
Extreme world weather events. Projections.</td></tr>
<tr><td>⚠️</td><td colspan="2">Requires strong artistic intention.</td></tr>
<tr><td>🔗</td><td colspan="2">030, 031, 055, 056, 065, 071, 076, 095, 103, 107, 111, 112, 116, 117, 120, 121, 125, 151, 153, 157, 158, 159, 168, 176–179, 181, 182, 183, 192, 196.</td></tr>
</table>

167 Desert(ed) Island

	'The world, that understandable and lawful world, was slipping away' (William Golding – British novelist, poet and playwright) *Lord of the Flies.*
⚇	All ages. Mixed groups of 4 upwards.
⚑	**Workshops/games**; *Control games. Fear.* Create an isolated space. Perhaps a lit/staged area, or a suitable outside space. Teacher in role with younger students. They are on an island with no immediate hope of rescue (yours to embellish!). A reading from chapter one of Golding's *Lord of the Flies* is a good start. Lighting for bright sunlight/greenery and heat and suitable SFX help create the mood/atmosphere. Younger students may want to be in a group on their island. Older students can explore loneliness with monologue/soliloquy.
☼	If you had to write one message in a bottle, who would you write to? What would you say? Take the 'Desert Island Discs Challenge' BBC Radio4. Describe loneliness on your island. List the pros and cons of living on a desert island.

Stimulus		
	☠	A letter folded up in a bottle.
	📖	*Lord of the Flies:* William Golding. *The Blue Lagoon:* Henry de Vere Stacpoole. *Robinson Crusoe:* Daniel Defoe.
	✍	*The Lake Isle of Innisfree:* W. B. Yeats.
	🎭	*Neville's Island:* Tim Firth. *Lord of the Flies (Acting Edition):* Adapted by Nigel Williams. *The Tempest:* William Shakespeare.
	🎞	*Cast Away:* 2000 (12). *Robinson Crusoe:* 1997 (PG-13). *Lord of the Flies:* 1963 British original or 1990 US re-make.
	🎵	*Message in a Bottle:* Sting.
	🎨	*The Ninth Wave:* Ivan Aivazovsky. *The Gulf Stream:* Winslow Homer

🎭	Lots of physical work. DV8. Some great opportunities for set design and lighting. Monologues.
⚠	Students may be influenced/side tracked by *Love Island* and some celebrity/reality shows.
🔗	025, 034, 042, 048, 054, 065, 074, 076, 084, 084, 088, 089, 094, 095, 103, 110, 111, 112, 123, 149, 155, 161, 182, 183.

168   Chaos

		'You must have chaos within you to give birth to a dancing star' (Friedrich Nietzsche – German philosopher).
♟♟		12+ Suits large groups.
⚑		**Workshops/games**: *Control. Energy games.* Ensemble/group building games, moving as one, finding moments of stillness. Lots of energy and pace. Experiment with calm and chaos, with the chaos in improvised comedy, dance and music. Chaos in nature. The butterfly effect. Chaos theory was first defined by James Yorke and T.Y. Li in 1975.
☀		**Look at the language**: Strike causes chaos! A life in chaos. Total chaos. Chaos and destruction. They appear to be mainly negative. **Research**: The chaos theory in mathematics and physics. **Look at**: Chaos/Magic in The Marvel universe.
Stimulus	☠	Projection of the butterfly effect.
	📖	*Chaos: Making a New Science*: James Gleick. *Does God Play Dice? The New Mathematics of Chaos*: Ian Stewart. *Lord of Chaos*: Robert Jordan.
	✍	*The World in Chaos*: Nosheen Irfan.
	🎭	*Disco Pigs*: Enda Walsh. Theatre of the Absurd (disorderly chaos).
	🎬	*Chaos Theory*: 2007 (PG-13). *The Butterfly Effect*: 2004 (15). *The Secret Life of Chaos*: 2010 (Documentary).
	🎵	*Chaotic*: Tate McRae. *Dazed and Confused*: Led Zeppelin.
	🎨	Images of fractals. The conflict of chaos and harmony in art.
🎭		Great ensemble piece, choreographed physical theatre/unison and coordinated movement. DV8, Frantic Assembly. Gecko, mime work. Pig Iron. Multimedia, projections of the butterfly effect/fractals . . . SFX, music. Dance based on images of fractals. Acrobatics, Parkour.
⚠		Risk assess the very physical work . . . Onstage what seems like chaos should be carefully choreographed.
🔗		025, 026, 038, 055, 056, 061, 071, 074, 076, 097, 103, 113, 114, 116, 121, 125, 146, 151, 154, 156, 162, 163, 166, 169, 170, 177, 196.

169   Science v Religion

<table>
<tr>
<td></td>
<td colspan="2">'Science without religion is lame; (and) religion without science is blind'
(Albert Einstein – German-American physicist).</td>
</tr>
<tr>
<td>⚭</td>
<td colspan="2">14+ Small groups.</td>
</tr>
<tr>
<td>⚑</td>
<td colspan="2">Workshops/games: The pointing game. Control games
Project images of the milky way onto a ceiling/wall. On another (or in turn), project images of The Sistine Chapel. Do we have to choose one? Darwin or Genesis? Faith v Reason. Allegorical or literal?
Discuss.</td>
</tr>
<tr>
<td>💡</td>
<td colspan="2">The Fitzwilliam Museum.cam.ac.uk Endless Forms: Charles Darwin, Natural Science and the Visual Arts (an Exhibition).
The Natural History Museum London (The Darwin Collection) view online.
Research: Newspaper headlines for 24 November 1854. The Scopes Monkey Trial.
Search for: Charles Darwin – BBC News
Many faiths have other versions of the creation. Check the similarities and differences.</td>
</tr>
<tr>
<td rowspan="7">Stimulus</td>
<td>☠</td>
<td>Search for: Images of Evolution of Man. Then images of Adam and Eve.
These work as a great visual starting point.
A microscope. A Bible.</td>
</tr>
<tr>
<td>📖</td>
<td>The Origin of Species.
The Book of Genesis.
Evolution vs. Creationism: Eugenie C. Scott.
Science and Earth History: Arthur Strahler.
God's Own Scientists: Christopher Toumey.</td>
</tr>
<tr>
<td>✍</td>
<td>If Only We Had Taller Been: Ray Bradbury.</td>
</tr>
<tr>
<td>🎭</td>
<td>The Mysteries: Tony Harrison (and other Mystery plays).
The Creation of the World and Other Business: Arthur Miller.
Trumpery: Peter Parnell.</td>
</tr>
<tr>
<td>🎬</td>
<td>A Matter of Faith: 2014.
Creation: 2009 (PG).
God's Not Dead: 2014 (PG).
The Monkey Suit: The Simpsons, Season 17, E21.
Charles Darwin and the Tree of Life: A 2009 David Attenborough Documentary.</td>
</tr>
<tr>
<td>🎵</td>
<td>Horrible Histories 'Charles Darwin Evolution Song': YouTube.
Missa Charles Darwin: Gregory Brown.
Part Man, Part Monkey: Bruce Springsteen.
It Began in Africa: The Chemical Brothers.</td>
</tr>
<tr>
<td>🎨</td>
<td>Look at Darwin's sketches and the works of Conrad Martens.
Did Darwin influenced 'Modernism'?
Charles Darwin: Victor Molev. The Creation of Adam: Michelangelo. The Garden of Earthly Delights: Hieronymus Bosch.</td>
</tr>
<tr>
<td>🎦</td>
<td colspan="2">Allow for both science and faith, to exist on the same stage. Audience participation. Forum.
Puppets work well with some interpretations.
Frantic Assembly, highly choreographed.</td>
</tr>
<tr>
<td>⚠</td>
<td colspan="2">Be sensitive to different faiths/beliefs and cultures.</td>
</tr>
<tr>
<td>🔗</td>
<td colspan="2">007, 025, 026, 027, 028, 032, 038, 048, 050, 056, 064, 076, 107, 111, 119, 125, 132, 152, 162–165, 178, 196.</td>
</tr>
</table>

170   Time

		'Time waits for no one' (Proverbial wisdom).
⚎⚎	All age groups and abilities. A great open topic.	
🚩	**Workshops/games:** *Energy games.* Listen to *Time* by Pink Floyd. Project images of time/clock faces. Discuss the things you do with time. The words 'spend' and 'waste' come up a lot! What happens to time we waste? **Look at the language:** How many idioms are there which include the word time? Improvise a short scene based on some of them. For example; 'Time waits for no man', or 'Time and time again'.	
🔆	Nature.com The illusion of time. **Research:** The history of recording time. The history of putting the clocks forward/back. From sundial to Alexa. What's the time? Why does time only move forwards?	
Stimulus	💀	A clock, an egg timer, a sundial, a digital alarm clock the time on your mobile phone, the speaking clock, SFX clocks ticking.
	📖	*Thief of Time:* Terry Pratchett. Consider time as a literary device. Most novels and plays have a chronological, linear timeline, consider the effect of flashbacks and flashforwards.
	📝	*Days:* Philip Larkin.
	🎭	*Time and The Conways:* J. B. Priestley. Look at *flashback/forward* as a theatrical device. The play *100* is set in the present with flashbacks into each character's past. *A Memory of Lizzie* flashes forward from the 1890s.
	🎬	*Deja Vu:* 2006 (12). *Groundhog Day:* 1993 (PG). *Edge of Tomorrow:* 2014 (12A).
	🎵	*Time:* Pink Floyd. *Time:* David Bowie. *Time is on My Side:* The Rolling Stones.
	🎨	*The Persistence of Memory:* Salvador Dali. *The Black Marble Clock:* Cezanne. *Clock of the Académie Française:* Andre Kertéz (Photograph).
🎭	For young students, a physical representation of time passing, with the sounds of a clock ticking throughout a performance ending with an alarm clock: Ensemble-Le coq. Older students can look at one event but with a focus on how differently it would be viewed through the juxtaposition of time. Physical: Frantic Assembly.	
⚠️	Not to be confused with Unit 171 Time Travel.	
🔗	004, 007, 019, 027, 038, 055, 056, 057, 068, 076, 084, 107, 119, 120, 123, 125, 137, 151, 163, 171, 176, 179, 190, 192.	

171 Time Travel

		'If time travel is possible, where are the tourists from the future?' (Stephen Hawking – British theoretical physicist, cosmologist, and author).
⚑		A favourite with all ages/groups.
⚑		**Workshops/games**: *Energy games. Repetition exercises.* **Questionnaire**: If you could go anywhere in history, where would you go? And the future? What rules would you write? Design/draw your time machine. What would it feel like? What good could you do? What would be the dangers?
💡		**Research**: Traversable wormholes, cosmic strings and Alcubierre drives! Time travel, you're doing it right now! Does the past still exist? All time is happening at the same time! **What the papers say**: Crazy stories in the press from claims that Michael Jackson could time travel to puzzling Charlie Chaplin time travel film where a man passes the camera in 1928 seemingly speaking on a mobile phone! See also wired.com/tag/time-travel/ The series *Genius* by Stephen Hawking, Episode 1 'Can we time travel?'
Stimulus	🕰	Clocks/watches/hour glasses. SFX Clocks ticking. Projections/pictures of time travel fiction from 'The Tardis' *Dr Who* to 'The Wave Rider' *Legends of Tomorrow*.
	📖	*The Time Traveller's Wife:* Audrey Niffenegger. *The Time Machine:* H. G. Wells. *The End of Eternity:* Isaac Asimov.
	✍	*A Vision:* Simon Armitage.
	🎭	*Time And The Conways:* J. B. Priestley. *Throwback Thursday:* Justin Flowers. *A Snitch in Time:* Claire Demmer.
	🎬	*Time after Time* 2018 (12). *Project Almanac:* 2015 (12A). *Back to the Future:* 1985 (PG). *Dr Who:* Long running TV series 1963 to present.
	🎵	*Travellers in Time:* Uriah Heep. *Twilight:* ELO. *Time Travel:* Damien Marley. See Video, *Time Travel:* Midnight CVLT and Le Duke on YouTube.
	🎨	Ancient works of art which suggest time travellers have been here already. Several religious paintings depict strange objects. See the *Crucifixion Fresco* from Svetitskhoveli Cathedral Georgia, C16th, or *The Expected One* by Ferdinand Waldmüllerin, 1860. **Look at**: The works of Salvador Dali, *The Persistence of Memory* (Melting Clock) and others.
🎭		Wonderful sets complete with time machines! Using moving projections to show audiences you have travelled back to the time of the dinosaurs. Projections/flashing lights and SFX Fantasy. Flashback/forward.
⚠		Ensure your students return to present time before the end of the lesson!
🔗		49, 109, 114, 161, 173, 178, 196.

172   The Visitor

	'We are the visitors in the lives of others; we visit them and we disappear!' (Mehmet Murat ildan – Turkish playwright).
👥	11+ Works well with mixed groups of 4–5.
🚩	**Workshops/games**: Roleplay Improv, A family at breakfast. Decide who is who (max 4). Hand out an archetype card to each. Engage as the family for a minute or two to establish characters. A visitor arrives. . . . The visitor is free to improvise their story, the others should engage and carry the story forward. (Even the inevitable silly ideas.) The group should each have an opportunity to play the visitor and take their scenario through to a conclusion.
💡	There are good and bad visitors. The loved Grandmother, hated aunt. A police officer with news! **Look at the language**: An unwanted visitor, a welcome visitor, a frequent visitor, I'm just a visitor here, a visitor from outer space! Get students to list possible types of visitors. What is the visitor's story/purpose/news? Encourage them to share their own stories. Mary Poppins, Inspector Goole. Or it could be you're the visitor in a strange new land.

Stimulus		
	💀	A suitcase, a pair of dark sunglasses, a sealed envelope, an umbrella.
	📖	*The Visitor (A short Story)*: Roald Dahl. *The Visitor*: Ray Bradbury.
	📝	*A Constable Calls*: Seamus Heaney.
	🎭	*An Inspector Calls*: J. B. Priestley. *Entertaining Mr Sloane*: Joe Orton. *The Birthday Party*: Harold Pinter.
	🎬	*ET*: 1982 (U). *Mary Poppins*: 1964 (U).
	🎵	*Guess Who's Coming to Dinner*: Black Uhuru. *Someone's Knocking at the Door*: Paul McCartney and Wings. *Knock at the Door*: An English Children's Nursery Rhyme and song.
	🎨	*Adoration of the Shepherds*: Bartolome Esteban Murillo. *The Visit – Couple and Newcomer*: Ernst Ludwig Kirchner.

🎭	Character work, Stanislavski. Storytelling. Older/more able students can use physical theatre and experiment with exaggerated movement and reaction, creating a more surreal piece. Complicité. Lecoq.
⚠️	With young groups the visitor could be teacher in role. However, you should leave the piece as soon as possible.
🔗	008, 016, 028, 031, 034, 035, 040, 041, 042, 047, 049, 055, 057, 064, 076, 085, 088, 089, 109, 114, 122, 155, 160, 161, 171, 176, 178, 181, 184, 187, 190, 192, 196.

173 UFO's and Aliens

	'I'm sure the universe is full of intelligent life. It's just been too intelligent to come here!' (Arthur C. Clarke – British science fiction writer).
	All ages (groups of 4 or 5). Popular with younger students.
	Workshops/games: *Energy games. Alienation. Body sculptures.* **Questionnaire**: Do you believe in the existence of aliens? Draw what you think an alien might look like. Compare around the group, are there similarities. If you met an alien what would you do? Run? Stay and try to communicate, take a selfie? Split into pairs **A** and **B**. **A** can only communicate in random numbers and **B** letters. Think of other ways to communicate. If you were the alien visiting a strange planet, what would you want?
	If you **search for** 'images of aliens' there is a very obvious 'look'. The same happens with images of UFOs. Where does that look originate and does it have a basis in truth, comic book or the movies? Why are aliens so often represented in fiction as hostile? **Research**: 'Ancient Aliens'. **What the papers say**: Research reported sightings in the media. A little village school in Pembrokeshire, West Wales, got a mention in the international press in 1977, when many of the children independently reported seeing UFOs over the fields. Sci Fi is one of the most popular genres in literature and the movies. **Look at**: World UFO day, 2 July and Roswell, New Mexico, 1947. Nassa's UFO report.

Stimulus		
		Alien masks. Drawings, newspaper articles. Comic books.
		To Sleep in a Sea of Stars: Christopher Paolini. *Contact: A Novel*: Carl Sagan. *War of the Worlds*: H. G. Wells.
		The Alien: Greg Delanty.
		Return to the Forbidden Planet and *The Tempest*. There is very little theatre based on aliens from outer space, but being human, yet alien is quite a theme.
		Independence Day: 1996 (12). *Close Encounters of the Third Kind*: 1977 (A). *Arrival*: 2016 (12A).
		Starman: David Bowie. *Rocket Man*: Elton John. *Planet Claire*: The B-52s.
		The Baptism of Christ: painted in 1710 by Aert De Gelder (look in the sky!). **Look at**: Ancient cave paintings of what could be aliens.

	First encounters as dance pieces. Non-naturalistic, stylisation, use of rhythm and music, mask, the grotesque, robotics, biomechanics. Meyerhold. Character based first encounters. Great costume/makeup and SFX/lighting challenges.
⚠	There are hundreds of movies about aliens. Not all of them are suitable.
🔗	026, 040, 055, 064, 076, 088, 102, 114, 125, 132, 153, 160–163, 169, 171, 172, 184, 190, 197.

174   Human Rights

	'The rights of every man are diminished when the rights of one man are threatened' (J. F. Kennedy – American President).
👥	All ages. Small groups.
🚩	**Workshops/games;** *Status. Control games* I used Amnesty International's simplified version of the UDHR (Universal Declaration of Human Rights) and the group selected 4 or 5 of the (30) articles that they considered most important. Small group of 3–4 students put into their own words a sentence/statement, which they believed their chosen article meant. They then improvised a scene to demonstrate this.
💡	'Human rights belong to each and every one of us equally' UNICEF. *Universal Declaration of Human Rights*, United Nations 1948. UNESCO. United Nations. ECHR, (The European Convention on Human Rights).

Stimulus	💀	Poster showing the 30 articles of the UDHR. Logos connected with civil rights. For example, Amnesty International's powerful image. What does it say to you?
	📖	*The Help:* Kathryn Stockett. *Fearless Fighter:* Vera Chirwa. *Taking a Stand: The Evolution of Human Rights:* Juan E Mendez.
	📝	*I Know Why the Caged Bird Sings:* Maya Angelou.
	🎭	*Death and The Maiden:* Ariel Dorfman. *Upon the Fragile Shore:* Caridad Svich. *Ubu and the Truth Commission:* Handspring Puppet Company.
	🎞	*Morgan Freeman: The Power of Words:* An Amnesty International Video (Youtube). *Beasts of No Nation:* 2015 (15). *Five Broken Cameras:* 2011 documentary (15).
	🎵	*A Hard Rain's a-gonna Fall:* Bob Dylan. *We Shall Overcome:* Joan Baez. *Blk Girl Soldier:* Jamilla Woods.
	🎨	**Look at:** Amnesty International's *Universal Declaration of Human Rights in pictures.*

🎭	Strong character work. Proxemics. Theatre of the Oppressed. Boal. Theatre of Cruelty, movement, gesture and dance, masks and puppets, shocking the audience. Shocking action and images, striking costumes, minimal dialogue and symbolic objects. Artaud.
⚠️	Searches may bring up disturbing images and stories.
🔗	001–025, 029, 043, 044, 053, 058, 064, 066, 068, 069, 071, 079, 085, 090, 091, 092, 101, 106, 107, 108, 111, 112, 119, 121, 124–133, 137, 138, 141, 142, 146, 147, 149, 156, 175, 181, 183, 186, 187, 194, 196, 199, 200.

175 That's not fair!

	'Fairness does not mean everyone gets the same. Fairness means everyone gets what they need' (Rick Riordan – American author).
👥	Small groups/pairs. Works well with younger students.
🚩	**Workshops/games**; *Mirror image. Lying. Levels of tension.* **Questionnaire**: What do you consider unfair? Everyone in the circle gets to say 'That's not fair' but it must be given a new tone/meaning each time. Next begin with an improv (in pairs) based on the same line. So what is fair?
💡	**Look at the language**: Fair enough. Fair weather. Fair game. Fair and square. Fair trade. Fair play. All's fair in love and war. 'Fair is foul, and foul is fair.' Life's not fair. Fair of face. Look at Synonyms and Antonyms for Fairness. **More controversial**: Is life fair?
Stimulus	💀 Scales/justice.
	📖 *Amazing Grace*: Mary Hoffman (Young students). *Animal Farm*: George Orwell. *To Kill a Mockingbird*: Harper Lee.
	✍️ *It's Not Fair*: Someone.
	🎭 *Animal Farm*: George Orwell (adapted by Ian Wooldridge). *The Tempest*: Shakespeare. *The Caucasian Chalk Circle*: Brecht.
	🎞️ *12 Angry Men*: 1957 (U). *The Crucible*: 1996 (12). *Gattaca*: 1997 (15).
	🎵 *Nobody*: Ry Cooder. *You Can't always Get What You Want*: The Rolling Stones. *It Should Have Been Me*: Ray Charles.
	🎨 *Justice Scales*: Emory Douglas.
🎭	Brecht. Narration, song, break the fourth wall. Soundscapes/chanting. Ensemble. Physical, stylised, highly choreographed scenes work well.
⚠️	Avoid allowing younger students to make it too personal.
🔗	001–013, 015–021, 023, 024, 025, 027, 032, 034, 043, 052, 053, 057–064, 069–075, 077, 100, 101, 102, 105, 106–112, 117, 119, 124, 126–142, 144–150, 172, 176, 178, 183, 186, 189, 191, 192, 194, 196, 198.

176   The stories behind great paintings

		'Art is not what you see, but what you make others see' (Edgar Degas – French artist).
♟		Any age. Small groups. Work of art will dictate group size, age and makeup.
▣		**Workshops/games**; *Body sculpture.* A Famous painting (should include people). Project it onto a wall. Focus on small sections details. Students give people in the scene a history, a story, objectives, wants. Role on wall. Use Stanislavski's techniques to build a character based on the painting as a whole.
☼		The theatre of digital art exhibition of Van Gogh. Immersive websites. Not necessarily a story about what is happening in the painting, it can be influenced by the artist themselves or the time in which it was painted. The relationship between the painter and the subject.
Stimulus	☗	The painting itself is the obvious artifact. But objects from paintings too. For example, a chair from a Van Gogh. A pearl earring. A Scream Mask. An artist's pallet and brush. Set up a large table then tableau 13 people in the positions of daVinci's *The Last Supper.*
	📖	*Girl with a Pearl Earring:* Tracey Chevalier. *I Mona Lisa:* Jeanne Lakogridis. *Sunflowers:* Sheramy Bundwick.
	✍	*Cézanne's Ports:* Allen Ginsberg
	🎭	Look how the characters from Literature and Art are used in Caryl Churchill's *Top Girls.* DULL GRET. *Journey's End:* R. C. Sherriff. Paul Nash's painting, *The Menin Road*
	🎞	*Girl with a Pearl Earring:* 2003 (12A). The mask from the 2000 Movie *Scream* and Edvard Munch's painting *The Scream.* *Shutter Island:* 2010 (15), and Gustav Klimt's *The Kiss.* For costume. Look at Thomas Gainsborough's *The Blue Boy* and *Django Unchained* 2012 (18), *Pan's Labyrinth* 2006 (15) and Goya's *Saturn Devouring His Son*
	🎵	*Mona Lisa:* Nat King Cole. 'Do you smile to tempt a lover or just a way to hide your broken heart?' There's a story there! *Vincent:* Don Maclean.
	🎨	The works of Bruegel, Hieronymus Bosch, Van Gogh, Albrecht Durer. See the theatre of digital art exhibition of Van Gogh. *The Last Supper:* Leonardo da Vinci.
🎦		Immersive piece with projections of works on the walls and ceilings. Great costume and makeup opportunities. Sets can be complicated or as simple as you wish. Naturalism meets multimedia. *Katie Mitchell.* Consider Site Specific Theatre.
⚠		There is a temptation to make work very story based, with older students try to encourage more creative physical work:
🔗		074, 084, 107, 119, 123, 178.

177   Dance

		'Dancing is poetry with arms and legs' (C. Baudelaire – French author).
♥		Any age. Small groups (they don't have to be dancers!) Know your students. Use dancers to inspire others.
⚑		**Workshops/games**: *Energy games. Mirror imaging.* A powerful impulse that has to be released or a choreographed art practised by professionals? **Questionnaire**: Can you dance? Do you dance? Are you trained/training? 'What does it feel like when you're dancing?' Forms of dance . . . Dance to tell a story, dance for the pure joy of it . . . Ancient, human, sensual. How many types of dance can you name?
☼		The V & A London has a dance section in their Theatre and Performance collection. Museum of Dance and Hall of Fame, Saratoga, New York. Look at dance in different cultures/faiths. 'I am the Lord of The Dance.' Many ancient civilisations had dance rituals. International Dance day is 22 April. 5 elements of dance: Body, Action, Space, Time and Energy. *Strictly* is never far from the news!
Stimulus	☠	The list of dance costume/clothing/shoes is vast. If you're lucky enough to have a dance studio, use it.
	📖	*Dancer:* Colum McCann. *Swing Time:* Zadie Smith. *A Time to Dance:* Padma Venkatraman.
	✍	*Everybody Is Doing It:* Benjamin Zephaniah.
	🎭	*Virgins:* John Retallack. *Paper Flowers:* Egon Wolff. *Billy Elliot:* Lee Hall. *Fosse:* The Musical.
	🎞	*Footloose:* 1984 (12A) *Black Swan:* 2010 (15). *Billy Elliot:* 2000 (15). *Hairspray:* 2007 (PG).
	🎵	*Electricity:* from *Billy Elliot.* *Just Dance:* Lady Gaga. *Twist and Shout:* The Beatles. *Dancing in The Dark:* Bruce Springsteen. Listen to various types of *Dance Music*: Tango, Salsa, Baroque, Jazz etc. . . .
	🎨	**Look at**: The International Dance day video 2022 in front of The Guernica (YouTube). *'The Dance'*: Roy Lichtenstein.
🎭		Great opportunities for Grotowski based physical pieces. Other influences like Frantic Assembly. The Late Great DV8 (resources still available). The work of Eddie Ladd and dance ensemble work. Ballet, Jazz and Tap. Watch the DV8 video 'To be straight with you' Rehearsal Footage
⚠		With so much raw dance talent and training among students, it is important to have a clear artistic intent from the start. Often pieces become a series of solos which although entertaining, can become disjointed.
🔗		025, 029, 032, 033, 047, 055, 056, 060, 087, 090, 107, 116, 123, 149, 163, 179, 181, 191, 196.

178   Literature

	'Great literature is simply language charged with meaning to the utmost possible degree' (Ezra Pound – American poet).
	All ages but suits younger students. Groups of 4–6.
	Workshops/games*: Story circle.* **Questionnaire:** What is your favourite story, and why? Great literature is storytelling. Choose a story they are familiar or studying in English/Lit. Take a moment/passage from the text and treat it as a beginning/end of a new story. Invite students to get in role and ask them to re-tell that moment, improvise a key section.
	Look at the language: Of Literature, how it has deeply influenced media and media reporting. Common expressions have their roots in great literature; *'The best laid plans of mice and men'*, *'The lady doth protest too much'*, *'After all, tomorrow is another day'*, *'Do not go gentle into that good night'*. *'Frankly my dear, I don't give a damn'*.

Stimulus		Use the imagery of the chosen text/texts. Plenty of costume and mask to mix it up!
		For younger students I have used *Skellig*: David Almond and *The Nature of The Beast*: Janni Howker. For older students I have taken classical literature, *Jane Eyre*, *Silas Marner* or some Dickens. Historical novels are great fun for character work.
		Many great plays began life as a novel. *39 Steps, Lord of the Flies, The Curious Incident of the Dog in the Night-Time, Cabaret, War Horse, Wicked!* (Adaptations).
		Films which have been adapted from books can give a new angle on the novel. The *Harry Potter* series. *War of the Worlds*: 2005 (PG13). *Lord of the Flies*: 1963.
		Theme tunes from the MCU and DC movies. The *Harry Potter* Score. Wagner's *Flight of the Valkyries* – in *Apocalypse Now*.
		Ophelia, Sir John Everett Millais inspired by Shakespeare's *Hamlet*. *Mad Tea Party*, Salvador Dalí, inspired by Lewis Carol's *Alice in Wonderland*. *Don Quixote*: Pablo Picasso, inspired by Cervantes's *Don Quixote de la Mancha*. *The Lady of Shalott*: John William Waterhouse, inspired by Tennyson's poem '*The Lady of Shalott*'.

	Students took familiar characters and gave them new stories. Great physical theatre. Narration. Opportunities for work with mask/puppet. Emma Rice, Polly Teal, Marianne Elliot. See also the use of Rosetti's Goblin Market in Unit 097
	Keep it simple. Don't retell the entire story. Look at a moment and take it somewhere else. Younger students need a strong framework.
	006, 029, 032, 039, 044, 047, 049, 076, 088, 101, 109, 123, 129, 139, 149, 157, 167, 171, 173, 176, 181–184, 186, 190, 191, 192, 196, 197, 198.

179 Music

	'Music is the shorthand of emotion' (Tolstoy – Russian writer).
👥	All ages. Mixed groups.
🚩	**Workshops/games**: *Energy games. Mirror imaging* Move/dance to different types of music and reflect/discuss how each piece makes you feel. From the movements, write a stream of consciousness and made sketches. Choose any contrasting pieces (I keep it to 4). There are suggestions in the music/song section below.
💡	Music has been documented by man since the early Palaeolithic period. BBC Howard Goodall's *Story of Music: The age of Discovery* (YouTube). Naxos records has produced a great resource on the history of classical music. Use the music specialists in your school/college. **Look at**: How directors like Baz Luhrmann and Quentin Tarantino use music in their movies.
Stimulus	

	🎛	Musical instruments, borrowed from the music department. Encourage students to experiment with the sounds and suggest moods for different instruments/sounds. Sheet music.
	📖	*The Gunners*: Rebecca Kauffman. *Song of the Lark*: Willa Cather. *Norwegian Wood*: Haruki Murakami.
	✍	*Ode to a Nightingale*: John Keats.
	🎭	*Twelfth Night*: William Shakespeare. I have always used music in school productions, even when none is called for. It should be chosen sensitively, to complement without distracting or overpowering.
	🎞	*Fantasia*: 1940 (U). *The Piano*: 1993 (15). *The Devil's Violinist*: 2013 (15). *Amadeus*: 1984 (PG). But also consider the sound scores from famous movies. Why were they chosen?
	🎵	*Listen to the Music*: The Doobie Brothers. *Music Is Healing*: Florida Georgia Line. *Your Song*: Elton John. Research major movie score writers such as: Alan Silvestri, Ennio Morricone, John Williams, Hans Zimmer, Howard Shore, Gustavo Santaolalla and Michael Giacchino.
	🎨	**Look at**: Art works inspired by Music: *Music Pink and Blue no 2* by Georgia O'Keefe. *Colour and Music* by Marc Chagall, *One: number 31* by Jackson Pollock, *Music* by Matisse. Also consider some of the great album covers.

🎪	Pieces based on music should be as result of selecting one or two pieces and really listening and moving to them. Some students like to play musical instruments in their pieces whereas others want only recorded music. Dance and choral movement theatre are often a result of allowing music to be the main stimulus. DV8. Brecht, Marianne Elliot, Joan Littlewood.
⚠	The unit is based on music without lyrics. Students are inspired by the sound and not a message or story contained within a song. See unit 181.
🔗	007, 012, 026, 057, 061, 068, 078, 107, 120, 151, 168, 177, 181, 188, 196.

180   Using other Plays/texts

		'The play's the thing / Wherein I'll catch the conscience of the king. (Hamlet – Shakespeare's Prince of Denmark).
👥		Any age. Works best with smaller groups 2–5.
🚩		**Workshops/games:** *Story circle* and *Body sculpture.* Devising based on a key extract from a performance text. Begin with a line or piece of action from a play (known texts are a good starting point). Improvise what happens next. Explore what is happening in the given text. Interpreting, creating, developing and polishing (Deconstruction). Looking for layers. Pick lines that are stimulating in themselves . . . '*What drawn and talk of peace? I hate the word . . .*' Think about a style in which to present this line. Think of a theme. What does your character want?
🔆		This is not about creating a character, rather developing it. Try a monologue. How would you finish it? Explore your performance space as your character.
Stimulus	💀	Prepared scene/line of text which is cut at a crucial moment . . . It's good to have a suitable prop/piece of costume on hand. SFX if you wish too.
	📖	*For Whom the Bell Tolls;* Ernest Hemingway. *Of Mice and Men:* John Steinbeck. *Something Wicked This Way Comes:* Ray Bradbury.
	📝	*Brave New World:* Aldous Huxley.
	🎭	*Rosencrantz and Guildenstern Are Dead:* Tom Stoppard. *After Juliet:* Sharman Macdonald. *The Threepenny Opera:* Bertolt Brecht. *The Lion King:* Stage musical. *Games and After Liverpool:* James Saunders.
	🎞️	*A Streetcar Named Desire:* 1951 (PG).
	🎵	Use these sections throughout the book to match themes with possible songs.
	🎨	*Journey's End:* R. C. Sherriff. *Ophelia:* Sir John Everett Millais.
🎭		Choose a style/practitioner that challenges the original text. Storytelling. Narration. Multi role with just 2 or 3 performers is interesting!
⚠️		Have scripts/texts in mind.
🔗		006, 008, 020, 027, 042, 044, 057, 071, 107, 115, 123, 130, 160, 178, 184, 190.

181   Song

	'A good song takes on more meaning as the years pass by' (Bruce Springsteen – American singer).
♣♀♂	Mixed groups. All ages.
⚑	**Workshops/games:** *Energy. Control games. Mirror imaging* As this unit is about song, it is entirely appropriate that the devising is influenced by the lyrics. **Questionnaire:** What's your favourite song? Why? Do you know what it's really about? Songs about love and heartbreak take up a vast part of our collections. Any theories on why? Why do we listen to songs? Do we sing along? Why does it make us feel good? Take a song apart. The music, rhythm, lyrics. Write your own!
☼	**Research;** UK Music Hall of Fame. The Kennedy Centre Honours awards. The Musical. Singing as a form of worship (in many cultures). The healing power of song. How do we listen to music today and are we being told what to listen to? **What the papers say:** How does the press cover events like Glastonbury or The Eurovision song contest?

Stimulus		
	☠	iPod, The HMV Dog, Sony, MTV, NME, *Rolling Stone Magazine*. And the idols, from Elvis Presley, The Beatles and The Rolling Stones to Adele, Amy Winehouse and Prince (put your own images together).
	📖	*Nick and Norah's Infinite Playlist:* David Levithan and Rachel Cohn. *This Song Will Save Your Life:* Leila Sales. *The Magic Strings of Frankie Presto:* Mitch Albom.
	✑	*My Lost Youth:* H. Longfellow.
	🎭	*Hannah and Hanna:* John Retallack. *Too Fast:* Douglas Maxwell. The musicals! *Blood Brothers, Billy Elliot, Mamma Mia, Hairspray, The Lion King, 42nd Street . . .* **Research:** Mumford and Sons, and Shakespeare. Their first Album 'Sigh no More'.
	🎞	*Rocketman:* 2019 (15). *8 Mile:* 2002 (15). *Yesterday:* 2019 (12A). *Almost Famous:* 2000 (15).
	🎵	*Sultans of Swing:* Dire Straits. *Your Song:* Elton John. *American Pie:* Don McLean.
	🎨	**Look at:** Some of the great album covers. Consider songs inspired by artists: Vincent (*Starry, Starry Night*), and artists inspired by songs.

🎦	Two distinct areas. Devised work based on the lyrics alone and work which looks at our love of songs: to listen to, sing along to, to move to. A lot of physical/dance-based ideas arise from songs. If students sing: focus on phrasing; pace and timing; projection, pitch and emotional range. Choral/ensemble work can be very challenging and pleasing.
⚠	A vast subject. Needs careful thought about artistic intent right from the start. Try to avoid talent shows!
🔗	006, 017, 025, 028, 030, 042, 045, 051, 062, 074, 081, 089, 096, 103, 109, 126, 144, 151, 153, 154, 170, 179, 186, 190, 198.

182   Autobiographical monologues

	'I find that there is no speech that is not soliloquy. And yet always, I sense an audience' (Randolph Stow – Australian author).
♀♂	More suited to older students 15+. Students work well in pairs who can direct/assist one another.
⚑	**Workshops/games:** *Story circle, Third person narration. Body sculpture.* A good way to get students talking/thinking about an autobiographical monologue is for them to remember a special moment/event (photographs help). Ask the class to sit with blank paper and pencil and write/draw whatever thoughts/feeling and memories they have of that moment. Focus on feelings and all the senses. What could you hear, see, smell, feel . . . From the words (stream of consciousness) build a scripted monologue and include detailed notes/stage directions. Try it out on your partner and get feedback. Always with a sense of audience.
☼	Consider a wide range of famous autobiographies and select small pieces as examples of style/ genre. *I Am Malala*: Malala Yousafzai. *Long Walk To Freedom*: Nelson Mandela. *The Collected Autobiographies* of Maya Angelou. *The Diary of a Young Girl*: Anne Frank. As an extension you could look at someone else in the first person. Write a soliloquy for a famous/notorious figure from history just before a specific event.

Stimulus		
	👁	This is personal to each individual student. Photographs, perhaps an item of clothing they were wearing. Use a mirror and think of your self-portrait.
	📖	Find examples of good monologues/first person narratives in literature; The opening chapter (Part 1) of *Wonder* by R. J. Palacio. Mina's journal in *My Name is Mina* by David Almond. Loll's description of his first day at school from Laurie Lee's *Cider with Rosie. Boy:* Roald Dahl
	✍	*Death of a Naturalist:* Seamus Heaney.
	🎭	*The Curious Incident of the Dog in the Night-Time.* Mark Haddon (adapted by Simon Stephens). *Five Kinds of Silence:* Shelagh Stephenson. *Adrian Mole 13¾:* Sue Townsend. *Blackout:* Davey Anderson.
	🎬	*The Shawshank Redemption:* 1994 (15). *Diary of a Wimpy Kid:* 2010 (PG). *American Beauty:* 1999 (18).
	🎵	*Rehab:* Amy Winehouse. *Collide:* Ed Sheeran. *Family Portrait:* Pink.
	🎨	In many ways an artist's autobiography is their self-portrait. **Look at:** The self-portraits of Freda Kahlo, Van Gogh, Da Vinci, Claude Monet, Gustave Courbet, Gauguin.

🎭	A monologue/soliloquy is still a performance. It seldom works when delivered by a motionless body. Frantic Assembly. Kneehigh. Some students like to take events from history and describe being there.
⚠	Sometimes the memory they wish to work with can be more personal; for example, a relationship, doubt or fear. Know your students.
🔗	008, 010, 020, 033, 051, 060, 075, 084, 097, 109, 122, 134, 139, 150, 156, 167, 178, 180, 190, 197, 199, 200.

183   The Letter

		'To write is human, to receive a letter: Devine!' (Susan Lendroth – American children's author).
⚥		Works well as paired work. Any age.
⚑		**Workshops/games**: *Levels of tension.* Tension and expectation. Reacting . . . Begin with impro work. Receiving a letter. Students in a given scenario, the content of the letter is written by you and they run with it, or they improvise the content with a partner. Life changing letters/Famous letters. **Look at**: The types of news. Good/bad. Blackmail/ransom. A lost letter from many years ago.
☼		**Search for**: Famous love letters. *The greatest letters ever written*: A collection belonging to Albin Schram. **Look at**: The letters of the famous: Dylan Thomas, Van Gogh, Ted Hughes, Tolkien . . . Letters from soldiers at war, people on death row, at sea, in love, dying, running away, saying goodbye . . . You've got mail! Is an email less personal? Why? **Research**: The 21 letters Tadeusz Korczowski wrote during the 16 months he was imprisoned in Auschwitz.
Stimulus	🐌	Letters, pens, envelopes. Old letters from relatives . . .
	📖	*Love Letters of the Great War*: Mandy Kirkby (Editor). *Dear Mr. You*: Mary-Louise Parker. *Dracula*: Bram Stoker.
	✍	*Come up from The Fields. Father*: Walt Whitman.
	🎭	Think about Juliet's letter to Romeo. What if he had received it? *Letters*: Mrs. Evelyn Merritt.
	🎬	*The Letters*: 1973 (TV Movie). *P.S. I Love You*: 2007 (12A). *Beaches*: 1988 (15).
	♫	*Please Read the Letter That I Wrote*: Robert Plant and Alison Krauss. *Letter From America*: The Proclaimers. *Stan*: Eminem.
	🎨	*A Lady Painting*: Vermeer. Look at Vermeer's paintings, many contain a letter! Look at how emojis are replacing words in emails.
🎭		Character work. Enact scenes from well-known plays as though the main characters had written to one another, narration/storytelling. Look at the story behind the letter . . .
⚠		Avoid actual letters which are personal to students and their families.
🔗		003, 006, 010, 021, 030, 051, 059, 077, 085, 119, 131, 140, 142, 155, 167, 171, 172, 178, 186.

184   Disguise

		'Be not caught by the cunning of those in disguise' (Horace – Roman lyric poet).
👥	14+ All group sizes from solo to large ensemble.	
🏁	**Workshops/games:** *Control games. Status.* Why are Fancy Dress parties so popular? Are we bolder when in disguise, more honest, liberated, more evil? Historically the person in disguise appears to have sinister intent. **Look at the language:** Synonyms of disguise, see sinister, hide, mask, camouflage, conceal, cover.	
💡	Masks were used in Greek Theatre to show the actor's feelings more clearly! **More controversial:** Think about how faceless people can be when online. The faceless bully. **Search for:** Museum of theatre masks. **Look at:** Images of Noh, Hannya, Oni, Greek and Roman masks.	
Stimulus	💀	A mask, a pair of dark glasses, a wig, a big overcoat, a hat. Standard disguises.
	📖	Consider disguise as a literary device; Think about the boys in Golding's *Lord of the Flies*. With painted faces they became savages. (*Alias*) *Madame Doubtfire*: Anne Fine. Bronte's *Jane Eyre*, when Mr Rochester disguises himself as a gypsy woman.
	📝	*The Mask*: Maya Angelou.
	🎭	The place of disguise/costume and in particular, the mask in theatre. *Volpone*: Ben Jonson. Or the faceless freedom of the characters in *Chatroom*: Enda Walsh. *Accidental Death of an Anarchist*: Dario Fo. *'Disguise I see thou art a wickedness'*. VIOLA *Twelfth Night*. Shakespeare.
	🎞️	Think about the moral ambiguity of the Terminator in the movie of the same name. We cannot see his eyes. In the second film, when he removes his sunglasses, we know he's good. A simple trick but so effective. *The Master of Disguise*: 2002 (PG). *Face Off*: 1997 (18). *Mrs Doubtfire*: 1993 (U). Ethan Hunt's face in the *Mission Impossible* films. And then the hidden identities of Batman, Superman, and co.
	🎵	*Brilliant Disguise*: Bruce Springsteen. *Devil in Disguise*: Elvis Presley. *Behind the Mask*: Michael Jackson.
	🎨	Instagram became inundated with images of classic paintings adorned with masks during the pandemic. Henry Moore's *Mask*.
🎪	Reasons for hiding your identity. Mask work. When your face is hidden, how you convey meaning through gesture. Mime work. Plain white masks and Trestle theatre masks. Ensemble work, Berkoff/ Lecoq, Greek chorus.	
⚠️	Remember that masks tend to muffle the voice.	
🔗	024, 025, 033, 041, 054, 074, 086, 102, 134, 156, 165, 176, 192, 195, 197.	

185   100 likes

		'It takes discipline not to let social media steal your time' (Alexis Ohanian – American internet entrepreneur).
⚥		All age rages. Differentiate!
🏳		**Workshop/games:** *Mirror images. Stereotypes. Third person narration.* A projected computer screen. Flicking through Facebook, YouTube, WhatsApp, Instagram, TikTok, Snapchat, 'X' (Twitter) etc. . . . **Questionnaire:** How many of these do you use? Is it healthy to spend 5 hours+ per day; tweeting, blogging, image sharing, gossiping, networking, media sharing, microblogging, bookmarking and generally not getting out much? Is it less about staying in touch and more about comparing and judging?
🔅		**Research:** Put together a timeline from all the social media platforms. **Look at:** Reader's Digest.ca *10-Step Digital Detox.* **Search for:** 'Help with social media addiction.' Weareteachers.com have a great unit on *digital stress and social media addiction.* Out for a meal, at the theatre, in the cinema and there it is the light of the smart phone!
Stimulus	💀	The logos of the most popular social media platforms. Their Icons.
	📖	*The Circle:* Dave Eggers. *Crudo:* Olivia Laing. *Friendship:* Emily Gould. *How to Get Rid of Social Media Addiction:* Anthea Peries.
	📝	*When Les Linked In:* Brian Wilson.
	🎭	*Chatroom:* Enda Walsh. *Mobile Phone Show:* Jim Cartwright. *Me, My Selfie and I:* Jonathan Dorf.
	🎞	*Love, Guaranteed:* 2020 (Netflix PG). *#Realityhigh:* 2017 (15). *The Social Dilemma:* 2020 (Netflix Documentary).
	🎵	*Perfect Illusion:* Lady Gaga. *The Social Media Song:* Shimona Kee. *New Friend Request:* Gym Class Heroes.
	🎨	*Social Media:* Vinnie Nauheimer.
🎦		Extreme naturalism juxtaposed with extensive use of multimedia. Set should be simple and uncluttered. Projections/multimedia. Katie Mitchell. Gareth Fry. Forum pieces which encourage use of audience smartphones
⚠		Students should be encouraged to keep personal online data safe and not share contact details outside of their friendship groups.
🔗		071, 081, 083, 089, 097, 114, 155, 161, 162, 163, 164, 165, 182, 183, 186, 193.

186   Words can hurt

	'Words can inspire. And words can destroy. Choose yours well' (Robin Sharma – Canadian writer).
👥	All ages/groups.
🚩	**Workshop/games:** *Soundscapes. Alienation. Get out of my way!* **Look at the language:** Of racism/sexism/ageism/bullying and how words make you feel. How some words and phrases are inflammatory or worse and have a history of oppression deeply ingrained in our language. The sounds of the words a bully uses. Listen for the sound as well as the meaning. Discordant and plosives, how they give a different message. Listen to the open sound of the word 'love' with BENVOLIO, MERCUTIO, ROMEO. Now compare with the closed sound of 'hate' with TYBALT! Watch how the face changes with these sounds. Build a good and bad sound/word chart. Consider opposite connotations, i.e. unique/weird, confident/arrogant, dedicated/stubborn.
🔅	**Research:** 'Language and Power.' Persuasive speaking. Vocabulary and audience. Transactional language. **What the papers say:** Compare the different language of broadsheets and tabloids.
Stimulus	A montage of words that exclude/divide people. 'Master bedroom, blacklist, sold down the river, master and slave (in electronics and software/hardware), chicken, pig, snake. *Mockingbird:* Kathryn Erskine. *The Book Thief:* Markus Zusak. *Jake's Tower:* Elizabeth Laird. *The Weight of a Word:* K. S. McKinney. Shakespeare's works are almost completely void of stage direction. The performer must hear the clues within the lines they speak. Often the sound of a word will inform the actor how to perform it, both vocally and physically. *Dead Poets Society:* 1989 (PG). *Born on the Fourth of July:* 1989 (18). *The King's Speech:* 2010 (12A). *Words:* The Bee Gees. *Words Are Weapons:* D12. *My Words Are Weapons:* Eminem. **Look at:** The work of artists like: Jenny Holzer, Ed Ruscha, Mel Bochner, Adam Pendleton, Christopher Wool and Kay Rosen.
🎭	The use of word play in Shakespeare. Double entendre and puns. Dialogue based. Projected words and mime, exaggerated movement and stillness with levels of tension to show meaning and misinterpretation of meaning. The sounds of words corrupting bodies/faces/meaning.
⚠	When experimenting with the sounds of words, students like to include the forbidden! Set your own ground rules, expectations and exceptions.
🔗	002, 008, 016, 017, 019, 021, 024, 032, 053, 060, 061, 068, 070, 073, 075, 101, 106, 107, 112, 126, 135, 100, 190, 191.

187   Surveillance society (A Case study unit, see Chapter 5)

	'Under observation, we act less free, which means we effectively are less free' (Edward Snowden – American whistle-blower).
👫👤	14+ Small mixed groups.
🏳	See details in Case study, Unit 187, Chapter 5.
🔆	Mass surveillance of telephone metadata started after the 911 attacks on the US. CCTV became widely used in department stores in the late 70s and 80s in an attempt to reduce loss through theft. **What the papers say:** BBC article by Ivana Davidovic dated 18/11/2019, *'Should we be worried by ever more CCTV cameras?'* **Look at** CCTV being used to curb antisocial behaviour. **Look at** your government's explanations of how CCTV is used in your community. Government data collection. **Search for:** Citizenship teaching resources with a focus on Surveillance Society. Speak to the citizenship tutor in your centre. Consider also inverse surveillance, where citizens can keep tabs on their governments. **More controversial:** Did mass surveillance during the Covid pandemic help to keep us safe or just to raise cash? Are traffic cameras for our safety of to raise money? Do you really need to know so much about me? What is the public support
Stimulus	

Stimulus		
	💀	CCTV camera, footage of Highstreet cams, Dash Cams, school security footage. A laptop/tablet/smartphone. Images of CCTV systems in operation signs. Roadside traffic cameras. A copy of George Orwell's *1984*.
	📙	*1984:* George Orwell. *The Circle:* Dave Eggers. *Little Brother:* Cory Doctorow. *The Bunker Diary:* Kevin Brooks. Non-fiction: *Surveillance Society:* David Lyon. *The Transparent Society:* David Brin. *The Digital Person:* Daniel J. Solove.
	✍	Poem: https://joemcalister.com/webcam-poetry/
	🎭	*Brave New World:* Aldous Huxley (adapted by David Rogers). *The Nether:* Jennifer Haley. *After the Blast:* Zoe Kazan. *1984:* Robert Ike and Duncan Macmillan (adaptation of Orwell's *1984*) Shakespeare: *'Oh what fools these mortals be'* Puck *A Midsummer Night's Dream*.
	🎞	*1984:* 1984 (15). *Minority Report:* 2002 (12). *The Truman Show:* 1998 (PG). *Enemy of the State:* 1998 (15). *Rear Window:* 1954 (A). TV: *Black Mirror:* 2011–2019 (Netflix series). *Person of Interest:* 2012–2017 series (15). Documentary: *7 Billion Suspects: The Surveillance Society.* 2020.
	🎵	*Every Breath You Take:* The Police. *Somebody's Watching Me:* Michael Jackson. *Watching Me:* Jill Scott. *Satellite:* Nine Inch Nails.
	🎨	**Research:** The work of Trevor Paglen (Photographer). **Look at:** Surveillance Art. artandsurveillance.com

🎦	See details in Case study, Unit 187, Chapter 5.
⚠	Obtain permissions before recording and showing students on the school premises. Check your school/college policy.
🔗	033, 040, 063, 076, 092, 094, 109, 125, 138, 139, 149, 152, 156, 157, 164, 174, 175.

188   Advertising

<table>
<tr>
<td></td>
<td></td>
<td colspan="2">
'Advertising is legalized lying'
(H. G. Wells – English writer).
</td>
</tr>
<tr>
<td>♟♟</td>
<td colspan="3">14+ Able groups.</td>
</tr>
<tr>
<td>⚑</td>
<td colspan="3">
Workshops/games: Control games.
Questionnaire: What is your favourite TV advert and why?
Think of the emotions used by advertisers to sell us stuff! List as many as you can.
How advertisers form a relationship between you and the brand. Associate an emotion/feeling with a product/brand.
</td>
</tr>
<tr>
<td>☼</td>
<td colspan="3">
Look at: The history of advertising. Newspapers were where advertising first flourished.
Look at: Advertising standards and false advertising.
Research: Transactional' language.
TES have produced 'An Introduction To Advertising' 7–11.
kennedycentre.org has a unit 'Media Awareness'.
Look at: How Alexa and friends make buying so easy.
More controversial: Look at how sex, and in particular the female form, has been historically used in advertising.
</td>
</tr>
<tr>
<td rowspan="8">Stimulus</td>
<td>◉</td>
<td colspan="2">Logos (many sheets available online). How many can you name?</td>
</tr>
<tr>
<td>📖</td>
<td colspan="2">
Syrup: Max Barry.
Ogilvy on Advertising: David Ogilvy.
Buyology: Truth and Lies about Why We Buy. M. Lindstorm.
</td>
</tr>
<tr>
<td>✑</td>
<td colspan="2">Look at: How poetry (verse) is used in advertising</td>
</tr>
<tr>
<td>🎭</td>
<td colspan="2">
Tabletop: Rob Ackerman (docudrama).
The Creation of the World and Other Business: Arthur Miller.
Shakespeare and his works have been used in advertising for a very long time. From chewing tobacco, cars, beds, burgers, jeans, gin and mobile phones.
</td>
</tr>
<tr>
<td>🎞</td>
<td colspan="2">
The Social Network: 2010 (12A).
How to Get Ahead in Advertising: 1989 (15).
The Greatest Movie Ever Sold: 2011 (Documentary) (12A).
</td>
</tr>
<tr>
<td>🎵</td>
<td colspan="2">
The Sounds of Silence: Simon and Garfunkel.
Feel Good Inc: Gorillaz.
Lost in the Supermarket: The Clash.
Look at popular songs used in media advertising.
</td>
</tr>
<tr>
<td>🎨</td>
<td colspan="2">
The work of Alphonse Mucha, Norman Rockwell and Andy Warhol.
Da Vinci's Last Supper used by Paddypower.com as a gambler's table. The same has been done with the following: Van Gogh's Self Portrait to sell glasses, Magritte to sell insurance, Rodin for vitamins, Dali for investments, Picasso for cars and to promote yoga!
</td>
</tr>
<tr>
<td>🎪</td>
<td colspan="2">
Multimedia (Katie Mitchell). Immersive with a lot of audience participation.
Colourful and loud!
Interactive, Forum, T.I.E.
</td>
</tr>
<tr>
<td>⚠</td>
<td colspan="3">Be aware of the age appropriateness of some advertising campaigns.</td>
</tr>
<tr>
<td>🔗</td>
<td colspan="3">029, 030, 045, 051, 055, 070, 092, 099, 125, 152, 164, 181, 189.</td>
</tr>
</table>

189 Propaganda

		'Propaganda is amazing, people can be led to believe anything' (Alice Walker – American author and activist).
⚱		12+ Mixed small groups (or large ensemble pieces).
⚑		**Workshops/games**: *Status. Control games. Alienation. Brown Eyes/Blue Eyes.* Can the Blue and Green eyed students convince the Brown and Hazel eyed ones that they are better in every way? What words/rhetoric would they use. How would this be countered?
☼		The Museum of International Propaganda. Political Propaganda at the British Museum. **What the papers say:** Consider the propaganda used during Brexit. Where did the papers stand? See Fake News Unit 102. **Research**: Jane Elliott's blue eye, brown eye experiment.
Stimulus	☠	Famous examples would be Uncle Sam, Lord Kitchener. War propaganda is usually quite obvious.
	📖	*1984*: George Orwell. *Brave New World:* Aldous Huxley. *Necessary Illusions:* Noam Chomsky.
	✍	Compare Jessie Pope's poem *Who's for the Game* with Wilfred Owen's *Dulce et Decorum Est.*
	🎭	Drama is by nature not propagandist, however, plays have been interpreted/directed to make political points. Miller's *Death of a Salesman* or *The Crucible.* Brecht's *The Resistible Rise of Arturo Ui* which uses allegory and satire to make a political point.
	🎬	*Red Dawn:* 1984 (15). *The Triumph of the Will:* Leni Riefenstahl (Nazi propaganda film) 1935 (E). *The War you Don't See:* 2010 (Documentary) (12°).
	🎵	*Tomorrow Belongs to Me:* (Watch the scene from the movie *Cabaret* on YouTube). *American Idiot:* Green Day. *The Revolution Will not be Televised:* Gil Scott-Heron.
	🎨	Art as propaganda. Art with a message. Graphic design and propaganda. Read Propaganda Art in the 21st century by Jonas Staal. **Look at:** Powerful/famous propaganda art work. For example, Jim Fitzpatrick's iconic poster of Che Guevara. Or the work of Valentina Kulagina (Russia 1930).
🎭		A great opportunity for large ensemble pieces with movement directed by forces seen or unseen. Grotesque masks and exaggerated movement (Berkoff/Lecoq). Chorus.
⚠		Historic propaganda is often racist and insensitive.
🔗		005, 006, 012, 015, 040, 064, 079, 092, 102, 119, 121, 147, 160, 174, 178, 188.

190   Storytelling

	'You're never going to kill storytelling, because it's built in the human plan. We come with it' (Margaret Atwood – Canadian writer).
♣♀	Any age. Works well as monologue/soliloquy and chorus work in small groups.
⚑	**Workshops/games**: *Story circle. Soundscapes.* **Questionnaire**: What's your favourite story? Why? Ask students to sit with the group and simply tell a story from the point of view of a character. Not read, just told. It should be of their own creation and need last no more than a minute or two. It could be based on a book they have studied or an event in history. Try to add gesture, vocal tone and range to the story. Or try telling a shared story round the circle; one line each. In pairs, one narrates their story and the other enacts it. Involve the narrator/storyteller, swapping roles.
☀	Think of a story passed down in your family. Can you re-tell it. Take a news item and tell the story of an involved person/witness. Storytelling is an ancient tradition and artform. Stories have been passed down for hundreds of years in many cultures. For example, the Aboriginal Dreamtime or Native Americans, North and South.

Stimulus	🎨	Ask students to bring in an artifact relevant to their story.
	📖	*100 Years of Solitude:* García Márquez. *The Bluest Eye:* Toni Morrison. *The Storytelling Animal: How Stories Make Us Human:* Jonathan Gottschall.
	📝	*Annabel Lee:* (Narrative verse) Edgar Allan Poe.
	🎭	*Private Peaceful:* Morpurgo and Reade. *Sparkleshark:* Philip Ridley. *Collected Grimm's Tales:* Carol Anne Duffy and Tim Supple.
	🎞	*Holes:* 2003 (PG). *Big Fish:* 2003 (PG-13). *Forrest Gump:* 1994 (PG-13).
	🎵	*Love Song:* Taylor Swift. *Hurricane:* Bob Dylan. *Hotel California:* Eagles.
	🎨	**Look at:** The painting, think of the story behind it. *The Siege of Tournai:* Pierre L'Enfant. *Till Death Us Do Part:* Edmund Blair Leighton. *The Burial of Manon Lescaut:* Pascal-Adolphe-Jean Dagnan-Bouveret

🎭	Minimalist set (works well in the round). Good work with mask/puppet and backlighting. Musical instruments. Designers like Gareth Fry. Narration, Physicalisation. Emma Rice, Polly Teal, Marianne Elliot. Waterwell.
⚠	Remind students to respect shared stories and privacy within the drama space.
🔗	003, 007, 008, 034, 036, 039, 055, 084, 089, 090, 106, 114, 139, 161, 175, 178, 180, 181, 182, 183, 196, 197.

191 Kid's games

	'Play is the highest form of research' (Albert Einstein – German-American physicist).
⚐	All ages. Mixed groups.
▶	**Workshops/games**; *Energy games. Stereotypes.* Show the scene from *Blood Brothers* '*Kid's Game*'. Available online. **Questionnaire**: What were your favourite games as a small child? What did you like about them? What social skills do games teach us? Sportsmanship, numeric skills, leadership, parenting, fighting, diplomacy and problem solving, but can you name the game?
☼	The history of toys and children's games. Consider how they have changed through the ages. The schoolrun.com has produced an excellent resource on the history of toys. *TIME* Magazine's 100 Greatest Toys. The Smithsonian collection of toys, puzzles and games. Learning Though Play, UNICEF. **Research**: Theories on children's play by Piaget, Vygotsky and Montessori. Toys have changed through time, but some toys just seem to have always been with us. Toys like weapons and dolls. What does this tell us? Children don't play together outside as much as they did. What might this mean for future generations?

Stimulus		
	💀	A selection of toys (or images).
	📖	*Trapped in a Video Game:* series Dustin Brady. *Slay:* Brittney Morris. *The Power of Play: Learning What Comes Naturally*: David Elkind.
	✍	The Lyrics to *Kid's Game* from Willy Russell's *Blood Brothers*.
	🎭	*A Memory of Lizzie:* David Foxton. *Blue Remembered Hills:* Dennis Potter. *Blood Brothers:* Willy Russell.
	🎬	*Toy Story 1–4:* 1995–2019 (PG). *Tag:* 2018 (15). *The Power of Play:* YouTube documentary.
	🎵	Consider the songs young children sing whilst playing as well as songs about playing. *Ring around the Rosie:* Unknown. *Where Do the Children Play?:* Yusuf/Cat Stevens.
	🎨	*Children's Games:* Bruegel the Elder. *The Little Cowboy:* Karyn Robinson. *Stitching A Patch:* Edmund Adler.

🎦	Playing is like acting! Explore a child's 'willingness to suspend disbelief'. Imagination and empathy. Parody, the good and the bad. From cigarettes and war to childcare and love. **More controversial**: Domestic Violence A Child's Game. Disturbing and thought provoking.
⚠	Don't let this get bogged with an educationalist's view point. Look instead at how play mimics real life and as practice for adult life.
🔗	014, 034, 081, 083, 165, 192, 193, 195, 197.

192   Sayings

<table>
<tr>
<td></td>
<td colspan="2"> 'Don't Judge a Book by its Cover'
(English idiom). </td>
</tr>
<tr>
<td>🐦</td>
<td colspan="2">All ages. Any group size.</td>
</tr>
<tr>
<td>🚩</td>
<td colspan="2">Workshop/games: Gestus. Stereotypes.
Begin by giving students (pairs) a short saying and challenge them to improvise a story around it. There are at least 2,500 in the English Language. Their origin and meaning can be the inspiration for some great devised work. For example, 'Caught Red-Handed!'</td>
</tr>
<tr>
<td>💡</td>
<td colspan="2">Use the Phrase Finder at phrases.org.uk
What the papers say: Look at the phrases commonly used by the press: The eleventh hour. A witch hunt. A Whistle blower. Red letter day. A house of cards.
Can you invent a new expression to cover an aspect of modern life/events?
Look at modern phrases made popular by social media.</td>
</tr>
<tr>
<td rowspan="6">Stimulus</td>
<td>💀</td>
<td>Put up a list of sayings. Can they add to them or know of variations (regional).</td>
</tr>
<tr>
<td>📖</td>
<td>For younger students.
The Illustrated Book of Funny Old Sayings: Everyday phrases and their origins: Sally Mooney.
For older students.
Sayings and their Meanings: Don't Judge a Book by its Cover: R. J. Clarke.</td>
</tr>
<tr>
<td>📑</td>
<td>The Old Man's Complaints and How He Gained Them: Robert Southey.</td>
</tr>
<tr>
<td>🎭</td>
<td>Collected Grimm's Tales: Carol Anne Duffy and Tim Supple.
Barber Shop Chronicles: Inua Ellams.
Shakespeare gave us many well known phrases. All that glisters is not gold (The Merchant of Venice). Eaten me out of house and home (2 Henry IV). Wear one's heart on one's sleeve (Othello). Wild-goose chase (Romeo and Juliet).</td>
</tr>
<tr>
<td>🎞</td>
<td>Look at the sayings we have gained from the movies.
'I'm going to make him an offer he can't refuse', The Godfather: 1972 (X).
'A boy's best friend is his mother', Psycho: 1960 (15).
'With great power comes great responsibility.' Spider-Man: Marvel Comics.
'There's no place like home', The Wizard of Oz: 1939 (A).</td>
</tr>
<tr>
<td>🎵</td>
<td>Look at sayings from music . . .
'Singing from the same hymn sheet.' 'Music to my ears.' 'Pull out all the stops.'
'Blowing your own trumpet.' 'Like a broken record.'
'Change your tune.' 'All that jazz.' 'Don't harp on about it.'</td>
</tr>
<tr>
<td></td>
<td>🎨</td>
<td>'With her Mona Lisa smile.'
'15 minutes of fame'. Andy Warhol.
'It's like Dante's Inferno in here.'</td>
</tr>
<tr>
<td>🎦</td>
<td colspan="2">From the starting point of improvising a well-known saying, students develop stories that explore how the meanings of many have altered over the years and through different cultural influences.
Story telling using narration to accompany on-stage action.
Character based. Stanislavski. 'Cat got your tongue' led to some great theatre using expressionism/physical theatre. (Lecoq and Artaud.)</td>
</tr>
<tr>
<td>⚠</td>
<td colspan="2">Some old sayings contain outdated cultural notions and language.</td>
</tr>
<tr>
<td>🔗</td>
<td colspan="2">16, 17, 18, 19, 20, 21, 140, 166, 168, 178, 180, 181, 183, 184, 188, 189.</td>
</tr>
</table>

193 eSports

		'Stay inside the bubble' (eSport saying).	
♣♥	Of interest to all ages. Small groups (pairs).		
⚑	**Workshops/games**: *Energy. Control games.* eSports is the short name for electronic sports, where players play video games against each other with fans watching them. Some even claim it should be included in the Olympics! **Questionnaire**: What do you play? How often? How seriously do you take it? **Look at**: The way players become immersed in the game they are playing, compare it to acting. The willingness to suspend disbelief.		
☀	Why are fighting games and first person shooters still the most popular games? Make a list of the top 10 games. During the pandemic and lockdown, millions of people escaped by playing a role, becoming: assassins, fighting dragons, fighting zombies, going to war, in space, on earth, in another universe. Some didn't come back! According to an April 2018 Pew study, 83% of teenage girls play some form of video games – and 97% of boys! **Research**: The Rise of eSports.		
Stimulus	💀	A PC. Game station. Gaming controllers, gamepads. A joy stick. A PS5, an Xbox etc. . . .	
	📖	*Dragon Age: The Stolen Throne:* David Gaider (Bioware). *Assassin's Creed:* Oliver Bowden. *Life Is Strange: Dust:* Emma Vieceli.	
	✍	*The Games in My Room:* Kenn Nesbitt.	
	🎭	*Cotton:* Alex Benjamin. *Love and Information*: Caryl Churchill.	
	🎮	**Look at**: The movies based on games: Angry Birds, Sonic, Streetfighter, Mortal Kombat, Lara Croft (Tomb Raider), Resident Evil . . . There are many more.	
	🎵	**Search for**: Best Video Game Music Tracks. There is a Top 50!	
	🎨	**Research**: Creating Art with Video Games.	
🎦	Metatheatre (Metadrama). The play within the play! Look at the surreal world of gaming, fantasy/reality. Getting lost in those worlds. Dealing with reality outside of the game. Multi role. Absurd/fantasy. Stylised/dance.		
⚠	Some games are very graphic and realistic in their portrayal of fighting/shooting etc. Be aware of age restrictions.		
🔗	014, 071, 076, 092, 097, 151, 162, 164, 165, 191, 197.		

194   The clothes on our backs

		'Clothes make the man. Naked people have little or no influence on society' (Mark Twain – American Author).
♟		Works well with older students 14+. Groups of 3–6.
⚑		**Workshops/games:** *Status games. Stereotypes. Body sculpture.* **Questionnaire:** What do you want your clothes say about you? Do you judge people on how they dress? What did your parents wear when they were your age? Look at old family photos. Why do we like to dress up? How do different clothes make you feel? Confident, attractive, silly?
☼		UK https://www.vam.ac.uk/collections/fashion; USA https://www.fashionhistorymuseum.com/ **Research:** Fashion and sweat shops. Sexual identity and clothes. **More controversial:** Who made your clothes and were they paid fairly?
Stimulus	📰	Fashion magazines.
	📖	*The Pink Suit:* Nicole Mary Kelby. *Silk for the Feed Dogs:* Jackie Mallon. *Overdressed: The Shockingly High Cost of Cheap Fashion:* Elizabeth L. Cline.
	📝	My Old Clothes: Amos Russel Wells.
	🎭	*Di and Viv and Rose:* Amelia Bullmore. Jean Paul Gaultier's *Fashion Freak Show.*
	🎞	*Dior and I:* 2014 (12). *The Devil Wears Prada:* 2006 (PG). *Coco before Chanel:* 2009 (PG-13).
	🎵	*Sharp Dressed Man:* ZZ Top. *Cosby Sweater:* Hilltop Hoods. *Raspberry Beret:* Prince
	🎨	Clothes inspired by art: *Piet Mondrian* by Yves Saint Laurent or *Pablo Picasso* by Moschino. *Organza Dinner Dress with Painted Lobster:* A collaboration between Elsa Schiaparelli and Salvador Dalí.
🎭		Traverse Stage (Catwalk). Lots of lighting effects. A chance to use that wardrobe! Ensemble piece using costume and mask. Costume and symbolism. Artaud.
⚠		Possible bullying issues.
🔗		021, 033, 053, 070, 090, 095, 101, 115, 120, 160, 176, 184, 192, 196, 198, 199, 200.

195 Clowns

		'Nobody likes a clown at midnight' (Stephen King – American Author).
👥	11+ Mixed groups.	
🚩	**Workshops/games**: *Energy games. Stereotypes.* We watched a classic circus clown routine. Then flashed up on the same screen still images of the clown from Stephen King's 'It'. Discuss reaction. **Look at the language**: Loveable clown, always clowning around, the class clown, send in the clowns. If they are objects of fun, why are they so frightening?	
💡	*Bozo, Coco, Krusty, Pennywise, The Joker, Harley Quinn, Charlie Chaplin and Ronald Macdonald.* **Look at**: 'Scary clown sightings' in 2016. The Clown attack craze. **Research**: The Dorian Mimes Troupe. The history of the clown. Consider the sadness of the clown paradox. Why so serious? They make us laugh, cry, scream, and buy cheese burgers! **What the papers say**: Reporting the 'Killer Clown Craze' . . .	

Stimulus		
	💀	Clown costumes and equipment. Circus posters and general clown images. **Research**: The clowns' egg registry. Try painting your own personal clown face.
	📖	*The Farmer and the Clown*: Marla Frazee. *The Clown of God*: Tomie dePaola. *Harleen*: (a graphic novel) by Stjepan Sejic.
	📝	*Cloony the Clown*: Shel Silverstein.
	🎭	*Accidental Death of an Anarchist*: Dario Fo. *Clown's Play*: Reginald F. Bain. **Research**: Theatre clowning, Pantomime, mime, Commedia dell'arte. **Shakespeare**: FESTE in *Twelfth Night*. TOUCHSTONE in *As You Like It* or King Lear's FOOL.
	📽	*Clown*: 2014 (18). *Fear of Clowns*: 2004 (R). *Joker*: 2019 (15). BBC Documentary *Clowns Part 1* on YouTube.
	🎵	*Send in the Clowns*: Judy Collins. *Everybody Loves a Clown*: Gary Lewis. *The Tears of a Clown*: Smokey Robinson. **Search for**: 'Circus Music', in particular *The Circus March* and *Screamer*.
	🎨	*Acrobat and Young Harlequin*: Pablo Picasso. *Sympathy for Cyclops*: Romare Bearden. **Search for**: Picasso and Clowns (images).

🎭	Circus clown performance is very demanding. Some students juggle and this is a start but does not make for great theatre on its own! ERS The sadness behind the smile catches students' imaginations. Physical work with mirrors and masks. The subtle clowning, the Spass/'Tickle and Slap'.	
⚠	Beware of adult content. Some infamous serial killers have used clown costumes and make up. There is a phobia (fear) of clowns and it can be extreme. Coulrophobia.	
🔗	025, 033, 042, 055, 064, 074, 083, 129, 143, 177, 180, 184, 191, 196, 198.	

196   Tradition

	'The less there is to justify a traditional custom, the harder it is to get rid of it' (Mark Twain – American author).
✿♀	11+ Mixed groups of 3 or more.
⚑	**Workshops/games:** *Status. Repetition exercises.* Form a 'traditional' drama class circle! Round the circle name a good and bad tradition. Look at the stories behind them. Mime a tradition. **Questionnaire:** Does your family have any traditions? How important are they? Use the stories behind some traditions and question if they are still relevant/appropriate today, or indeed if they ever were!
☼	Every culture has its own traditions, customs and beliefs that are passed down through the generations. **Look at the language:** A traditional song. a traditional punishment, a harmless tradition, a dangerous tradition, a great tradition, an ancient tradition, a lovey tradition, a vile tradition. Institution. Theatrical tradition. Military tradition. Literary tradition. A traditional celebration. Traditional games. A traditional restaurant. A traditional prayer. A traditional Christmas . . . Ritual. Habit. **More controversial:** Child marriage, a harmful traditional practice in some cultures. Maundy Thursday, when the Queen gives money to 'selected' pensioners.

Stimulus		
	🕯	List artifacts with a traditional symbolic meaning. A lit candle, for example.
	📖	*A Suitable Boy:* Vikram Seth. *The Invention of Tradition:* Eric J. Hobsbawm. *The Night of Las Posadas:* Tomie dePaola.
	✑	*Henry V:* Verse IV i 116, 'Upon the king . . .' Shakespeare.
	🎭	*At the Black Pig's Dyke:* Vincent Woods. *Translations:* Brian Friel.
	🎬	*Coco:* 2017 (PG). *Lost in Translation:* 2003 (15). *Brave:* 2012 (PG).
	🎵	*Tradition:* From *Fiddler on the Roof.* *Auld Lang Syne:* Traditional Scots! *Something Old, Something New:* The Fantastics.
	🎨	Traditional art.

▥	Commedia dell'arte; tradition of the comic relationship between master and servant. Stylise robotic movement to emphasise ritual and repetition. Freeze frame and story within a moment.
⚠	Should not seek to undermine traditions, only to view them in the modern day.
⌗	016, 029–034, 068, 078, 079, 084, 089, 096, 105, 119, 120, 130, 138, 143, 151, 160, 177, 178, 179, 181, 184, 192.

197   Superheroes

	'I wear a mask, and that mask is not to hide who I am, but to create who I am' (Batman – DC superhero).
⚉	Popular with all age ranges.
⚐	**Workshops/games**: *Energy games. Mirror imaging* **Questionnaire**: List the superpowers . . . Choose which super power you would have. Draw/describe your own super hero. What makes a super hero. Can ordinary people be superheroes? Your Mum/Dad?
☼	The costumes are worth a mention. Think about some of those images and look at how they've altered to keep up with fashion and trends. Even characters like Captain America and Thor have made subtle alterations to their costumes. **More controversial**: Have superheroes been over-sexualised in the past and are we now getting past that? The secret identity. Is it really to protect the loved ones, or is there something about a mask?

Stimulus	💀	The Logos; Superman, Batman, The Flash, Captain America, Wonder Woman, Spiderman, Black Panther, The Avengers, Captain Marvel.
	📖	*Miles Morales: Spider-Man:* Jason Reynolds. *Soon I Will Be Invincible:* Austin Grossman. *Akata Witch:* Nnedi Okorafor.
	📝	*If I Was a Superhero*: Sally Gray.
	🎭	*The Playboy of the Western World:* J. M. Synge. *Manic Pixie Dream Girl:* (A graphic novel play) Katie May. *The Continued Adventures of Super Dan and Super Kelli*: Eric Pfeffinger.
	🎬	*The Dark Knight:* 2008 (PG-13). *Avengers End Game:* 2019 (PG-13). *The Incredibles:* 2004 (U).
	🎵	*Holding out for a Hero:* Bonnie Tyler. *Flash:* Queen. *Heroes:* David Bowie. *Superman Main Theme:* John Williams.
	🎨	**Look at**: The works of Anthony Lister, Roy Lichtenstein and Andy Warhol. Simone Bianchi: *Villains and Superheroes*.

🎦	The super in hero and everyday heroes, like parents or doctors and nurses during the pandemic. Music plays a big part in ensemble pieces. Great costume opportunities. Physical theatre/stylised. Highly choreographed. Godber/Frantic Assembly.
⚠	Some superhero movies are for adults.
🔗	001, 002, 026, 034, 037, 040, 044, 076, 088, 116, 132, 156, 173, 184, 190, 191, 198, 199, 200.

198   Fame

	'I don't think I could think of a single thing that's more isolating than being famous' (Lady Gaga – American singer, songwriter, and actress).
👥	13+ Groups of 2–4.
🚩	**Workshops/games**: *Status games.* **Questionnaire**: Who is the most famous person you can think of? Why are they famous? Do you want to be famous and if so why? Single one person out and get the group to invade their personal space, asking questions and pushing their phones close to their face. How did you feel? Imagine not being able to go out in public without feeling like this. Everyone agreeing with you, no matter what you say. The rumours and gossip. What does being famous mean? List 2 positives and 2 negatives. Compare across the group and discuss.
🔆	Most really famous people say lack of privacy is their biggest regret. **Look at the language**: A star is born. Superstar. A legend. In the public eye. Household name. Celebrity status. Rich and famous. **What the papers say**: How the media treat the famous. In 1968 Andy Warhol famously predicted; 'In the future everybody will be world famous for fifteen minutes'. Discuss whether with social media, this has become a reality. **More controversial**: The infamous! The man who shot . . .

Stimulus		
	📷	Iconic photographs of the very famous. Cameras and flashes! Red carpets. VIP signs.
	📖	*Crazy Rich Asians:* Kevin Kwan. *Charlie Chaplin's Own Story:* Charlie Chaplin. *Delayed Rays of a Star:* Amanda Lee Koe.
	📝	*Fame is a fickle food:* Emily Dickinson.
	🎭	*Like a Virgin:* Gordon Steele. *Fame:* (Musical) Richard McKee. *Galileo:* Bertolt Brecht.
	🎬	*Almost Famous:* 2000 (15). *Bohemian Rhapsody:* 2018 (PG-13). *Coco before Chanel:* 2009 (PG-13).
	🎵	*Candle in the Wind:* Elton John. *Applause:* Lady Gaga. *Miss America:* James Blunt.
	🎨	*Jimi Hendrix Purple:* David Lloyd Glover. *Lionel Messi and Cristiano Ronaldo:* Paul Meijering. *Diana, Princess of Wales:* (Photographs) Terence Donovan.

🎭	Artaud or Berkoff. Shock the audience, attack on the emotions, shocking action and images, striking costumes, minimal dialogue, symbolic objects.
⚠️	Impersonating fame is not the same as impersonating the famous!
🔗	001, 002, 004, 018, 054, 062, 070, 071, 076, 092, 097, 109, 110, 118, 119, 129, 131, 145, 160, 176, 185, 195, 197.

199   Man

<table>
<tr>
<td></td>
<td></td>
<td colspan="2">Vulnerability is tough, especially being a man
(Channing Frye – American professional basketball player).</td>
</tr>
<tr>
<td colspan="2">♟♟</td>
<td colspan="2">All ages. Mixed groups (although be prepared for some electing all male groups, which is fine.)</td>
</tr>
<tr>
<td colspan="2">⚑</td>
<td colspan="2">Workshops/games: Status games. Stereotypes.
Discuss gender equality
Questionnaire: Who are your heroes? How many are men?
Do boys tend to have male heroes? Is your dad your hero? What does it mean to be an adult male?</td>
</tr>
<tr>
<td colspan="2">☽</td>
<td colspan="2">Research: The changing definitions of 'manliness throughout time and in different cultures. Renaissance man.
Look at how advertising sells the image of the strong sensitive man. Compare this with 40 or 50 years ago.</td>
</tr>
<tr>
<td rowspan="7">Stimulus</td>
<td>🐌</td>
<td colspan="2">Find images of men's fashion in the 20s to 60s and the present day. Discuss the changes.
Do the same with present-day images of men in different cultures.</td>
</tr>
<tr>
<td>📖</td>
<td colspan="2">The Way of Men: Jack Donovan.
Iron John: A Book about Men: Robert Bly.
The Art of Manliness: Manvotionals: Brett McKay.</td>
</tr>
<tr>
<td>✍</td>
<td colspan="2">If: Rudyard Kipling.</td>
</tr>
<tr>
<td>🎭</td>
<td colspan="2">Rules for Being a Man: Alex Oates.
The Caretaker: Harold Pinter.
Hymns: Chris O'Connell.</td>
</tr>
<tr>
<td>🎬</td>
<td colspan="2">Stand by Me: 1986 (15).
The Book of Eli: 2010 (15).
Hacksaw Ridge: 2016 (15).</td>
</tr>
<tr>
<td>🎵</td>
<td colspan="2">The Man: The Killers.
Man in the Mirror: Michael Jackson.
One Man Can Change the World: Big Sean.
It's Raining Men: The Weather Girls.</td>
</tr>
<tr>
<td>🎨</td>
<td colspan="2">Young Man with a Flower behind His Ear: Paul Gauguin.
Michelangelo's David.</td>
</tr>
<tr>
<td colspan="2">🎦</td>
<td colspan="2">The image and physicality of manliness, Look at the men in Hymns by Chris O'Connell and Beautiful Burnout by Bryony Lavery, both Frantic Assembly. Physical theatre.
Also sensitive monologues/soliloquy HAMLET, or ASTON's large monologue at end of Act 2. Act 3 in Pinter's The Caretaker.</td>
</tr>
<tr>
<td colspan="2">⚠</td>
<td colspan="2">Be sensitive to male body image and identity issues. Don't allow the girls to be left out.</td>
</tr>
<tr>
<td colspan="2">🔗</td>
<td colspan="2">004, 018, 020, 028, 054, 066, 071, 073, 075, 078, 080, 107, 119, 126, 130, 160, 176, 177, 182, 192, 198, 200.</td>
</tr>
</table>

200   Woman

	'In a world that wants women to whisper, I choose to yell' (Luvvie Ajayi – Nigerian-American author).
🥂👤	All ages. Mixed groups (although be prepared for some electing all female groups, which is fine.)
🚩	Discuss gender equality. **Workshops/games:** *Status games. Stereotypes.* **Questionnaire:** Who are your heroes? How many are women? List famous women, your heroines. Why do you admire them? We want the students to engage with and research women who have made a difference. But also recognise those who mean something to them. It could be their Mum, Gran, a neighbour, teacher. Ordinary women not just the famous.
🔦	**Look up:** Women's History Month. International Women's Day goes way back to 1910. In 1908, 15,000 women marched through New York demanding better working conditions and pay. A year later the Socialist party of America declared the first National Women's Day. And before the boys kick off . . . yes there is an international Men's Day. **More controversial:** Women's rights under the Taliban. **What the papers say:** Do the tabloids sexualise and stereotype women?

💡	An apple, red roses, a mirror, a makeup bag, nail varnish. A gun, a stethoscope, boxing gloves. A nun's habit, a shawl, etc . . . (depending on age/maturity of group).

Stimulus

Let's just look at the characters. Can you name the book/play/TV series or film.
Jane Eyre, Hermione Granger, Enola Holmes, The Wife of Bath, Eowyn, Natasha Romanoff, Buffy, Veronica Mars, Nancy Drew, Matilda, Jo March, Elphaba, Laura Ingalls, , Karen Blixen, Madeline, Lisa Simpson, Ripley, Jessica Jones, Boudica, Peggy Carter, Teresa Mendoza, Red Reznikov, Eve Polastri, Beth Harmon, Elizabeth R, Mary Poppins, Lieutenant Uhura, Daisy Meredith, Lynda Carter, Michonne, Carrie Mathison, Olivia Pope, Claire Underwood, Clarice Starling, Aunt Polly, Kara Danvers, Hedda, Elektra, Eleven, Sabrina Spellman, Hannah and Hanna, The Doctor, Fennec Shand, Sara Lance, Caitlin Snow, Lagertha, Auntie Marlene, Sarah Connor, Wanda Maximoff, Ruth Langmore, Elizabeth Keen, Catherine Wood, Esther Shapiro, Lisbeth Sandler, (Adele, Mel, Carol and Nicky), Eva Peron, Dr Martha Livingston, Lyra Silvertongue, Princess Leia, Dorothy Gale, Phoebe Buffay, Maria Von Trapp, Scarlett O'Hara, Brienne of Tarth, Mulan, Annie Hall, Regina George, Felicity Smoak, Scully, Lizzie Borden, Lizzie Morden, Esme and Shaz. And not forgetting: Cordelia, Lady Macbeth, Viola, Beatrice, Juliet, Desdemona, Rosalind, Hermia, and Cleopatra.

And the songs: For Angie, Mandy, Roxanne, Billie Jean, Sharona, Delilah, Jolene, Eileen, Little Suzie, Rhiannon, Cecilia, Barbara Ann, Valerie, Rosalita, Alice, Mary.

And the art: Freda Kahlo, Suzanne Valadon, Sofonisba Anguissola, Hilma Klint. Tracey Emin, Sarah Maple. Fahren Feingold. The Mona Lisa!

🎭	Shifts in time. Projections. Minimalist. Clever lighting/sound or use of costume and props. Polly Teal. Shared Experience. Historical feminist.
⚠️	Artistic intent quickly and firmly established. Don't allow the boys to be left out. Be sensitive to body image and identity issues.
🔗	01, 18, 51, 70, 75, 77, 78, 86, 87, 88, 89, 90, 126, 130, 198, 199.

INDEX OF TOPICS

Note: The locators in this section refer to Units throughout the book.

INDEX OF PLAYWRIGHTS, PRACTITIONERS, COMPANIES AND STYLES

Note: The locators in this section refer to page numbers.

Playwrights

Practitioners

Companies

Styles